An Introduction to Global Media for the Twenty-First Century

An Introduction to Global Media for the Twenty-First Century

Ole J. Mjøs

BLOOMSBURY ACADEMIC
LONDON • NEW YORK • OXFORD • NEW DELHI • SYDNEY

BLOOMSBURY ACADEMIC
Bloomsbury Publishing Inc
50 Bedford Square, London, WC1B 3DP, UK
1385 Broadway, New York, NY 10018, USA
29 Earlsfort Terrace, Dublin 2, Ireland

BLOOMSBURY, BLOOMSBURY ACADEMIC and the Diana logo
are trademarks of Bloomsbury Publishing Plc

First published in Great Britain 2023

Cover design: Eleanor Rose
Cover image © Getty Images

A catalogue record for this book is available from the British Library.

Library of Congress Cataloging-in-Publication Data
Names: Mjos, Ole J., 1970- author.
Title: An introduction to global media / Ole J. Mjøs.
Description: New York : Bloomsbury Academic, 2022. | Includes
bibliographical references and index. | Summary: "A student-friendly
book that assesses how such trends as marketization, conglomeration,
digital convergence, personalization and competition, are transforming
the global media landscape"– Provided by publisher.
Identifiers: LCCN 2022015445 (print) | LCCN 2022015446 (ebook) |
ISBN 9781350348714 (hardback) | ISBN 9781350348707 (paperback) |
ISBN 9781350348745 (epub) | ISBN 9781350348738 (pdf) | ISBN 9781350348721
Subjects: LCSH: Mass media and globalization. | Communication, International.
Classification: LCC P94.6 M5455 2022 (print) | LCC P94.6 (ebook) |
DDC 302.2–dc23/eng/20220804
LC record available at https://lccn.loc.gov/2022015445
LC ebook record available at https://lccn.loc.gov/2022015446

ISBN: HB: 978-1-3503-4871-4
         PB: 978-1-3503-4870-7
       ePDF: 978-1-3503-4873-8
      eBook: 978-1-3503-4874-5

Typeset by Integra Software Services Pvt. Ltd.
Printed and bound in Great Britain

To find out more about our authors and books visit www.bloomsbury.com
and sign up for our newsletters.

To Mari and Frida.

Contents

Case Studies

Tables

About the Author

Ole J. Mjøs is Professor in Media Studies at the Department of Information Science and Media Studies, University of Bergen, Norway. He specializes in the fields of international communication and global media. He is co-author of *The Media Welfare State: Nordic Media in the Digital Era* (2014) and author of *Music, Social Media and Global Mobility: MySpace, Facebook, YouTube* (2012) and *Media Globalization and the Discovery Channel Networks* (2010). He has been a visiting scholar at the Center for Global Communication Studies, Annenberg School for Communication, University of Pennsylvania, USA, and visiting researcher at the Centre for Mobilities Research, Lancaster University, UK. He holds a PhD from the University of Westminster, UK.

Acknowledgments

This book draws on my work and research in the field, including previously published material. The main concept of the book first appeared in my article "International communication and global media: Continuity of critical concerns" (2015; *Communication Research and Practice*, 1, 3: 267–74). The book specifically uses previously published material from two of my books, *Media Globalization and the Discovery Channel Networks* (2010; London: Routledge) and *Music, Social Media and Global Mobility: MySpace, Facebook, YouTube* (2012; London: Routledge). Pages 28–31, 33, 34, 108, 109, 111–13, 156, and 157 are previously published in *Media Globalization and Discovery Channel Networks*. Pages 23, 24, 38–41, 56–9, 60–2, 63, 64, and 74–6 are previously published in *Music, Social Media and Global Mobility: MySpace, Facebook, YouTube*. Permission to reuse the material has been obtained from the publisher, and I thank them for giving such permission. Where possible, URLs from the previous edition text have been updated to ensure that they still work. However, some instances of URLs from the previous edition no longer work, and cannot be restored. These have been left as they are, for transparency.

This book cites data from statista.com, and provides the original URLs to the articles on their website. However, statista.com is continually updated, meaning that the exact data cited in this book is no longer easily displayed. For clarity, the dates on which these links were initially accessed have been included.

Many thanks to Hallvard Moe, Trine Syvertsen, Vilde S. Sundet, Gunn Enli, and Espen Ytreberg for fruitful discussions and valuable feedback during the very early stages of the development of the book's concept.

I am grateful for the financial support from The Norwegian Non-fiction Fund for this book project.

I also wish to thank Katie Gallof, Stephanie Grace-Petinos, and Jonathan Nash at Bloomsbury Academic, and Judy Napper for her copy-editing of the manuscript.

Introduction

The global digital shift is accelerating throughout the twenty-first century. We adopt global digital media and communications services, devices, and products at unprecedented speed, for all purposes: communication, entertainment, education, health, civic, and lifestyle. Digitization of society, geopolitical shifts, constant technological innovation, and a global pandemic have speeded up this process and are shaping global media and communications in unforeseen ways. This book will present and explain the key changes taking place, but will also show how the field of global media is shaped by a continuity of themes and critical concerns throughout its history up until today. This phrase refers to the aims of the book: to draw attention to the massive changes, but also the continuity of scholarly and theoretical perspectives, themes, and concerns within the field.

The book thus first introduces the emergence and consolidation of an international and global media and communications industry and landscape. It then discusses key theoretical traditions and concepts of the field and aims to explain these developments and their consequences. The book shows how the field of international communication and global media consists of several theoretical traditions and concepts that emerged at certain historical periods then became the focus of discourses and defined the field. These traditions consist of the perspectives, themes, and concerns that emerged which were considered by many to accurately theorize major developments in global media and communications and society. They correspond with historical theoretical developments and shifts within the wider media studies discipline.

However, a focus on historical periods may lead to a certain compartmentalization, and the omission of perspectives, thoughts, and concepts for understanding the present. This is not to say that this book suggests we move back to the future, so to speak, nor does it take a revisionist approach, but the point is to also explore the existence of a certain continuity of themes and scholarly concerns from when these themes emerged up until the present time.

Before we move on to look at the content and approach of the chapters in the book, we need to keep a few important points in mind when dealing with perspectives and concepts that make up theoretical traditions. This will help explain how theories evolve, become adopted and criticized, and sometimes fade, within a chosen field or discipline.

First, theories do not emerge out of nowhere. Whether we talk about historical or current theoretical approaches, we need to understand the context in which they appear. Theories or concepts do not appear in a vacuum but reflect and address the concerns of the time. They emerge as scholars attempt to comprehend and explain developments in society. We should consider definitions of theoretical concepts in relation to a context as it "reflects a historical moment, a cultural setting, a geographical location" (Scholte, 2005: 53). The point is neither to search for a "universally endorsable definition" nor expect all to agree on "a single view," but to develop perspectives that can be shared and discussed with others (2005: 53).

Second, it follows from this that definitions are not absolute. The production of knowledge is an ongoing activity, with new discoveries and the constant testing and reevaluation of existing explanations and meanings. As such, a definition is "in motion rather than fixed," and our task is to encourage debates and analyses that lead to new insights and new definitions (2005: 53).

Third, the book introduces several concepts and terms that are presented, defined, and applied in the relevant parts and discussions of the chapters. As definitions may change over time, this book's historical approach attempts to address these issues throughout the book. Two fundamental terms of the book are "international" and "global." While they refer to similar developments, they can be distinguished. The term "international" has a longer history within the field and refers to the various forms of links, flows, ownership structures, and collaborations between parties from two or more national media and communications players, companies, and their audiences, or regulatory bodies. The term "global" has increasingly become part of the field's terminology over the past decades, much in response to the global expansion of the online infrastructure and media and communications companies, services, and organizations increasingly aiming to attract and reach audiences and users across the world (Mjøs, 2015).

However, the focus on the "the global" has been increasing exponentially since the 1960s, although for much of this period "global" was conflated or confused with "international" (Robertson, 2020). During the 1990s, "the global" became more and more visible and "noticeable in virtually any sphere—in economics, finance, advertising, media as well as in culture, politics and social movements" (Nederveen Pieterse, 2021: 4). While the term "global" is not new in any of these spheres, the term's "salience is new" (Nederveen Pieterse, 2021: 4), and has become far more prominent. For example, we are witnessing a growing "global awareness" of global challenges and problems, such as climate change, epidemics, terrorism, poverty, and financial challenges (Nederveen Pieterse, 2021: 4). Media and communications are central in fostering such global awareness across these different spheres and sectors, and at the same time, it is also an industry that is becoming increasingly more global.

The concept of "connectivity" is central to our understanding of the evolvement and characteristics of the global media landscape. Communication wire cables across the Atlantic and throughout the world; global trade in media and cultural products; cable and satellite distribution of television and communication in the twentieth century; the worldwide take-up of the internet as the global digital shift accelerates throughout the twenty-first century; digital technology and globally expanding online services and products that have become central in everyday media use: these developments have all increased connectedness across the world (e.g., Chalaby, 2020; van Dijck, 2013; Flew, 2020; Flew et al., 2016; Mjøs, 2010; 2012; 2015; Nederveen Pieterse, 2021; Thussu, 2006; 2010; Thussu and Nordenstreng, 2021; Winseck and Pike, 2007). This book argues that we need to understand how this global connectedness is created and its characteristics: who constructs, shapes and benefits from it, and what are its limits, and for whom? There is a need for a "critical awareness of the politics of connectivity" in the digital era, not least in relation to Facebook and other major online players (van Dijck, 2011: 173).

The use of "global" regarding the media and communications industry and companies can be criticized both because of the traditional US skew of products and revenue of many of them, and their total number of subscribers, audience, and users. Even Netflix, one of the most "global" companies, still has just over 220 million subscribers worldwide, and national broadcasters and media outlets and their products continue to attract large shares of audiences. While the term "global" can refer to scale, for example, to a media company with a presence in over 100 territories, or Facebook with around 3 billion users, it can also refer to increased "interdependence" in the sector, as companies increasingly interact across borders and rely on one another for the design, manufacture, distribution, and marketing of a product (Chalaby, 2016: 36). Since the 1980s, global production and value networks and global supply chains have proliferated in retailing and other industries (Nederveen Pieterse, 2021: 3). This is also increasingly the case within the media and communications industry. "Global" can therefore also refer to the way that media production and distribution is increasingly organized across the world: "A handful of global firms and products do not make a system global," but the global value chains do as they link together national markets and companies, institutions, places and networks (Chalaby, 2020: 382). Furthermore, competition in the media and communications industry is becoming global, as local, regional, national, and the major globally expanding media and communications companies move online (e.g., recently Disney+), facing the internet-based giants, and as geopolitical shifts lead to the expansion of regional companies and networks (e.g., those in China). In terms of the relationship between the global, regional, national, and local, the role of the nation-state is a key part of the discussion. While some argue its position is diminishing in the face of the global (Castells, 2013; Chalaby, 2009; 2020), others emphasize its sustainability, persistence, and adaptability (Flew, 2020; Flew and Waisbord, 2015; Syvertsen et al., 2014) and its key role in negotiating and coordinating these complex relationships in the industry (Flew, 2020). In fact, some point out how the process of "glocalization," the way the global and local connect and interact (e.g., Facebook and its individual users, or the climate crisis and sustainability and individual citizens across the world), is key to understanding the current state of world society (Robertson, 2020).

The book introduces central industry developments and trends together with key theoretical traditions of the field of international communication and global media. It thereby aims to actualize and mobilize the empirical and theoretical history of the field to help explain how the global media and communications landscape is shaped by significant change, but also continuity. The concept of the global coexists with the regional, national, local, and individual media users, and this book aims to contribute to our understanding of their relationships, not least in terms of power, autonomy, influence, and democratic and sustainable development, in the context of media and communications.

Part One of the book consists of three chapters that focus on key historical phases and developments of the internationalizing and globalizing media and communications landscape. With a focus on industry developments, and through examples and case studies, it first focuses on the twentieth century, giving an introduction to the early development of an international telegraph and cable infrastructure, and the emergence of Western-based international news agencies utilizing the new possibilities for cross-national communication.

The development of US film exports as a major force is then discussed, with the establishment of television, a culturally and politically powerful medium in the national context, yet also of particular significance in the internationalization process, both in terms of distribution of foreign programming and advertising, and the expansion of cable and satellite television worldwide, and the early phase of digitization and an emerging internet. This leads to the second part of Part One: the twenty-first century. The global digital shift accelerates the digitization of the global media and communications sector, in particular through the expansion, commercialization, and popularization of the internet and digital infrastructure and connected devices, of which the smartphone is key. The consolidation of global online media and services such as social media, search engines, and streaming entities has increasingly shaped and contributed to redefining the media and communications sector. Technology companies entering the sector as content acquirers and distributors, and geopolitical developments characterized by the expansion of non-Western companies, contribute to reconfiguring the sector in the digital age in unforeseen ways.

Part Two of the book consists of four chapters that focus on key theoretical traditions of the field of international and global media. In line with the book's rationale of drawing attention to the continuity of themes and concerns within the field, this part traces the emergence of theoretical traditions that have shaped and continue to shape the field. The book focuses on four such traditions that all aim to explain the internationalizing and globalizing media landscape and key consequences of these developments up until today. The first tradition focuses on the recurring theme of the role of media and communications in modernizing, developing, and fostering social change across the world. The second tradition is about the power of media in an international and global context. This tradition is concerned with the uneven distribution of cultural, political, and financial influence and how major companies and the media and communications industry of certain Western and developed countries dominate and wield influence across the world, and how user data is collected and exploited by such players. The third tradition is preoccupied with the media audience and users' perspective and how they experience empowerment and influence within the media and communications landscape, and how they contribute to shaping it. The fourth tradition focuses on how the term "globalization" emerged and became prominent within the field. This tradition consists of and reflects different concerns and diverse opinions as to how globalization unfolds, its intensity and its possible consequences.

Part One: Key Developments: Industry, Infrastructure, Content, and Audiences

Chapter 2: This chapter traces the development of an international and global media landscape in the mid-nineteenth century up until the beginning of the twenty-first century. A key starting point is the emergence of the telegraph and undersea cables, creating the first international communications infrastructure, and the subsequent establishment of the first international, or according to some global, media companies, namely the Western news agencies, that exploited this new infrastructure (Boyd Barrett, 1998; Winseck and Pike, 2007: 16). The chapter then draws attention to the growing export of film from the first half of the twentieth century. The US industry was from the beginning a driver in this process, leading to its strong position across the world today (Miller and Maxwell, 2006; Miller et al., 2005; Segrave, 1997). The next part looks at the establishment of television across the world in the mid-twentieth century, and how the export of television and film programming, with the United States as the leading player, became a key driving force in shaping the world's media and communications sectors (Nordenstreng and Varis, 1974; Straubhaar, 2007). At the same time, national and regional media sectors were maturing, and in many ways represent a counterforce to US imports through domestic production and distribution, as well as increased flows within and between regional media centers in both the South and North (Mellor et al., 2011; Sinclair et al., 1996; Straubhaar, 2007; Syvertsen et al., 2014; Thussu, 2006). The expansion of US cable and satellite television channels across the world, beginning in the last decades of the twentieth century, is a further key development in the internationalization of this landscape (Chalaby, 2002; 2009; Mjøs, 2010). Toward the end of the twentieth century, digitization, and the emergence of the internet as a new cross-national media and communications infrastructure, impacting on the media and communications industry, and speculative investments drove the value of internet-based companies and services. The financial collapse in the value of these entities at the turn of the twentieth and into the twenty-first century did not end the development of the internet. The expansion and popularity of the internet was ensured, and its central position in the international and global media landscape became increasingly evident.

Chapter 3: This chapter looks at the emergence and consolidation of a global online environment and the expansion of key online companies and services dominating this landscape in the twenty-first century. The chapter explains how this environment functions through advertising and monetization of users, and how key companies and technologies are driving this development. These include both media and communications hardware, such as the smartphone and digital infrastructure in general, and the major services for online communication, navigation, and web searches. Throughout the twenty-first century, a major issue facing the industry is the demand for sustainable development, particularly in terms of electronic waste, recycling, and carbon emissions.

Coupled with deregulation, privatization, and commercialization, a key process both driving and resulting from the transformations within the global media and communications landscape is *convergence* (Castells, 2013; Iosifidis, 2011; International Telecommunication Union [ITU], 2021; Thussu, 2010; Thussu and Nordenstreng, 2021). The smartphone is at the center of global media and communications in the twenty-first century. It has revolutionized how we consume media and communicate, but increasingly, how we access other services within the fields of finance, health, and education. In fact, the smartphone should be seen as a key driving force in the processes associated with convergence. While Western smartphone producers used to dominate sales globally, Chinese producers have now taken the lead.

The global popularization of the online environment is much due to the sophisticated and extensive monetizing of online users and the general growth in digital advertising, reaching over 50 percent of all global advertising in 2020 (McStay, 2016; Sinclair, 2012; Spurgeon, 2008; Turow, 2011). Here, localization is key to the unprecedented expansion of online media companies in national and local contexts, and the catering for and monetization of individual users (Chalaby, 2009; Mjøs, 2012). Still, localization has not enabled US and Western media and communications companies to enter China's enormous domestic media and communications sector and the online market, with the most internet users in the world and Chinese-owned search engines, social media, and streaming and cloud services (Thussu, 2018; Thussu and Nordenstreng, 2021; Zhu and Keane, 2021). Global media and communications are also characterized by dominance, as a handful of companies and services, such as Google, Amazon, Apple, Facebook, and Microsoft, have achieved superior positions. Increasingly, private, corporate, public, and civic life is dependent on—and influenced by—a few online platforms, and we see the emergence of platformization in society. The platform economy is mainly driven by these US companies, and only Chinese companies such as Baidu, Alibaba, and Tencent can compete with their own platforms, although mainly within China's domestic market (van Dijck et al., 2018; de Kloet et al., 2019; Poell et al., 2019).

Chapter 4: This chapter focuses on media companies in a global digital context in the twenty-first century. Digitization, convergence, and the worldwide popularization of the internet have had a major impact on these companies. It explores the global media players, how audiovisual content is produced and distributed, and the role of media branding.

While the traditional export of television, film, and media content to national media outlets continues to grow, the globally expanding legal and illegal streaming services, such as Netflix, Amazon Prime, and Popcorn Time, are redefining the audiovisual media sector. The arrival of new players from outside the media sector is prompting major mergers and acquisitions. The new global online media content players are making inroads into national audiences across the world and thereby represent fierce competition for traditional national media and broadcasters, who seek to adapt. Global value chains for media production and distribution interlink companies, institutions, and services across the world. China, with an enormous domestic market with the world's largest internet population, but also the other BRICS (Brazil, Russia, India, China, and South Africa) countries, are emerging on the global scene. Together, these developments represent major drivers of change (Chalaby, 2016; 2020; Chalaby and Plunkett, 2020; Cunningham and Silver, 2013; van Dijck et al., 2018; Lobato, 2019; Thussu and Nordenstreng, 2021). In the digital era, where global, national, and local media outlets proliferate and compete, and media content is distributed across borders at unprecedented pace and scale, the need to be noticed and attract audiences is more challenging than ever. Therefore, media branding has become a key phenomenon throughout the global media and communications sector. The chapter discusses the significance of media branding and how such strategies are employed in relation to media outlets, content, and services (Arvidsson, 2006; Chalaby, 2002; 2009; Lopera-Mármol et al., 2021; McStay, 2016; Sinclair, 2012).

Part Two: Key Theoretical Traditions: The Continuity of Themes and Concerns

Chapter 5: Throughout the twenty-first century, public, private, and civic stakeholders increasingly agree on ICT (information and communications technology) and digital media and communications as among the most significant factors for achieving development and social change in the world. This chapter discusses how scholars, policy makers, and practitioners have for decades explored and debated how media, communications, and technology can contribute to development. The chapter details key theoretical concepts and perspectives that have shaped this tradition within global media, often broadly referred to as "development communication."

Beginning with the early influential "top-down" modernization theory tradition (e.g., Lerner, [1958] 1962; Schramm, 1964), the chapter moves on to the emergence of the more "bottom-up," participatory approach in development communication which followed as a reaction (e.g., Beltran, 1975; Freire, [1970] 2000). The technology-focused approach termed "telecommunication for development" then emerged, which was a forerunner to the current, highly influential "information communication technologies for development" paradigm. Scholars, politicians, and organizations emphasize how ICT and digital media and communications clearly play a significant role in development (e.g., ITU, 2003; Thussu and Nordenstreng, 2021; World Bank, 2016; World Economic Forum, 2020). However, many also emphasize that there remain major global digital divides and gaps in connectivity in the world, and, importantly, a number of factors other than access to ICT are crucial for successfully closing the digital divide and achieving development (e.g., van Dijk, 2005; ITU, 2018; 2021; Norris, 2001; Ragnedda and Muschert, 2013; Wessels, 2013). Critics also draw attention to how the world's largest ICT companies originated in the West, mostly in the United States, or developed and industrialized Eastern countries such as Japan and Korea and, increasingly, China. These global technology companies and digital media and communications companies (e.g., Apple, Huawei, Samsung, Google, and Facebook) have enormous market power and can be accused of seeing development as mainly market opportunities. In fact, some argue that it is the companies and governments of the developed world that benefit from the expansion of ICT in the developing world (Mosco, 2009; Unwin, 2017). The rise of China has created geopolitical tension and competition for influence with Western countries, and the United States in particular, as Chinese authorities have launched a number of major technology and digital infrastructure initiatives and partnerships with developing countries across the world (Hillman, 2021; Lisinge, 2020; Thussu, 2018; Thussu and Nordenstreng, 2021).

Chapter 6: The corporatization and commercialization of the global digital media and communications landscape, and worldwide expansion of US companies, fronted by Google's and Facebook's dominant positions in search and social media markets, and Netflix's and other streaming services' rapid growth worldwide, raise concerns among scholars, the public, policy makers, and regulators. There is a concern about dominance, competition for the national media audiences and advertising market, exploitation of user data, and reduced national autonomy regarding regulation, privacy of citizens, and the public sphere. The rise of China also leads to geopolitical tensions and new competition for power and influence across the global media and communications landscape. However, several of these current concerns mirror those of the past. The distribution of US films, television programming, and cultural products and the parallel international growth of media companies triggered and motivated the emergence of a theoretical tradition concerned with the uneven structural power and asymmetry in influence within these processes and the consequences of this development. While the development of communication approaches viewed media and communications as a force for societal change and improvement, the new tradition was concerned with the harmful effects of imported media and foreign media companies' activities. In the 1960s, 1970s, and 1980s, a number of concepts and terms, such as "cultural imperialism" (Schiller, [1976] 2018), "media imperialism" (Boyd Barret, 1977), and "cultural synchronization" (Hamelink, 1983), were introduced to support this argument and became central to this tradition. Several of these terms achieved prominence in academia and were also adopted in politics and in public. This chapter first traces the emergence of this tradition and its concepts and discusses the presence of similar concerns today. The continuing preoccupation with, for example, the term "imperialism," through recent concepts such as "platform imperialism" (Jin, 2015) and "regional imperialism" (Boyd-Barret, 2015), along with terms such as "digital colonialism" (Kwet, 2019), "data colonialism" (Couldry and Mejias, 2019), "algorithmic injustice" (Birhane, 2021; Birhane and Cummins, 2019), "micro-targeting propaganda" (Boyd Barrett, 2020), and "global personalization" clearly shows that concerns of uneven power, exploitation, and dominance remain strong throughout the twenty-first century. This chapter will therefore trace the manifestations of such critical thinking and theories throughout the history of international communication and global media.

Chapter 7: Throughout the twenty-first century, the worldwide adoption of the internet, and the popularization of smartphones and other digital devices and services, have given unprecedented opportunities for media users to communicate, consume, and distribute media products across the world. Scholarly interest in digital media audiences and users has increased significantly. However, the preoccupation with understanding the media audience and user is not new. The previous chapter shows how the critical political economy tradition—concerned with asymmetric power relations, exploitation of user data, and dominance—stretches from the 1960s up until today. However, already in the 1970s, scholars began criticizing this tradition for having major weaknesses.

It did not give attention to the media audiences. It did not explore how audiences actually engage with media content nor ask the audiences of their opinion of media content they had watched. A tradition emerged that aimed to explore these questions, and it argued that the media audience was far from passive and powerless, but active, interpretive, and selective in their media use. Scholars within the field of cultural studies pioneered such studies of the media audience: "If, for much of the 1970s, the audience was largely ignored by many media theorists in favour of the analysis of textual and economic structures which were presumed to impose their effects on the audience, the 1980s, conversely, saw a sudden flourishing of 'audience' (or 'reception') studies" (Morley, 1991: 2). As scholars explored media audiences across the world and their ability to interpret and make choices according to their background and cultural and linguistic preferences, theoretical concepts focusing on unequal media flows and structural inequalities were increasingly "criticized as overly simplistic" (Straubhaar, 1991: 39). This chapter first traces the emergence of this audience-centered tradition and moves on to discuss how today's audience is conceptualized, studied, and understood in the context of digital global media and communications. The recent emergence of numerous media audience- and user-centered approaches and concepts such as "participatory culture" (Jenkins, 2006), "produsage" (Bruns, 2008), "creator power" (Cunningham and Craig, 2019), "mass-self communication" (Castells, 2013), "global mobility" (Mjøs, 2012; Urry, 2007), "co-creation" (Kornberger, 2010), and "crowdsourcing" (Howe, 2006) clearly underline the continuing preoccupation with the media audience and user throughout the twenty-first century. This chapter will therefore trace the manifestations of such audience-centered thinking and theories throughout the history of international communication and global media.

Chapter 8: In recent decades, globalization has been one of the most popular, discussed, and influential terms and concepts in general, and particularly in relation to media and communications. The term "globalization" was soon incorporated into the field of international communication and global media and many scholars central in shaping the field consider globalization to be a key concept.

Despite the widespread adoption and use of the term, the meaning, significance, and nature of globalization are fiercely contested by these scholars. This chapter does not aim to find an all-encompassing definition of the term. Instead, it narrows its inquiry with the aim to theoretically explore the diverse views and understandings of how we can understand globalization in the context of media and communications.

The chapter emphasizes how the concept of connectivity, or interconnectivity, is central to the wider understanding of the term "globalization" (e.g., van Dijck, 2013; Mjøs, 2012; 2015; Nederveen Pieterse, 2021; Robertson, 2016; Thussu and Nordenstreng, 2021; Tomlinson, 1999). In fact, Robertson, suggests, "I would speculate that about 80 percent or even more of writings or pronouncements on globalization have defined it as centered upon the phenomenon of connectivity (interconnectedness)" (Robertson, 2016: 16).

Global trade in media and cultural products, cable and satellite distribution of television and communication in the twentieth century, and the global digital shift accelerating across the world throughout the twenty-first century, with the popularization of the internet and the emergence of online-based services and companies and the general digitization and maturing of the industry across the world, have created increased connectedness across the world.

The term "globalization" in the context of media and communications attempts to capture, conceptualize, and explain this connectedness. This increased connectedness has contributed to triggering and motivating the development of theoretical concepts and approaches associated with globalization, and the term itself over the past few decades. Therefore, this chapter explains key concepts and terms that help define and describe the nuances and contested nature of the concept of globalization—how it unfolds and its consequences—in relation to media and communications.

On the one hand, some argue that globalization is not necessarily something new, but rather more of the same. In fact, media scholar McChesney (1999) argues that globalization should be viewed as stronger and more totalizing than the earlier concepts of media and cultural imperialism. While the global and local or national were considered to be in opposition, now, globally expanding media localize their operations and collaborate with local media (McChesney, 1999). Furthermore, if definitions of globalization lack a critical stance they "pose a threat to constructing mythologies that only see positive sides of globalization and ignore the negative consequences of contemporary globalization processes" (Fuchs, 2011: 164). We should therefore pay attention to aspects of continuity in terms of power and influence, as old concepts like *imperialism* and *capitalist empire* continue to be of significance and relevance, Fuchs argues: "the notions of imperialism and capitalist empire have gained importance in critical globalization studies" (2011: 165). A key recent example is "platform imperialism," exemplified by the US-based global digital platforms, fronted by Facebook and Google: "In the 21st century, again, there is a distinct connection between platforms, globalization, and capitalist imperialism" (Jin, 2013: 167; 2020). A handful of platforms "dominate the global order" and this has led to the accumulation and concentration of capital: "This is far from a globalization model in which power is infinitely dispersed" (2013: 161).

On the other hand, many argue that globalization is something new and constantly evolving. Globalization is a much more unpredictable, "far less coherent or culturally directed process" in society compared with the earlier concept of "cultural imperialism" (Tomlinson, 1991: 175). This process is again made up of a range of interrelated processes, developments, and concepts.

One key concept signifying change is the process of "cultural hybridization"— the mixing of media genres and cultural forms across borders. Some consider it the very logic of globalization (Kraidy, 2005; Nederveen Pieterse, 2004; 2021). The related terms "glocalization" and "localization" are also considered key terms in the globalization discourse as they signify how the global and local are connected in myriad ways (Robertson, 1992; 1995). In fact, Robertson argues, the "glocal turn" characterizes the current state of globalization analysis (Robertson, 2020). Others point to how globalization is characterized by the related process of "counter-flow" of media and cultural products from non-Western regions to the West (Thussu, 2006; 2010).

Some emphasize how the process of globalization of media and communications leads to increased autonomy and power for the digital media users (e.g., Cunningham and Craig, 2019; Jenkins, 2006). Others emphasize the process of "deterritorialization": how cross-national electronic media challenges conventional connections between the territorial, and culture and social life (Morley and Robins, 1995). The process of "deterritorialization" is, among others, present in transnational television, global streaming services, and global competition and production in the media sector (Chalaby, 2003; 2020; Lodz, 2020). A related concept is that globalization entails time and space compression (Robertson, 1995), a process mainly created by the global expansion of media and communications, with consequences for our perception of the world and how we live our lives.

Others argue how globalization is increasingly being shaped by geopolitical shifts and this may lead to the splitting up and reconfiguration of the global media and communications landscape. The rise of China and India, and also the BRICS constellation as a whole and individually, may lead to the "de-Americanization" and even "Sino-globalization" of global media and communications. This may have fundamental consequences for our understanding of globalization (Thussu, 2021; Thussu and Nordenstreng, 2021).

References

Arvidsson, A. (2006) *Brands: Meaning and Value in Media Culture*. New York: Routledge.

Beltran, L. R. (1975) Research ideologies in conflict. *Journal of Communication*, 25, 2: 187–93.

Birhane, A. (2021) Algorithmic injustice: A relational ethics approach. *Patterns*, 2, 2: 1–9.

Birhane, A. and Cummins, F. (2019) Algorithmic Injustices: Towards a Relational Ethics. Presented at the Black in AI workshop, @NeurIPS2019, arXiv:1912.07376 (accessed April 21, 2021).

Boyd-Barrett, O. (1977) Media Imperialism: Towards an International Framework for an Analysis of Media Systems, pp. 116–35 in J. Curran, M. Gurevitch, and J. Woollacott (eds.) *Mass Communication and Society*. London: Edward Arnold.

Boyd-Barrett, O. (1998) "Global" News Agencies, pp. 19–34 in O. Boyd-Barrett and T. Rantanen (eds.) *The Globalization of News*. London: SAGE.

Boyd-Barrett, O. (2015) *Media Imperialism*. London: SAGE.

Boyd-Barrett, O. (2020) Media and Cultural Imperialism: Genealogy of an Idea, pp. 11–30 in O. Boyd-Barrett and T. Mirrlees (eds.) *Media Imperialism: Continuity and Change*. Lanham, MD: Rowman & Littlefield.

Bruns, A. (2008) *Blogs, Wikipedia, Second Life, and Beyond: From Production to Produsage*. New York: Peter Lang.

Castells, M. (2013) *Communication Power*. Oxford: Oxford University Press.

Chalaby, J. K. (2002) Transnational television in Europe—The role of pan-European channels. *European Journal of Communication*, 17, 2: 183–203.

Chalaby, J. K. (2003) Television for a new global order. *Gazette*, 65, 6: 457–72.

Chalaby, J. K. (2009) *Transnational Television in Europe*. London: I. B. Tauris.

Chalaby, J. K. (2016) Television and globalization: The TV content global value chain. *Journal of Communication*, 66, 1: 35–59.

Chalaby, J. K. (2020) Understanding Media Globalization: A Global Value Chain Analysis, pp. 373–84 in S. Shimpach (ed.) *The Routledge Companion to Global Television*. New York: Routledge.

Chalaby, J. K. and Plunkett, S. (2020) Standing on the shoulders of tech giants: Media delivery, streaming television and the rise of global suppliers. *New Media & Society*. https://doi.org/10.1177/1461444820946681

Couldry, M. and Mejias, U. A. (2019) Data colonialism: Rethinking big data's relation to the contemporary subject. *Television & New Media*, 20, 4: 336–49.

Cunningham, S. and Craig, D. (2019) *Social Media Entertainment: The New Intersection of Hollywood and Silicon Valley*. New York: New York University Press.

Cunningham, S. and Silver, J. (2013) *Screen Distribution and the New King of the Online World*. Basingstoke, UK: Palgrave Pivot.

Flew, T. (2020) Globalization, neo-globalization and post-globalization: The challenge of populism and the return of the national. *Global Media and Communication*, 16, 1: 19–39.

Flew, T. and Waisbord, S. (2015) The ongoing significance of national media systems in the context of media globalization. *Media, Culture & Society*, 37, 4: 620–36.

Flew, T., Iosifidis, P., and Steemers, J. (2016) Global Media and National Policies: The Return of the State, pp. 1–15 in T. Flew, P. Iosifidis, and J. Steemers (eds.) *Global Media and National Policies*. London: Palgrave Macmillan. https://doi.org/10.1057/9781137493958_1

Freire, P. ([1970] 2000) *Pedagogy of the Oppressed*. Thirtieth Anniversary Edition. New York: Continuum.

Fuchs, C. (2011) *Foundations of Critical Media and Information Studies*. London: Routledge.

Hamelink, C. J. (1983) *Cultural Autonomy in Global Communications*. New York: Longman.

Hillman, J. (2021) Competing with China's digital silk road. February 9. https://www.csis.org/analysis/competing-chinas-digital-silk-road (accessed May 6, 2022).

Howe, J. (2006) The rise of crowdsourcing. *Wired*, June 1. https://www.wired.com/2006/06/crowds (accessed June 2, 2022).

Iosifidis, P. (2011) *Global Media and Communication Policy*. Basingstoke, UK: Palgrave.

International Telecommunication Union (2003) *Declaration of Principles. Building the Information Society: A Global Challenge in the New Millennium*. December 12. https://www.itu.int/net/wsis/docs/geneva/official/dop.html (accessed June 14, 2021).

International Telecommunication Union (2018) *Measuring the Information Society*. https://www.itu.int/pub/D-IND-ICTOI (accessed April 1, 2021).

International Telecommunication Union (2021) *Measuring Digital Development: Facts and Figures 2021*. International Telecommunication Union (ITU): Geneva. https://www.itu.int/en/ITU-D/Statistics/Documents/facts/FactsFigures2021.pdf (accessed May 25, 2022).

Jenkins, H. (2006) *Convergence Culture: Where Old and New Media Collide*. New York: New York University Press.

Jin, D. Y. (2013) The construction of platform imperialism in the globalization era, *tripleC*, 11, 1: 145–72.

Jin, D. Y. (2015) *Digital Platforms, Imperialism and Political Culture*. London: Routledge.

Jin, D. Y. (2020) *Globalization and Media in the Digital Platform Age*. New York: Routledge.

de Kloet, J., Poell, T., Zeng, G., and Chow, Y. F. (2019) The platformization of Chinese society: Infrastructure, governance, and practice. *Chinese Journal of Communication*, 12, 3: 249–56. https://doi.org/10.1080/17544750.2019.1644008

Kornberger, M. (2010) *Brand Society: How Brands Transform Management and Lifestyle*. Cambridge, UK: Cambridge University Press.

Kraidy, M. M. (2005) *Hybridity: Or the Cultural Logic of Globalization*. Philadelphia: Temple University Press.

Kwet, M. (2019) Digital colonialism: US empire and the new imperialism in the Global South. *Race & Class*, 60, 4: 3–26.

Lerner, D. ([1958] 1962) *The Passing of Traditional Society: Modernizing the Middle East*. New York: Free Press.

Lisinge, R. T. (2020) The Belt and Road Initiative and Africa's regional infrastructure development: Implications and lessons. *Transnational Corporations Review*, 12, 4: 425–38.

Lobato, R. (2019) *Netflix Nations: The Geography of Digital Distribution*. New York: New York Press.

Lodz, A. (2020) In between the global and the local: Mapping the geographies of Netflix as a multinational service. *International Journal of Cultural Studies*, 24, 2: 195–215.

Lopera-Mármol, M., Jiménez-Morales, M., and Bourdaa, M. (2021) Televertising Strategies in the Age of Non-advertising TV, pp. 154–88 in L. Mas-Manchón (ed.) *Innovation in Advertising and Branding Communication*. New York: Routledge.

McChesney, R. (1999) The Media System Goes Global, pp. 78–118 in R. McChesney, *Rich Media, Poor Democracy: Communication Politics in Dubious Times*. Champaign: University of Illinois Press.

McStay, A. (2016) *Digital Advertising*. Second edition. London. Palgrave.

Mellor, N., Ayish, M., Dajani, N., and Rinnawi, K. (2011) *Arab Media: Globalization and Emerging Media Industries*. Cambridge, UK: Polity.

Miller, T., and Maxwell, R. (2006) Film and Globalization, pp. 33–52 in O. Boyd-Barrett (ed.) *Communications Media, Globalization, and Empire*. London: John Libbey.

Miller, T., Govil, N., McMurria, J., Maxwell, R., and Wang, T. (2005) *Global Hollywood 2*. London: British Film Institute.

Mjøs, O. J. (2010) *Media Globalization and the Discovery Channel Networks*. London: Routledge.

Mjøs, O. J. (2012) *Music, Social Media and Global Mobility*. London: Routledge.

Mjøs, O. J. (2015) International communication and global media: Continuity of critical concerns. *Communication Research and Practice*, 1, 3: 267–74.

Morley, D. (1991) Where the global meets the local: Notes from the sitting room. *Screen*, 32, 1: 1–15.

Morley, D. and Robins, K. (1995) *Spaces of Identity: Global Media, Electronic Landscapes and Cultural Boundaries*. London: Routledge.

Mosco, V. (2009) *Political Economy of Communication*. Second edition. London: SAGE.

Nederveen Pieterse, J. (2004) *Globalization and Culture: Global Melange*. Lanham, MD: Rowman and Littlefield.

Nederveen Pieterse, J. (2021) Global Why, pp. 1–11 in *Connectivity and Global Studies*. London: Palgrave Macmillan. https://doi.org/10.1007/978-3-030-59598-2_1

Nordenstreng, K. and Varis, T. (1974) *Television Traffic, a One Way Street? A Survey and Analysis of the International Flow of Television Programmes Material*. UNESCO Reports and Papers on Mass Communication 70. Paris: UNESCO.

Norris, P. (2001) *Digital Divide: Civic Engagement, Information Poverty, and the Internet Worldwide*. Cambridge, UK: Cambridge University Press.

Poell, T., Nieborg, D., and van Dijck, J. (2019) Platformisation. *Internet Policy Review*, 8, 4. https://doi.org/10.14763/2019.4.1425

Ragnedda, M. and Muschert, G. W. (2013) Introduction, pp. 1–15 in M. Ragnedda and G. W. Muschert (eds.) *The Digital Divide: The Internet and Social Inequality in International Perspective*. London: Routledge.

Robertson, R. (1992) *Globalization: Social Theory and Global Culture*. London: SAGE.

Robertson, R. (1995) Glocalization: Time-space and homogeneity-heterogeneity, pp. 23–44 in M. Featherstone, S. Lash, and R. Robertson (eds.) *Global Modernities*. London: SAGE.

Robertson, R. (2016) Global Culture and Consciousness, pp. 5–20 in R. Robertson and D. Buhari-Gulmez, *Global Culture: Consciousness and Connectivity*. London: Routledge.

Robertson, R. (2020) The Glocal Turn, pp. 25–38 in I. Rossi (ed.) *Challenges of Globalization and Prospects for an Inter-civilizational World Order*. Cham, Switzerland: Springer. https://doi.org/10.1007/978-3-030-44058-9_2

Schiller, H. ([1976] 2018) *Communication and Cultural Domination*. First edition. Abingdon, UK and New York: Routledge.

Scholte, J. (2005) *Globalization: A Critical Introduction*. Second edition. Basingstoke: Palgrave.

Schramm, W. (1964) *Mass Media and National Development: The Role of Information in the Developing Countries*. Stanford, CA: Stanford University Press.

Segrave, K. (1997) *American Films Abroad: Hollywood's Domination of the World's Movie Screens from the 1890s to the Present*. Jefferson, NC: McFarland.

Sinclair, J. (2012) *Advertising, the Media and Globalization: A World in Motion*. London: Routledge.

Sinclair, J., Jacka, E., and Cunningham, S. (1996) *New Patterns in Global Television*. Oxford: Oxford University Press.

Spurgeon, C. (2008) *Advertising and New Media*. New York: Routledge.

Straubhaar, J. (1991) Beyond media imperialism: Asymmetrical interdependence and cultural proximity. *Critical Studies in Mass Communication*, 8, 1: 39–59.

Straubhaar, J. D. (2007) *World Television: From Global to Local*. Los Angeles: SAGE.

Syvertsen, T., Enli, G., Mjøs, O. J., and Moe, H. (2014) *The Media Welfare State: Nordic Media in the Digital Era*. Ann Arbor, MI: University of Michigan Press.

Thussu, D. K. (2006) *Media on the Move: Global Flow and Contra-flow*. London: Routledge.

Thussu, D. K. (2010) Introduction, pp. 1–10 in D. K. Thussu (ed.) *International Communication: A Reader*. London: Routledge.

Thussu, D. K. (2018) Globalization of Chinese Media: The Global Context, pp. 17–33 in D. K. Thussu, H. de Burgh, and A. Shi (eds.) *China's Media Go Global*. New York: Routledge.

Thussu, D. K. (2021) BRICS De-Americanizing the Internet? pp. 280–301 in D. K. Thussu and K. Nordenstreng (eds.) *BRICS Media: Reshaping the Global Communication Order?* Abingdon, UK: Routledge.

Thussu, D. K. and Nordenstreng, K. (2021) Introduction, pp. xv–xvi in D. K. Thussu and K. Nordenstreng (eds.) *BRICS Media: Reshaping the Global Communication Order?* Abingdon, UK: Routledge.

Tomlinson, J. (1991) *Cultural Imperialism: A Critical Introduction.* London: Continuum.

Tomlinson, J. (1999) *Globalisation and Culture.* Cambridge, UK: Polity.

Turow, J. (2011) *The Daily You: How the New Advertising Industry Is Defining Your Identity and Your Worth.* New Haven, CT: Yale University Press.

Unwin, T. (2017) *Reclaiming Information and Communication Technologies for Development.* Oxford: Oxford University Press.

Urry, J. (2007) *Mobilities.* Cambridge, UK: Polity.

Van Dijk, J. (2005) *The Deepening Divide: Inequality in the Information Society.* Thousand Oaks, CA: SAGE.

Van Dijck, J. (2011) Facebook as a tool for producing sociality and connectivity. *Television & New Media.* https://journals.sagepub.com/doi/full/10.1177/1527476411415291

Van Dijck, J. (2013) *The Culture of Connectivity: A Critical History of the Social Media.* Oxford: Oxford University Press.

Van Dijck, J., Poell, T., and De Waal, M. (2018) *The Platform Society: Public Values in a Connective World.* Oxford: Oxford University Press.

Wessels, B. (2013) The Reproduction and Reconfiguration of Inequality: Differentiation and Class, Status and Power in the Dynamics of Digital Divides, pp. 17–28 in M. Ragnedda and G. W. Muschert (eds.) *The Digital Divide: The Internet and Social Inequality in International Perspective.* London: Routledge.

Winseck, D. R. and Pike, R. M. (2007) *Communication and Empire: Media, Markets, and Globalization, 1860–1930.* Durham, NC: Duke University Press.

World Bank (2016) *World Development Report 2016: Digital Dividends.* Washington, DC: World Bank.

World Economic Forum (2020) *Accelerating Digital Inclusion in the New Normal.* Geneva: World Economic Forum. http://www3.weforum.org/docs/WEF_Accelerating_Digital_Inclusion_in_the_New_Normal_Report_2020.pdf (accessed May 25, 2021).

Zhu, Y. and Keane, M. (2021) China's Cultural Power Reconnects with the World, pp. 209–22 in D. K. Thussu and K. Nordenstreng (eds.) *BRICS Media: Reshaping the Global Communication Order?* Abingdon, UK: Routledge.

Part One

Key Developments:
Industry, Infrastructure, Content, and Audiences

2

The Emergence of a Global Media and Communications Landscape

From the Telegraph to the Internet

This chapter traces the development of an international and global media landscape from the mid-nineteenth century up until the beginning of the twenty-first century. A key starting point is the emergence of the telegraph and undersea cables—creating the first international communications infrastructure—and the following establishment of the first international or, according to some, global media companies, namely the Western news agencies, which exploited this new infrastructure. The chapter then draws attention to the growing export of film from the first half of the twentieth century. The US industry was from the beginning a driver in this process, leading to its strong position across the world today. The next part of the chapter looks at the establishment of television across the world in the mid-twentieth century, and how the export of television and film programming, with the US industry as the dominant player, became a key driving force in shaping the world's media and communications sectors. However, the national and regional media sectors began maturing, and represented a counterforce to US imports through domestic production and distribution. The expansion of US cable and satellite television channels across the world, beginning in the last decades of the twentieth century, is a further key development in internationalizing this landscape. Toward the end of the twentieth century, digitization and the emergence of the internet as a new cross-national media and communications infrastructure began to develop and gradually impact on the media and communications industry. Speculative investments drove the value of internet-based companies and services, yet the collapse in the value of these entities at the turn of the twentieth and twenty-first centuries only delayed the popularization of the internet.

Wiring the World: Telegraph, Cables, and News Agencies

The creation of an international communications infrastructure beginning in the mid-nineteenth century was a key formative development: "Nearly a century and a half before the World Wide Web and a glut of fiber-optic cables were weaved around the planet, another global communication infrastructure was being put into place" (Winseck and Pike, 2007: 16). Telegraph and cable revolutionized communication internationally as they enabled for the first time the distribution of information more rapid than the speed of people travelling. This also led to growth in trade and the commercial value of information and news (Herman and McChesney, 1997: 12). The first large communications companies were formed in this phase. These achieved powerful positions and their services influenced world politics and power:

> After printing, the next revolution came with the invention of the telegraph: the wire age (1844–1900) culminated in the establishment of the first international and multinational communication companies. The international cable telegraph companies were now possessors of power. This new medium enabled the powerful nations like Great Britain to maintain contact with their far-flung colonies. Then came wireless telegraphy (1901–1926).
>
> (Woods, 1992: 1)

Some draw parallels to contemporary powerful media and communications corporations, claiming that the "British-based Eastern Telegraph Company was the Microsoft of its age." As late as 1929, it represented half of the cable networks of the world (Winseck and Pike, 2007: 4). A handful of news agencies came to exploit these new technologies and thereby pioneer international media expansion from the second half of the nineteenth century to the first third of the twentieth century:

> This was an oligopolistic and hierarchical structure of the global news market controlled by Reuters, Havas, and Wolff at the top tier, in partnership with an ever-increasing number of national agencies. Each member of the triumvirate had the right to distribute its news service, incorporating news of the cartel, to its ascribed territories: these territories were determined by periodic, formal agreements. With some exceptions, the members of the triumvirate were prohibited from selling their news to clients in the others' territories, although they could gather news independently from those territories if they wished. The triumvirate of Reuters, Havas and Wolff supplied world news to national

news agencies in return for a service of national news and payment of a subscription fee by the national agencies. In general [...] the national agencies had exclusive rights to the distribution of cartel news in their territories, and the cartel had exclusive rights to the national agency news services.

(Boyd Barrett, 1998: 27)

While the members of the cartel were established as national news agencies, their international operations made them "the first significant form of global media" (Herman and McChesney, 1997: 12). The cartel was later reorganized when the American Associated Press (AP) and United Press (UP) news agencies became part of it, and the members divided global markets for news (Boyd Barrett, 1998: 27; Winseck and Pike, 2007: xvi). As some argue, these Western news agencies "were, in effect, the global media until well into the twentieth century, and even after the dawn of broadcasting their importance for global journalism was unsurpassed" (Herman and McChesney, 1997: 12).

In the late 1920s, after the introduction of commercial radio in the United States and the launch of radio by the British public service broadcaster BBC (1922), shortwave bands enabled radio broadcasting worldwide. The US commercial broadcasters NBC and CBS, and the BBC rebroadcast their national programming for an international audience, and the former two saw it as an opportunity to enter national radio markets with US commercial advertising, and Latin America in particular (Woods, 1992: 1). However, these early commercial approaches overseas proved unsuccessful. Instead, it was the political opportunities international radio broadcasts created that were to have major significance. The start of the Second World War "brought about the first explosion of international propaganda broadcasting; it was a powerful weapon of war for all participants" (Woods, 1992: 2). Parallel to the development of national and local markets populated by both commercial and public radio stations, the role of radio continued to be a major means of international propaganda throughout the Cold War as radio stations transmitted from the Western and Eastern blocs; each "demonstrated commitment to their respective ideologies" (Somerville, 2012; Woods, 1992). From the West, the US-backed Voice of America, Radio Liberty, and Radio Free Europe, the latter two funded by the Central Intelligence Agency (CIA), broadcast into the Eastern European states and the Soviet Union. From the East, the Soviet Union's Radio Moscow transmitted both domestically and internationally (Somerville, 2012: 56).

The Emergence of Film and Television in a Global Context: Programming Export, Television Systems, and Cable and Satellite Television

In the beginning of the twentieth century—prior to the First World War—US films were only dominant in Germany and Britain. In 1911, the main producers of US films had a presence in the UK, and US films had a 50 to 60 percent market share between 1910 and 1914. In contrast, Italian, French, and British film was popular throughout the European market. For example, around 1913, around one-third of films released in Germany were US produced, slightly less were from Italy, and around 20 percent of films in the German market were split between the UK and Germany (Segrave, 1997: 4). However, this was to change:

> When World War I began in August 1914, the U.S. Industry received the final impetus and advantage necessary to take control of the world film market. [...] [N]ew production was drastically receded throughout Europe. Shipping problems from Europe to other areas played havoc with what little product remained. Yet, exhibitors around the world needed product to fill their screens.
>
> (Segrave, 1997: 12)

In fact, between 1915 and 1916 the export of US films increased from 36 million feet of film to 159 million, while film imports to the United States was more than halved: from 16 million to 7 million feet by the mid-1920s. At the time, Hollywood took advantage of the increased popularity of the feature film format and exported to Asia and Latin America. As a consequence, US films were "almost wiping out Brazilian productions" (Miller and Maxwell, 2006: 36). The international expansion became institutionalized, so from 1919 income from foreign markets was included in the budget of Hollywood productions (Miller and Maxwell, 2006: 36). At the start of the 1920s, US films had conquered the world's cinemas, as national markets were destroyed by war:

> American movies clearly and totally dominated the world film market. There was nobody close enough to even be in the running for number two. All the former serious rivals had been decimated by the war. Such nations did not return to normal the day after hostilities ceased. Many more years were needed to reconstruct their societies; filmmaking was rarely a top priority.
>
> (Segrave, 1997: 18)

In the wake of the Second World War, as national cinema markets around the world were demolished or at least dramatically reduced, US film reestablished their dominance in world markets. By the late 1940s, US films had a dominant market share globally, and in 1949, they had over half the market share of the European and the Middle Eastern film market, nearly two-thirds of the South American film market, and as much as three-quarters of the Pacific, and Mexican and Central American film markets (Schatz, 1997: 303, referred to in Miller and Maxwell, 2006: 37).

The US film industry exploited the impact of the two World Wars on national film markets and the demand for film after these wars. However, the organization of the US film sector was also a major reason for the global presence of US films. Since the 1920s, the major film studios had been organized in cartels, and although these cartels were reorganized in subsequent decades, the industry is characterized by stability and an oligopolistic structure. In addition, the vertically integrated industrial organization and the size of the US market, along with various forms of support from US authorities and strong industry bodies, were key to cementing the historical and contemporary dominant position of the US film industry (Miller and Maxwell, 2006; Miller et al., 2005; Segrave, 1997).

Television was a "national-bound medium in its organization and regulation," and "each country developed its own national broadcasting structure" (Sinclair, 2012: 27). From the outset, there were three main television systems. Throughout the 1950s and 1960s, European countries established television services as part of existing public service regimes—either "directly or indirectly state-controlled" (2012: 27). The license fee–funded British public service broadcaster, BBC, and the Scandinavian public service broadcasters, for example, introduced television with no advertising, while the public service broadcasters in, for example, Spain and Finland supplemented public funding with advertising (Sinclair, 2012: 64; Syvertsen et al., 2014). In most of Asia, the Middle East, and Africa, television was launched by the state as "governments acted to ensure its role in controlling a powerful medium" (Straubhaar, 2007: 64). Only a few countries, such as Taiwan and South Korea, permitted private television channels, but these were co-owned and controlled by the state (Straubhaar, 2007: 64).

In the United States, commercial television emerged out of the commercial media model already established. The majority of Latin American countries "adopted the US's commercial model of broadcasting at an early stage, as distinct from the public service model instituted in most European countries" (Sinclair and Straubhaar, 2013: 1), many with technical assistance and television programming from US television operators (Sinclair, 2012: 27). The introduction of television in the media system is of key significance for media's role in society: "Television has differed crucially from music, film, radio, newspapers, and newer media in several crucial ways, some of which focus on the interest and the power of many nation-states to control or even own and operate television to ensure or at least pursue several key national goals" (Straubhaar, 2007: 61).

As newspapers and books were in the nineteenth century, and later radio, television was "a crucial medium to unify geographically and ethnically dispersed and diverse peoples into a sense of nationhood" (Straubhaar, 2007: 61). The national nature of broadcasting is in the case of public service broadcasters tied to their role of "nation-building," particularly in European countries. They were major media policy instruments that aimed to uphold cultural and linguistic diversity, while at the same time fostering a national arena for debate and the national distribution of culture and information outside of the influence of market forces (Straubhaar, 2007; Syvertsen et al., 2014). The political aim was therefore to utilize television to tie the nation's population together in "imagined communities" (Anderson, 1992). As such, since its inception, television has been regulated or controlled by national authorities in most parts of the world, in line with their political and ideological systems and goals.

US versus National: Production and Distribution of Television and Film Programming

Despite the differences in broadcasting systems, one key dynamic characterizes these systems and thereby the history of television across the world. This is the dichotomy between the national and the foreign, or more specifically, the export and distribution of US television programming globally, and the national and domestic production and distribution of television programming.

International television export began in the 1950s, between the UK and France, and prior to this, British films were shown in the United States. However, as within the film industry, the United States soon also became the key player within television programming. While the number of television sets in the United States outnumbered the rest of the world until 1962, that year there were more television sets outside the United States—53 million compared with 50 million in the United States. This development represents a shift in television history that propelled export of US programming:

> The need for imported programmes in the new television countries was more or less an artificial one, a product of the technology itself. Having introduced TV and made a large capital investment, countries felt obliged to make use of this equipment, which in turn created the need for foreign imported programmes. Limited funds and inexperience usually kept local production very low while

the more experienced and wealthy American producers took advantage of this opportunity to penetrate into foreign television.

(Nordenstreng and Varis, 1974: 31)

The export of US television and film programming intensified, as these imports were far less costly compared with domestically produced programming. In fact, toward the end of the 1960s and into the beginning of the 1970s, most countries imported the majority of television programming that were distributed domestically from the United States (Nordenstreng and Varis, 1974)

Still, while the United States' export increased throughout the 1970s, at the same time "a nationalization of programming swept a number of regions" (Straubhaar, 2007: 162). For example, from 1962 to 1972 in Latin America, nationally produced programs in prime time increased from 70 to 86 percent, and in Mexico from 63 to 68 percent. In the same period, both in Australia and the UK the share increased from 26 to 38 percent. In Hong Kong, the share increased from 23 to 64 percent, in South Korea from 73 to 80 percent, and in Japan from 81 to 95 percent. Still, the development was uneven: in Chile, for example, the share went from 63 to 54 percent, and in Italy from 99 to 79 percent (Straubhaar, 2007: 261).

In Brazil, from 1962 to 1972, the share of US-produced programs in prime time was reduced from 30 to 14 percent, while its total broadcast day share increased from 31 to 44 percent. In this period in Mexico, the US programming share in the total output was reduced from 38 to 26 percent and in the UK it increased from 13 to 14 percent. In Hong Kong, it was reduced from as much as 69 to 28 percent and in Taiwan from 36 to 21 percent, while in Japan it increased from 7 to 9 percent, and in Lebanon it increased from 23 to 41 percent.

While it was far cheaper to acquire imported television programming, especially for newly launched television channels, the point made here is that by the 1980s "studies began to show an increase in national productions in several parts of the world" (Straubhaar, 2007: 61). In addition, in many markets, "regional imports" were favored compared with American television programming. This was the case in Brazil, where television programming from within the region was scheduled in prime time. Still, at the time, the regionalization was not as strong in other regions. In several East Asian countries, after four decades of television, the import of US programming showed a "small but noticeable decrease," and increasingly came to include expensive television and film productions. In some African countries and in Europe, there was an increase in national television programming, particularly in prime time, but US imports "were still used heavily in key genres that were not widely produced nationally" (Straubhaar, 2007: 179).

The United States has dominated global sales of television, with an estimated 75 percent share by the end of the 1980s, and this continued throughout the 1990s within all television genres (DCMS, 1998: 41). Their dominant position in the global television programming market is explained by several competitive advantages:

- the multiplication of channels outside the United States, which greatly increases the demand for programming
- first-mover advantages in program development and marketing, abetted by the polyglot US audiences, which requires common-denominator programming readily acceptable in most foreign markets
- the worldwide trend toward an increased demand for the escapist fiction of the type long associated with the United States (Hoskins and McFadyen, 1991)
- the advantages of having a large home market
- the advantage of English as first language and production language
- the geographical clustering of production in Hollywood (Flew, 2013; Hoskins et al., 1997).

Historically, the dominant position of the United States within television export, then, has also to do with the increased demand for programming as television systems in many parts of the world went from being a "national, protected industry" to more deregulated and competitive television systems that were opened to "flows of capital and programming" (Waisbord, 2004: 360). The launch of globally expanding cable and satellite television channels was to further increase the demand for television programming.

Cable and Satellite Television in a Global Context

By the mid-1980s, cable and satellite channels began to challenge the terrestrial broadcasters, as: "Part of the Reagan administration's agenda was to *de*-regulate businesses and the media were no exception" (Croteau and Hoynes, 2001: 43). A number of technological, political and economic factors contributed to the changing of the media and communications sector. The traditional broadcasting networks' position gradually weakened as the expansion of cable, new video-delivery technology, as well as rapid VCR penetration increased the fragmentation of the American media audience (Owers and Wildman, 1992: 196; Litman, 1998: 137; Crandall, 1992: 211). These developments had a radical impact as

American broadcast networks saw their audience share slide from 90 percent to under 50 percent in the period from 1978 to 1997 (Owers et al., 1998: 35). In the early 2000s, the "big four" broadcasting networks, ABC, NBC, CBS and Fox, had an audience share of less than 50 percent, and were experiencing continuing decline (Croteau and Hoynes, 2006: 131). The US-originated cable and satellite channels and their owners had the "capital, corporate ethos, expertise and content library," needed to expand outside the US (Chalaby, 2002: 187).

In the 1980s and 1990s, national deregulation, privatization, and liberalization of cross border activity and ownership rules were the dominating trends in the European broadcast industry (Curran, 2002; Dahlgren, 2000; Tunstall and Machin, 1999). These developments opened up for an influx of US-originated cable and satellite television channels, as well as pan-European operators. Still, although cable and satellite technology did challenge the national terrestrial television systems all over the world, it proved difficult for the early pan-European and pan-Asian television services alike to become profitable (Sinclair, 2012). While the television operators, and global advertisers and advertising agencies saw the potential, they were faced with difficulties. In Europe, the cultural and linguistic diversity of the European television audience proved to be problematic for the early commercial pan-European operators. The pioneering pan-European satellite television channels Super Channel and Sky Channel in the 1980s experienced major difficulties in generating large enough advertising revenues (Collins, 1990). A key technological development was the splitting of video signals that allowed for the targeting of national markets within larger culturally and linguistically diverse regions. In Europe, pan-European television channels could increasingly insert programing and advertising for specific countries, in contrast to the whole European territory. This had consequences for both the media and the advertising industry that restructured to exploit opportunities for transnational advertising campaigns (Chalaby, 2009: 83).

The emergence of cable and satellite television channels throughout the 1980s and 1990s contributed to the transformation of the targeting of the television audience across the world regions. In contrast to mass advertising through national broadcasting, narrowcasting became a vehicle for reaching segments of the television audience. The cable and satellite television channels pioneered the targeting of global or pan-European and pan-regional segments of the national television audiences through localization (Chalaby, 2009). Furthermore, in for example the Nordic region, they also contributed to the liberalization of television and the abolishing of the public service broadcaster monopolies and the subsequent establishment of national commercial television channels funded mainly by advertising (Syvertsen et al. 2014). One of the consequences of the privatization and deregulation of television across the world was the dramatic increase in television channels and the subsequent strengthening of television's reliance on advertising funding (see Case Study 2.1).

In the 1990s, most of Latin American countries began to deregulate their economies. This came as a result of trade pacts such as NAFTA and MERCOSUR and included a gradual liberalization of restrictions on cable and satellite television and foreign ownership of media. Several major American media enterprises expanded into Latin America, either by collaborating with large local Latin American media companies, or through acquisitions of local media players. News Corporation's pan-regional satellite network Sky became allied with Televisa in Mexico and Globo in Brazil. The US-based satellite platform DirectTV bought local companies in both countries (Straubhaar and Duarte, 2005: 225; Sinclair, 2005: 201). In the early 2000s, the American media conglomerates Time Warner, Discovery Communications, News Corp, Viacom, and Disney had rolled out many of their global television channels in Latin America. However, despite the American presence, the large Latin American media groups such as Globo (Brazil), Televisa (Mexico), and Cisneros (Venezuela) offered competition. Their television channels offered a large amount of local programing, and television channels created by 'local and national cable systems' represented competition to the American players (Straubhaar and Duarte, 2005: 241–2).

In 1991, Indian television consisted of one channel, Doordarshan. A combination of the emergence of satellite distribution technology, a growing national economy, and gradual integration into the global market, coupled with an expanding middle class with money to spend, made India a particularly large and attractive market also for US-originated satellite television channels. In 1998, almost 70 cable and satellite television channels had been launched in India. Among these were the large media and television operators STAR, BBC, Discovery, MTV, Sony, and Disney (Thussu, 1999). In the early 2000s, India had become one of the largest television markets in the world and Discovery's television channels formed part of the total of the more than 300 digital channels operating in India (Thussu, 2006). Several of these channels were part of joint ventures and collaborations between Indian and large global and international media conglomerates. One of the significant partnerships was formed in 2002 when Sony Entertainment Television and Discovery formalized "The One Alliance"—a major television joint venture for distribution of television channels.

The television industry in Asian countries has been subject to similar transformations in the form of deregulation and privatization as seen in Latin

America and Europe. In the early 2000s, transnational corporations expanded into these new markets through collaborations and joint ventures with national and regional media companies (Jin, 2007: 193). Although global television channels have entered and consolidated their presence in most countries in South East Asia, mainland China has proved a more difficult territory to enter. News Corporation's Star TV entered China in 1996 via investments in the joint venture Phoenix TV. Since then, Star TV has expanded, and launched a 24-hour television entertainment channel, Xing Kong Wei Shi, in Guangdong. This was made possible partly due to News Corporation's distribution of China Central Television's English-language channel, CCTV 9, on Fox Cable Network in the USA (Chan, 2005: 181–2). Chinese authorities gradually reduced control over the media system: International satellite channels are, to a certain degree, allowed to broadcast into China, and international media enterprises can invest in the Chinese media industry under certain conditions (Jin, 2007). However, Shi points out that at the time "the direct, legalized access to global media like CNN or MTV is restricted either to some peripheral 'experimental zones' (Guangdong province) or to privileged locations (such as five-star hotels)" (Shi, 2005: 34).

In general, transnational television received less attention in Europe than elsewhere in the world. In the Middle East, satellite channels such as Al-Arabya (formerly MCB), contributed to improving news journalism and the independent Al-Jazeera "unsettled governments." In South Asia, the satellite television operations Zee TV and Star TV represented players that contributed to "sweeping cultural change and radical transformations in the television industry" (Chalaby, 2009: 43).

Case Study 2.1 Television Advertising in a Global Context

The relationship between media and communications and advertising and commercialization is key in driving the global expansion of the consumer goods and service industries, but also the media and communications industries themselves. Advertisers pay media and communications companies to bring advertising to their media audiences—that is, potential customers. The advertising revenue funds media operations and profit creation for the media companies, including a large share of their media content and services (Sinclair, 2012).

The selling of media audiences to advertisers has been a central activity since print media in the 1920s not only offered "circulation guarantees or willingly submitting to circulation audits, but were actively devising ways to sell themselves to advertisers" (Leiss et al., 2005: 127). In the 1940s, commercial television was introduced in the United States, but in contrast to newspaper advertising, the adoption of commercial television across the world was far more uneven. Still, television was to become the key media vehicle for internationalizing advertising in media. Of the three different television systems internationally—public service broadcasting, state-controlled broadcasting, and commercial television—the latter was, by the 1980s and 1990s, the most popular form of television around the world, regardless of the initial television system (Sinclair, 2012; Syvertsen et al., 2014).

A key development of the commercialization of television as well as other advertising-carrying media was the expansion of US-based advertising agencies. As American companies expanded internationally, so too did advertising agencies such as McCann Erickson and J. Walter Thompson. In response to the corporate expansion, these agencies created international networks of affiliates (Bamossy and Johansson, 2009: 374). In the 1980s and 1990s, both the media and advertising industry experienced major consolidation and mergers. Global media conglomerates were formed, and within the advertising companies "Holding companies with multiple subsidiaries were created by merging previously independent agencies, many with their own already established global networks" (Bamossy and Johansson, 2009: 376). This gave rise to the establishment of global media buying and media planning agencies, the former responsible for coordinating where advertising campaigns appears, and the latter for negotiating the cost of placing advertisements with media companies, that is, broadcasters and publishers (Chalaby, 2009: 87).

In an international media context, the emergence of cable and satellite television channels from the 1980s and 1990s and onwards played a key role in transforming the targeting of the television audience first in the United States and then in other world regions, and the internationalization of advertising. In contrast to mass advertising through national broadcasting, narrowcasting became a vehicle for reaching international segments of the national television audience (Chalaby, 2002; 2009; Mjøs, 2010).

Narrowcasters used specific television program genres and relied on language localization of the television programming to reach the preferred audience. While Disney Channel attracts the youngest television audience segments of national audiences through animation programming, it adapted and reshaped the factual television genre to attract a male audience aged twenty-five to forty-five years across the world (Mjøs, 2010). Errol Pretorius, director of advertising sales at the News Corp–controlled factual television outlet National Geographic Channel, highlights the logic of narrowcasting: "Don't count the people you talk to, talk to the people who count. I'd rather talk to a thousand people who can afford to buy a new Volvo, than talk to a million people who can't" (Pretorius, quoted in Chalaby, 2002: 201). The advertising industry adapted to pan-regional television and began "to offer flexible local advertising windows and integrated communication solutions involving cross-format and cross-platform opportunities for advertisers" (Chalaby, 2008).

In the early twenty-first century, television advertising continues to represent a major part of the global advertising market in the twenty-first century. However, the following chapters show how the advertising models of television have been increasingly challenged and recently overtaken by, the new advertising strategies of the online environment, which represents new forms of targeted advertising.

Global Television Genres

The US export of fiction television programing and films increased parallel to the proliferation of commercial television channels in Western Europe throughout the 1980s. The imported programing was cheaper to buy for these new channels than domestically produced programing. However, domestic programing has had a growing presence especially in prime time on broadcasters throughout Europe, as in other regions of the world. This shift is amongst others due to the development of stronger domestic production communities: "as markets have matured, mainstream channels have sought to raise their profile and ratings with domestically produced drama or entertainment formats in peak time" (Iosifidis, et al., 2005; Steemers, 2004: 150). However, despite the reduced presence of US television fiction on European television channels, it still represented the largest quantity of acquired fiction programming across the world. The imported US fiction genre was still cheaper than domestic production and continues to perform financially for the television channels also outside prime time (Iosifidis et al., 2005: 138). Furthermore, the US's capability to finance program series increases the possibility for sales overseas, as they can be scheduled on television networks throughout the week (Steemers, 2004: 43). Another underlying economic factor that helps explain the American dominance of the exports of television programing is Hollywood's ability to sell the bulk of television programing on the back of films. If television distributors or channels want to buy the most sought-after feature films, they may have to buy television programing that they are not necessarily interested in from the Hollywood studio or distributor. Throughout the 1990s "output deals" became more and more common. These deals involve a contractual agreement over several years between Hollywood studios and buyers to take all programing produced over a particular period, as well as older programing (Havens, 2006: 29).

Although fiction is historically the most exported genre, animation and factual television represented a significant part of the global program market. Animation programing travels particularly well across borders, as it is very visual and less dependent on language or culture. Animation television programing is expensive to produce, but the genre can be easily localized to different territories and television markets by dubbing animation characters (Artz, 2005: 80).

There are several explanations for the export of the factual television genre and its ability to cross borders. First, the increase in the global sales of both animation and the factual television genre was due to the growth of thematic cable and satellite television channels, and the two genres are "seen as uniquely suited for global trade because replacing the speech of animated characters or voice-over narrators causes less of a disturbance for viewers than dubbing or subtitling live actors" (Havens, 2006: 44). Second, while most of the factual television is produced for local distribution, certain forms of factual television programs have more potential for cross-national distribution than others: historically "Ageless 'uncontroversial' programmes dealing with natural history, wildlife and science are in most demand internationally" (Iosifidis et al., 2005: 142). Third, in contrast to television fiction, it may be difficult to identify which country some of these programs are made in, and this makes them more attractive internationally (Iosifidis et al., 2005: 143; see also Case Study 2.2).

Case Study 2.2 The Discovery Channel and the Factual Television Genre

Discovery Communications' first cable television channel, the Discovery Channel, was launched in the United States in 1985, offering documentary programming to 156,000 subscribers. In 1993, the founder and chairman of the company, John Hendricks, pronounced, "We hope to blanket the world by late 1995 or early 1996" (Hendricks, quoted in Brown, 1993: 38). Fronted by the Discovery Channel, the company began to expand worldwide, and into the 2000s its tier of factual television channels and media brands—for example, Discovery Channel, TLC, Animal Planet, Discovery Kids, Discovery Home &

Health, Investigation Discovery—reached hundreds of millions of viewers across the world.

Discovery Channel has had a pioneering role in cable and satellite narrowcasting of popularized factual television themes such as science, engineering, technology, archeology, and wildlife. Since its launch, the television channel has targeted a segment of the television audience—adults aged twenty-five to fifty-four, and particularly men—while other Discovery-owned television channels have targeted different viewer segments such as females and children (Discovery, 2015). In the 2000s, Discovery Channel began to distribute originally produced series that soon became popular across the world: *MythBusters*, *River Monsters*, *Gold Rush*, *American Chopper*, and *Deadliest Catch*. Furthermore, Discovery and BBC Worldwide, the commercial arm of BBC, have through the largest factual television deal in history spanning fifteen years—1998–2013—introduced the blockbuster logic to the factual genre by creating global factual cross-media brands such as the *Walking with ...* media brands, and the natural history series *Blue Planet*, *Planet Earth*, and *Frozen Planet*. At the time of the rapid international expansion of Discovery, the founder of Discovery Channel, John Hendricks, stated:

> [A] principle is to think globally and to act locally. The new technologies give us the chance to span the world and tie it together in ways never before imagined. The goal is not to export one culture in an effort to dominate and denigrate others. It is to showcase a mosaic of influences—to venerate the best of many cultures in hopes of forming a truly global culture. (Hendricks, 1996)

What does Discovery consider as "the best" and "global culture" since its worldwide expansion? One must assume that "the best" and "global culture" are chosen according to the Discovery Channel's program policy and its targeted audience. The company has described itself in the following way: "Discovery produces content that appeals to a global audience, working across dozens of languages and cultures. We augment our global content with local productions and customized programming to increase relevancy and reach" (Discovery, 2015).

Although Discovery Channel emerged as a major global provider of factual information, the programs' accounts of the real world have a defined focus. This has also included a notion of "government-friendliness" (Hendricks, quoted in Thal Larsen, 2003: 8), and a certain limit of critical portrayal of the real world in many programs. However, this gives the global television channel a crucial ability to cross cultural, political, and religious boundaries unhindered. There is a certain presence of entertainment in Discovery Channel's programming represented by the spectacular: the biggest, the most dangerous, the heaviest, and so on. This indicates that—on one level—"the best of many cultures in hopes of forming a truly global culture" involves the worldwide search for the spectacular stories and themes in various forms and contexts, although within a certain scope of the real world.

There has been a tendency for the *spectacular* to serve as a connection between the local and the global. The television channel has attempted to target a global audience segment, in which the local in this context represents a segment of the national television audience. The Discovery Channel have thereby attempted to appeal to the preferences of a local *and* global audience through its form of factual television (Mjøs, 2010).

Geocultural Markets, Diaspora, and Contra-flows

While the United States dominated television programming export, a number of countries, such as Brazil, Mexico, China, Hong Kong, and South Korea, became centers of production and regional distribution strongholds with a presence in the global television market. For example, Japan became a considerable exporter of animation, Hong Kong made its mark within the action-adventure genre, and China, the UK, Japan, and Hong Kong produce various forms of historical drama. Australia is a significant producer and exporter of serial dramas (soap operas) (Straubhaar, 2007: 180; Flew, 2013).

In the mid-1990s, Sinclair et al., (1996) pointed out how the regionalization of television production and distribution through "geocultural" or "geolinguistic" markets can in many ways be seen as a counterweight to the influx of US export. Such geocultural markets had production centers such as Mexico and Brazil for Latin America, Hong Kong for the Chinese-speaking parts of the populations throughout Asia, Egypt for the Arab world, and India for the Indian populations in Africa and Asia (Hesmondhalgh, 2019: 383–4; Sinclair et al., 1996). There was an increased awareness of how cultural, linguistic, and societal commonalities developed over time: "define cultural markets, to which television responds. Populations defined by these kinds of characteristics tend to seek out cultural products, such as television programs or music, that are most similar or proximate to them" (Straubhaar, 2007: 43). Sinclair et al. pointed out how "satellite distribution has opened up regional and transcontinental geolinguistic markets" that also secured "distribution of television products to diasporic communities, notably those of Chinese, Arab, and Indian origin" (1996: 23). These are ethnic communities that are spread throughout the world. As such, these geocultural and geolinguistic markets extend across the world and consist of geographically dispersed people (Hesmondhalgh, 2019: 383–4).

In the early 1990s, the concept of "contra-flow" aimed to further show the nuances and explain the complexities of the global media and communications landscape (Boyd Barrett and Thussu, 1992; Thussu, 2006). It referred to how a deregulated television industry, digital technology, and increasingly affordable satellite television distribution facilitated flows of media content from the South to the West and other parts of the world. As such, the global media landscape is not just characterized by the dominant flows from the West and the United States in particular. The media industries in China, Japan, South Korea, Brazil, and India are key contributors to these contra-flows (Thussu, 2006: 23).

Still, by 2007, as much as 76 percent of the global market for "ready-to-air" programming was made by US producers, with the UK following with 7 percent (Steemers, 2014). However, we see how both cultural and financial factors have influenced the attractiveness of the various television genres within the global television program market. Buyers and television channel executives will consider the appeal and costs of an imported program in comparison to the appeal and costs of a program produced domestically (Havens, 2006: 44).

While the global trade and distribution of television programming was long characterized by "ready-to-air" programming, from the late 1990s a genre that had existed in the margins of the television trade since the 1950s began to revolutionize the television industry. *Big Brother, Idols, Survivor,* and *Who Wants to Be a Millionaire?* were the "super-formats" that drove the popularity of the television format (Chalaby, 2012: 37). The programming form is in essence "a show based in the format rights of an existing show, that is, a *remake produced under licence*" (Chalaby, 2016: 8). What distinguishes television formats from traditional ready-made television programming is their ability to insert local or national cultural content into a defined and copyrighted concept: "Domestic producers can incorporate local color and global audiences can paradoxically feel at home when watching them. Locality needs to be evicted so it can be reintroduced as long as it does not alter the basic concept" (Waisbord, 2004: 378). The impact of television formats on the television industry was considerable due to their ability to travel across the world both through standardizing and localizing. Their characteristics and logic are of particular interest in a global perspective (see Case Study 4.1).

As we move further into the twenty-first century, we see increased internationalization as media economies are maturing, and an increase in television production and distribution within and between world regions and countries (Thussu, 2021; Thussu and Nordenstreng, 2021; Thussu, de Burgh and Shi, 2018). This development will also be further explored in the following chapters.

The popularization of the internet is also a key driver of the internationalization of television. The distribution of television content online, Lobato argues, "changes the fundamental logics though which television travels, introducing new mobilities and immobilities" (Lobato, 2019: 5). The point is that "Internet television does not replace legacy television in a straightforward way; instead it adds new complexity to the existing geography of distribution." Lobato argues that despite the global trade of programming, prior to the internet, "television distribution did not yet have a strongly transnational dimension" (Lobato, 2019: 5).

To understand the internet's role in shaping not only the professional television industry but the very global media and communications landscape, we need to first examine the internet's formative development in the context of global media and communications into the twenty-first century.

The Emergence of the Internet in the Context of Global Media and Communications

Parallel to the development of a commercial cable and satellite television market in the mid-1990s, the Internet drew increased attention for its commercial potential (McStay, 2016). Throughout the 1990s, media conglomerates spent enormous sums of money on various Internet ventures and entities. At the turn of the millennium, most of these investments proved to be far less lucrative than initially thought. The dotcom bubble burst, as the unrealistically high value of internet-based enterprises plummeted. Similarly, such "speculative boom(s)" have been observed throughout history from tulipomania in the Netherlands in the 1630s to financial crashes on Wall Street. Such crashes are the result of "speculative investment [that] has risen like a rocket and come down again like a stick" (Lister et al., 2009: 188). This was certainly the case with numerous internet-based companies or dotcoms as the technology-heavy US Nasdaq stock exchange, in which many such companies were listed, rose and dropped at dramatic speed.

Perhaps the most spectacular casualty of the dotcom crash was AOL's (formerly America Online) acquisition of Time Warner. The internet service provider AOL bought the traditional media conglomerate Time Warner for more than

$150 billion in 2000. This deal became a symbol of the new era as it represented the merger of the "new" and the "old" as underlined by Stephen M. Case, a co-founder of AOL: "This is a historic moment in which new media has truly come of age" (quoted in Arango, 2010). However, as the dotcom bubble burst, the value of the new company AOL Time Warner diminished at dramatic speed (Arango, 2009). Again, in hindsight, some argue that the merger between AOL and Time Warner was "driven by the manoeuvres of the financial markets" and not the demands among the media audience and consumers: "Despite looking like the Holy Grail this particular example of corporate convergence became more of a poisoned chalice—falling victim at least in part to the disillusion with digital media that followed the dotcom crash" (Lister et al., 2009: 204).

Media conglomerates, then, were not untouched by these developments. These internet investments were partly to blame for the subsequent reorganization of companies like AOL Time Warner and Vivendi (Curran and Seaton, 2010: 271). The enthusiasm for the internet and the subsequent dotcom bubble and crash has numerous historical parallels. Key events in the development of the transport sector such as the railways in the 1850s and later the arrival of cars in the 1920s "were both followed by horrific stock market collapses in the US, but neither railways nor automobiles went away" (Hartley, 2002: 77, 78). In the long run, then, many predicted that the technological innovations underpinning the development of the Internet will result in a viable industry sector (2002: 78). Similarly, Klaus Schwab, founder of the World Economic Forum, argued around the time of the dotcom crash that information communication technologies had much promise for businesses, but also societal development:

> Animated discussion of the economic miracle heralded by information and communication technologies (ICTs) was ubiquitous in the late 1990s. Yet as the dust settles upon the era of the "new economy," and as the wilder claims regarding the resurgent power of new technologies die down, it is nevertheless clear that ICTs have become one of the key factors in all modern economies. Policymakers and business leaders increasingly recognize the need to create an enabling environment to support the development and adoption of technologies across all sectors. […] ICTs can help countries fulfill their national potential and enable a better quality of life for their citizens. (Klaus Schwab, quoted in World Economic Forum, 2002: ix)

Still, it is worth reflecting on some of the reasons why the dotcom crash took place. In hindsight commentators point out that throughout the 1990s and beginning of the 2000s, some investment funds tempted customers with 100 percent returns on investments. However, such "promise was based on little more than enthusiasm and technophilic passion—very few direct consumer service providers were able to demonstrate that their sites could actually maintain secure income streams" (Lister et al., 2009: 188). Furthermore, people began to realize that the development of "net retailing" would take both time and considerable investment, in contrast to the speculative approach that led to the dotcom crash in 2000 and 2001 (Curran and Seaton, 2010: 271). Some even pointed to this at the time of the dotcom boom: "What makes many internet company valuations baffling for seasoned observers is that many have yet to make a profit, and show little sign of ever doing so" (Hunt, 1999). While the hopes were high in the early phase of Internet development, the challenge for commercial ventures and companies was how to generate revenue and profit.

While the main task for marketers and advertisers remained the same as with all advertising—to get the audience to buy products or services—the online milieu represented something more, marketing people claimed:

> The new interactive arsenal would accommodate new ways to separate people into different lists according to lifestyles they expressed in viewing and computer use. One consultant exhorted marketers that "hundreds of thousands of names and addresses are floating on the internet, waiting to be listed, organized, sliced and diced." After all, he pointed out, "the internet is essentially one giant agglomeration of special interests." (Turow, 1997: 175)

However, the main challenges were to locate and reach the growing number of Internet users with targeted advertisements and other commercial messages and thereby monetize them to create a viable and stable commercial online environment. In fact, a technological invention introduced as early as 1994 was key to creating an online environment in which media content and services, websites owners, advertisers and the users are connected (see Case Study 2.3).

Case Study 2.3 Cookies—Connecting Users, Advertising, and Online Services

A technology called "cookie" was created in 1994 and introduced in the Netscape internet browser the same year (Schwartz, 2001; Elmer, 2004). This technology enabled the collection of data on parts of users' online activity. Cookies were therefore considered key in commercializing the online environment and in developing an audience that could be sold to, for example, advertisers. Today, cookies and related technologies are underpinning and facilitating growth in Internet advertising, and for online services like social media.

Cookies and related technology contributed to creating "a relatively stable platform for interactions" between users and the owners or controllers of a website. This meant that the cookies helped in "identifying repeat visitors to their websites" (Elmer, 2004: 118), and subsequently enabled the mapping of user activity and data that again facilitated the increased targeting of advertising and other commercial messages to individual users across borders. Still, the technology thereby also: "fundamentally challenge[d] the ability of users to remain anonymous on the Net" (Elmer, 2004: 118).

Cookies caused significant controversy, not least since companies controlling the web browsers Netscape and Microsoft (who owned Internet Explorer) "neglected to make public the use of cookie technology in 1995 and early 1996" (Elmer, 2004: 119). By informing the public about this technology from the outset, one could have avoided some of the criticism at the outset, and the continuing suspicion of the cookies technology (Elmer, 2004: 119). Law scholar and activist Lawrence Lessig claimed that the consequences of cookies have been devastating for the privacy of internet users. While the Web was "essentially private" prior to the launch and implementation of cookies, after the arrival of this technology, it has been turned into "a space capable of extraordinary monitoring" (Lessig, quoted in Schwartz, 2001). Similarly, others considered cookies as "one of the most common examples of on-line surveillance" as the technology allowed for the registration of "how users surf the internet, which websites they visit, how long they spend in a particular site, and which links they use" (Molz, 2006: 380).

It is clear that cookies and related technologies have opened up for controversial practices. Already at the beginning, it was difficult to detect the cookies at work, but one of the most noticeable ways in which this technology affects online use is when users try to obstruct them. Often, if users try to block cookies, they will not be able to fully use or even be prevented from accessing websites. The web browser and the cookie have enabled the "automating" of the gathering of information of Internet users. If users try to deny the "software's use of cookies," the user may be prevented from using various services and functions (Elmer, 2004: 112).

Throughout the twenty-first century, social media services and search engines have pioneered the utilization of such technologies to increase observation of media users and searches made by individuals, to develop ever more customized and individualized targeted marketing practices. The next chapter explores the popularization of the internet and digital communications technologies and the rise of internet-based services.

References

Arango, T. (2009) US media see a path to India in China's snub. *New York Times*, May 3. http://www.nytimes.com/2009/05/04/business/media/04media.html (accessed May 4, 2009).

Arango, T. (2010) How the AOL-Time Warner merger went so wrong. *New York Times*, January 11. http://www.nytimes.com/2010/01/11/business/media/11merger.html (accessed October 26, 2010).

Anderson, B. (1992) *Imagined Communities*. London: Verso.

Artz, L. (2005) Monarchs, Monsters, and Multiculturalism: Disney's Menu for Global Hierarchy, pp. 75–99 in M. Budd and M. H. Og Kirsch (eds.) *Rethinking Disney: Private Control, Public Dimensions*. Middletown, CT: Wesleyan University Press.

Bamossy, G. J. and Johansson, J. K. (2009) Global Communication, pp. 374–97 in M. Katobe and K. Helsen (eds.) *The SAGE Handbook of International Marketing*. London: SAGE.

Boyd-Barrett, O. (1998) "Global" News Agencies, pp. 19–34 in O. Boyd-Barrett and T. Rantanen (eds.) *The Globalization of News*. London: SAGE.

Boyd-Barrett, O. and Thussu, D. K. (1992) Contra-flow in Global News: International and Regional News Exchange Mechanisms. London: Published in association with UNESCO by J. Libbey.

Brown, R. (1993) New frontiers for Discovery: Network will expand original production as it reaches new outlets in Latin America, America, Europe and Asia. *Broadcasting & Cable*, 123, 40: 38–9.

Chalaby, J. K. (2002) Transnational television in Europe—the role of pan-European channels. *European Journal of Communication*, 17, 2: 183–203.

Chalaby, J. K. (2008) Advertising in the global age: Transnational campaigns and pan-European television channels. *Global Media and Communication*, 4, 2: 139–56.

Chalaby, J. K. (2009) *Transnational Television in Europe: Reconfiguring Global Communications Networks*. London: I. B. Tauris.

Chalaby, J. K. (2012) At the origin of a global industry: The TV format trade as an Anglo-American invention. *Media, Culture & Society*, 34, 1: 37–53.

Chalaby, J. K. (2016) *The Format Age: Television's Entertainment Revolution*. Cambridge, UK: Polity.

Chan, J. M. (2005) Trans-border Broadcasters and TV Regionalization in Greater China: Processes and Strategies, pp. 172–95 in J. K. Chalaby (ed.) *Transnational Television Worldwide: Towards a New Media Order*. London: I. B. Tauris.

Collins, R. (1990) *Satellite Television in Western Europe*. London: John Libbey.

Crandall, R. W. (1992) Cable Television, pp. 211–59 in B. Owen and S. Steven (eds.), *Video Economics*. Cambridge, MA: Harvard University Press.

Croteau, D. and Hoynes, W. (2001) *The Business of Media: Corporate Media and the Public Interest*. First edition. Thousand Oaks, CA: Pine Forge Press.

Croteau, D. and Hoynes, W. (2006) *The Business of Media: Corporate Media and the Public Interest.* Second edition. Thousand Oaks, CA: Pine Forge Press.

Curran, J. (2002) *Media and Power.* London: Routledge.

Curran, J. and Seaton, J. (2010) *Power without Responsibility.* Seventh edition. Abingdon, UK: Routledge.

Dahlgren, P. (2000) Key Trends in European Television, pp. 23–34 in J. Wieten, G. Murdock, and P. Dahlgren (eds.) *Television across Europe—A Comparative Introduction.* London: SAGE.

DCMS (1998) *The Report of the Creative Industries Task Force Inquiry into Television Exports.* Department for Culture, Media and Sport, Creative Industries Programme. March 20.

Discovery (2015) *30 Years of Bringing You the World: 2014 Annual Report.* Silver Spring, MD: Discovery Communications, inc. https://corporate.discovery.com/wp-content/uploads/2015/07/disca2014_download.pdf (accessed May 26, 2022).

Elmer, G. (2004) *Profiling Machines: Mapping the Personal Information Economy.* Cambridge, MA: MIT Press.

Flew, T. (2013) *Global Creative Industries.* Cambridge, UK: Polity.

Hartley, J. (2002) *Communication, Cultural and Media Studies: The Key Concepts.* Third edition. London: Routledge.

Havens, T. (2006) *Global Television Marketplace.* London: BFI.

Hendricks, J. (1996) The Worldview Address. Edinburgh International Television Festival, August 4.

Herman, E. S. and McChesney, R. (1997) *The Global Media: The New Missionaries of Corporate Capitalism.* London: Cassell.

Hesmondhalgh, D. (2019) *The Cultural Industries.* Fourth edition. London: SAGE.

Hoskins, C. and McFadyen, S. (1991) The US competitive advantage in the global television market: Is it sustainable in the new broadcasting environment? *Canadian Journal of Communication,* 16, 2. https://doi.org/10.22230/cjc.1991v16n2a602

Hoskins, C., McFadyen, S., and Finn, A. (1997) *Global Television and Film: An Introduction to the Economics of the Business.* Oxford: Clarendon Press.

Hunt, A. (1999) Stockmarkets: A crash to come? *BBC News,* December 30. http://news.bbc.co.uk/2/hi/business/582792.stm (accessed May 12, 2022).

Iosifidis, P., Steemers, J., and Wheeler, M. (2005) *European Television Industries.* London: BFI.

Jin, D. Y. (2007) Transformation of the world television system under neoliberal globalization, 1983 to 2003. *Television & New Media,* 8, 3: 179–96.

Leiss, W., Kline, S., Jhally, S., and Botteril, J. (2005) *Social Communication in Advertising Consumption in the Mediated Marketplace.* Third edition. New York: Routledge.

Lister, M., Dovey, J., Giddings, S., Grant, I., and Kelly, K. (2009) *New Media: A Critical Introduction.* Second edition. London: Routledge.

Litman, B. R. (1998) The Economics of Television Networks: New Dimension and New Alliances, pp. 131–50 in A. Alexander, J. Owers, and R. Carveth (eds.) *Media Economics: Theory and Practice.* Second edition. Mahwah NJ: Lawrence Erlbaum.

Lobato, R. (2019) *Netflix Nations: The Geography of Digital Distribution*. New York: New York Press.

McStay, A. (2016) *Digital Advertising*. Second edition. London: Palgrave.

Miller, T. and Maxwell, R. (2006) Film and Globalization, pp. 33–52 in O. Boyd-Barrett (ed.) *Communications Media, Globalization, and Empire*. London: John Libbey.

Miller, T., Govil, N., McMurria, J., Maxwell, R., and Wang, T. (2005) *Global Hollywood 2*. London: British Film Institute.

Mjøs, O. J. (2010) *Media Globalization and the Discovery Channel Networks*. London: Routledge.

Molz, J. G. (2006) "Watch us wander": Mobile surveillance and the surveillance of mobility. *Environment and Planning A*, 38, 2: 377–93.

Nordenstreng, K. and Varis, T. (1974) *Television Traffic, a One Way Street? A Survey and Analysis of the International Flow of Television Programmes Material*. UNESCO Reports and Papers on Mass Communication 70. Paris: UNESCO.

Owers, B. M. and Wildman, S. S. (1992) *Video Economics*. Cambridge, MA: Harvard University Press.

Owers, J., Carveth, R., and Alexander, A. (1998) An Introduction to Media Economics Theory and Practice, pp. 1–44 in A. Alexander, J. Owers, and R. Carveth (eds.), *Media Economics: Theory and Practice*. Second edition. Mahwah, NJ: Lawrence Erlbaum.

Schatz, T. (1997) *History of the American Cinema, Vol. 6: Boom and Bust: American Cinema in the 1940s*. New York: Charles Scribner's Sons.

Schwartz, J. (2001) Giving web a memory cost its users privacy. *New York Times*, September 8. https://www.nytimes.com/2001/09/04/business/giving-web-a-memory-cost-its-users-privacy.html (accessed June 21, 2022).

Segrave, K. (1997) *American Films Abroad: Hollywood's Domination of the World's Movie Screens from the 1890s to the Present*. Jefferson, NC: McFarland.

Shi, A. (2005) The taming of the shrew: Global media in a Chinese perspective. *Global Media & Communication*, 1, 1: 33–6.

Sinclair, J. (2005) International television channels in the Latin American audiovisual space, pp. 196–215 in J. K. Chalaby (ed.) *Transnational Television Worldwide: Towards a New Media Order*. London: I. B. Tauris.

Sinclair, J. (2012) *Advertising, the Media and Globalization: A World in Motion*. London: Routledge.

Sinclair, J. and Straubhaar, J. D. (2013) *Latin American Television Industries*. London: British Film Institute/Palgrave MacMillan.

Sinclair, J., Jacka, E., and Cunningham, S. (1996) *New Patterns in Global Television*. Oxford: Oxford University Press.

Somerville, K. (2012) *Radio Propaganda and the Broadcasting of Hatred: Historical Development and Definitions*. London: Palgrave Macmillan.

Steemers, J. (2004) *Selling Television: British Television in the Global Marketplace*. London: BFI.

Steemers, J. (2014) Selling television: Addressing transformations in the international distribution of television content. *Media Industries*, 1, 1: 44–9.

Straubhaar, J. D. (2007) *World Television: From Global to Local*. Los Angeles: SAGE.

Straubhaar, J. D. and Duarte, L. G. (2005) Adapting US Transnational Television Channels to a Complex World: From Cultural Imperialism to Localization to Hybridization, pp. 216–53 in J. K. Chalaby (ed.) *Transnational Television Worldwide: Towards a New Media Order*. London: I. B. Tauris.

Syvertsen, T., Enli, G., Mjøs, O. J., and Moe, H. (2014) *The Media Welfare State: Nordic Media in the Digital Era*. Ann Arbor, MI: University of Michigan Press.

Thal Larsen, P. (2003) Taking on the real world. *Financial Times*, September 23, pp. 8–9.

Thussu, D. K. (1999) Privatizing the airwaves: The impact of globalization on broadcasting in India. *Media, Culture & Society*, 21, 1: 125–31.

Thussu, D. K. (2006) *Media on the Move: Global Flow and Contra-flow*. London: Routledge.

Thussu, D. K (2021) BRICS De-Americanizing the Internet? pp. 280–301 in D. K. Thussu and K. Nordenstreng (eds.) *BRICS Media: Reshaping the Global Communication Order?* Abingdon, UK: Routledge.

Thussu, D. K. and Nordenstreng, K. (2021) Introduction, pp. 1–19 in D. K. Thussu and K. Nordenstreng (eds.) *BRICS Media: Reshaping the Global Communication Order?* Abingdon, UK: Routledge.

Thussu, D. K., de Burgh, H., and Shi, A. (eds.) (2018) *China's Media Go Global*. New York: Routledge.

Tunstall, J. and Machin, D. (1999) *The Anglo-American Media Connection*. Oxford: Oxford University Press.

Turow, J. (1997) *Breaking Up America: Advertisers and the New Media World*. Chicago: University of Chicago Press.

Waisbord, S. (2004) McTV: Understanding the global popularity of television formats. *Television & New Media*, 5, 4: 359–83.

Winseck, D. R. and Pike, R. M. (2007) *Communication and Empire: Media, Markets and Globalization*. Durham, NC: Duke University Press.

Woods, J. (1992) *The History of International Broadcasting*. London: Peter Peregrinus.

World Economic Forum (2002) *The Global Information Technology Report 2001–2002: Readiness for the Networked World*. New York: Oxford University Press.

3

The Popularization and Consolidation of the Global Online Environment

The Internet, Social Media, and Search Engines

This chapter looks at the emergence and consolidation of a global online environment and the expansion of key online companies and services dominating this landscape in the twenty-first century. The chapter explains how this environment functions through advertising and monetization of users, and discusses the players that are driving this development. These include both media and communications hardware and the major services for online communication, navigation and search, and content distribution.

A number of factors contributed to the global popularization of the online environment. Personal computers became cheaper and more powerful, an ever larger part of the world's population have access to the internet, and the capacity for transferring and distributing digitized media content and communication increased dramatically. Smartphones and other handheld digital devices enabled mobile internet, and the possibility for monetizing online users, digital advertising, services and media distribution created viable online business models and major financial investment opportunities.

A number of new forms of internet-based media and communications companies and services have emerged, but search engines and social media represent perhaps the two online phenomena that have had the most significant impact in developing the global online landscape. The former revolutionized search within the online environment, while the latter enabled unprecedented communication and distribution of media content. Both generate enormous revenues and make inroads into the national advertising markets across the world. Both have turned their operations into platforms that expand into new services and spheres in society. Increasingly, private, corporate, public, and civic life is dependent on—and influenced by—a few, dominating online platforms.

The Digital Infrastructure

In 2021, the number of individual internet users globally increased to an estimated 4.9 billion—around 63 percent of the world's population. This is an increase of 800 million since 2019. Still, around 2.9 billion of the world's population are not using the internet—of which 96 percent are living in the developing world (International Telecommunication Union [ITU], 2021a).

The connecting of broadband, mobile telephony, and the internet have—in addition to facilitating new possibilities for communication—given rise to numerous new audiovisual distribution possibilities through video-on-demand, online video streaming, and downloading of professional as well as user-generated media content. Coupled with deregulation of national television sectors, the privatization of state monopolies, and commercialization of the satellite industry, a key process both driving and resulting from the transformations within the media and communications landscape is *convergence* (Castells, 2013; Iosifidis, 2011; ITU, 2021; Thussu, 2010; Thussu and Nordenstreng, 2021). At a basic level, convergence refers to the "merging of the computing (information technology), broadcasting print and telecommunications sectors" (Iosifidis, 2011: 170). Technology development has enabled, for example, broadcasting and telecommunication to create cable networks to distribute television, and digitization and the internet have "accelerated the scope of convergence potential" (2011: 169).

In fact, there are at least four different levels of convergence of particular significance for the field of international and global media. First, *technological convergence* refers to the digitization of a whole media and communications industry. The creation of digital content, infrastructure, software, and hardware such as handheld devices contribute to this process. Second, *structural and industry convergence* refers to the consequences of collaboration, mergers, and joint ventures between and across previously separate parts and sectors, and traditional media companies and new digital and online players. Third, *producer-consumer convergence* refers to shifting audience and user patterns, and that "everyone" can "become a publisher or producer" (Iosifidis, 2011: 183).

There is also a fourth level of convergence: the consensus among public and private stakeholders that media and information and communications technologies (ICT) are key for societal progress and development. There is a powerful and persuasive argument for the centrality of information and communications technologies in the development of the world society—also increasingly expressed throughout the twenty-first century by supranational bodies such as the World Trade Organization (WTO) and the International Telecommunications Union (ITU):

ICTs have the potential to make the world a much better place – in particular for those who are the poorest and the most disenfranchised, including women, youth, and those with disabilities.

(ITU Secretary-General Dr. Hamadoun I. Touré, quoted in ITU, 2014)

Telecommunications are an essential prerequisite for a wide range of economic activities in any national economy, developing or developed, from agriculture, travel and tourism to mining and manufacturing. Opening telecommunications has been a win-win game," said Mr. Lamy.

(Pascal Lamy, Director-General WTO, 2008)

These four types of convergence have been key in driving change, developing and consolidating a global media and communications landscape. However, there are regional differences in how these developments take place across the world. This will be explored further in the next part of the chapter.

Globalizing Internet Access and Mobile Broadband

Throughout the twenty-first century, the increase in mobile broadband access in the developing world has been formidable. By 2021, more than 95 percent of the world's population have access to a mobile-broadband network, and nearly 88 percent have access to 4G networks (see Table 3.1).

Table 3.1 Global Population Coverage by Mobile Network, 2021 (%)

	4G	3G	2G
World	88	7	2
Developed	99		1
Developing	85	9	2
Europe	99		1
The Americas	92	4	
CIS	91	3	4
Arab States	70	25	2
Africa	49	33	7
Asia-Pacific	96	1	1

Source: ITU, 2021b.

Note: The values of 2G and 3G networks show the incremental percentage of population that is not covered by a more advanced technology network (e.g. 95% or the world population is covered by a 3G network, that is 7% + 88%).

However, there are still differences in terms of access between countries and within countries and continents. For example, only 49 percent of the population of Africa has access to 4G compared to 99 percent in the developed part of the world, and 18 percent of the population still do not have access to a mobile broadband network. In terms of broadband access, major "connectivity gaps" persist in rural areas. Practically all urban parts of the world have mobile broadband connections, but this is not the case in rural areas. By 2021, over 97 percent of global households in urban areas had access to 4G, compared with 75 percent in the rural parts of the world. In the urban part of Africa 88 percent of the population had access to 4G. In contrast, in the rural part of the African continent only 21 percent had 4G access and 50 percent had access to 3G networks, 11 percent had only access to 2G mobile networks, while 18 percent of the rural population did not have mobile network coverage. This means that close to 30 percent of the rural population on the African continent did not have access to the internet (ITU, 2021b). The differences in mobile network and internet access across the world were accentuated during the Covid-19 pandemic, prompting Houlin Zhao, the secretary-general of the UN organization ITU, to argue, "In the age of COVID-19, where so many are working and studying from home [...] accelerating infrastructure roll-out is one of the most urgent and defining issues of our time" (ITU, 2020b).

Growth in smartphone sales runs parallel to growth in mobile-broadband access. This market has been characterized by the expansion of Asian producers, and increasingly Chinese companies. In 2013, China became the world's largest smartphone market and by 2020, three of the top five mobile phone producers were Chinese (see Tables 3.2 and 3.3; Gartner, 2021a).

The Covid-19 pandemic is considered to be the reason for the drop in sales in 2020, but according to Gartner, a global research and advisory company, strong growth was expected from 2021. In fact, global sales of smartphones increased by

Table 3.2 Global Mobile Phone Producers—Market Share (%)

	2020	2019
Samsung	18.8	19.2
Apple	14.8	12.6
Huawei	13.5	15.6
Xiaomi	10.8	8.2
OPPO	8.3	7.7
Others	33.7	36.7

Source: Adapted from Gartner, 2021a.

Table 3.3 Global Mobile Phone Producers—Sales (Thousands of Units)

	2020	**2019**
Samsung	253,025	296,124
Apple	199,847	193,475
Huawei	182,610	240,615
Xiaomi	145,802	126,049
OPPO	111,785	118,693
Others	454,799	565,630
Total	1,347,869	1,540,657

Source: Adapted from Gartner, 2021a.

Table 3.4 Worldwide Smartphone Sales by Region, 2020–1 (Millions of Units)

	2020	**2021**
Eastern Europe	42,960	49,364
Emerging Asia-Pacific	336,897	365,891
Eurasia	43,473	47,261
Greater China	368,016	409,968
Latin America	116,301	134,349
Mature Asia-Pacific	26,311	30,457
Middle East & North Africa	71,477	79,112
North America	136,257	151,750
Sub-Saharan Africa	84,440	94,293
Western Europe	125,430	142,796
Japan	27,159	30,118

Source: Adapted from Gartner, 2021a.

as much as 26 percent in the first quarter of 2021 year over year, and 10 percent in the second quarter of 2021 (See Table 3.4; Gartner, 2021a; 2021b; 2021c).

As 5G networks expand across the world, increasing the market share of the total wireless infrastructure revenue fast, the sales of 5G smartphones are expected to follow, parallel to this development (Gartner, 2021d).

The smartphone is at the center of global media and communications in the twenty-first century. Its development has been rapid, and it has revolutionized how we use the mobile phone for media and communications, but increasingly other services such as finance, health, and education. In many ways, the smartphone epitomizes the unpredictable consequences of convergence, but at the same time should also be seen as a key driving force in the processes associated with convergence (see Case Study 3.1 and Case Study 3.2).

Case Study 3.1 The Rise and Fall of Nokia—Once the World's Largest Mobile Phone Producer

Nokia, once the world's market leader in sales of mobile telephones, exemplifies the speed of product development, competition, and volatility within the media and communications industry. In the mid-1990s, Nokia made a decision that was to transform the company. Nokia's decision to consider the mobile telephone as a consumer product and produce phones with fashionable and personalized features revolutionized mobile telephony worldwide. The Nokia 2100 series was the first phone to feature the characteristic Nokia tune ringtone, and while expected to sell 400,000 units, actually sold 20 million units. In 1998, the company produced new models monthly and in that year became the market leader in sales of mobile telephones, taking the top spot from Motorola (Andersson, 2000; Monaghan, 2013; Peters, 1992; Syvertsen et al., 2014). Although experiencing a drop in sales, the company maintained a 35 percent share of the global mobile phone market in 2004 and sold its billionth mobile phone in Nigeria in 2005 (Monaghan, 2013). However, the launch of Apple's iPhone in 2007 represented a surprising development for Nokia:

> While the Finnish mobile phone company had benefitted from a "first-mover advantage" in the late 1990s and early 2000s, this advantage was lost with the increasing dominance of smartphones. Smartphones provided online access and were therefore able to transfer pictures and video, display maps, and play music and radio. Not least, Nokia's setback was a result of Apple's launch of the first iPhone in 2007, which made the US company the market leader.
>
> (Syvertsen et al., 2014: 114)

As the then Finnish company's executive vice-president for mobile telephones pointed out, "if you go back a few years, the market changed suddenly, and we were not fast enough changing with it" (Oistamo, quoted in Ramnarayan, 2009). The arrival of smartphones revolutionized the mobile phone market and integrated mobile telephony in the media and communications industry. By 2012, Samsung became the world leader in mobile phones sales, with 93 million units in the first quarter compared with Nokia's close to 83 million (BBC, 2012). However, Nokia continued to be a major player in terms of sales of units in 2013, with 14.2 percent market share when taking the sales of all kinds of mobile phones into account.

However, if we look at the sales of smartphones, Nokia's fall was fast. In 2007, it had a dominant share of 49.4 percent, a position that was reduced to 3 percent by mid-2013. Nokia had rapidly been outperformed by the two South Korean companies Samsung and LG Electronics, Apple's iPhone, and the Chinese

Huawei and Lenovo's smartphones. In 2013, the worldwide sales of smartphones outperformed the sales of "feature phones" or "dumb phones" (Gartner, 2014; Lee, 2013).

In 2013, Microsoft bought Nokia's mobile operation for €5.44 billion—of which the mobile phone business was valued at €3.78 billion. It is difficult to predict Microsoft's plans for Nokia, but it gives Microsoft "a more solid foothold in the device market," and Nokia's cheaper smartphone ranges have been considered commercially promising in developing markets where the Nokia brand name is stronger (*Forbes*, 2014). Still, in 2014, it was announced that the Nokia Lumia smartphone would be rebranded Microsoft Lumia, although the cheaper phones would continue to have the Nokia brand name. In 2015, Microsoft had a mere 3 percent of the worldwide smartphone market and announced that it would reduce its workforce by 18,000 employees, of which the majority were from the Nokia team (Eadicicco, 2014; Lapowsky, 2015). In 2016, Microsoft sold its Nokia mobile phone assets and rights to the brand name to a Finnish start-up, HMD Global, with former Nokia management. The same year, it was announced that the company would produce Android mobile phones, branded with the Nokia name, and the year after a new range of Nokia mobile phones was on the market (BBC, 2016; HMD Global, 2022). While Nokia, along with other Western mobile phone producers, previously dominated the world market, today, three of the top five mobile smartphone producers are Chinese. Apple is the sole Western producer among the top five.

Case Study 3.2 Digital Media and Technology, E-Waste, and Sustainability

The UN's 193 member states adopted the 2030 Agenda for Sustainable Development in 2015. Key to the 2030 Agenda are seventeen Sustainable Development Goals (SDGs), with a total of 169 defined goals to solve the challenges the world is facing in terms of climate and sustainability (UN, 2021). There is a general strong belief in technology to succeed in creating a sustainable future, in line with the UN's SDGs. Technology is believed to play a role in neutralizing carbon emissions, creating economic growth through renewable energy, industry innovation, and the implementation of responsible and sustainable use of resources in production and consumption. While technology can arguably be linked to all of the SDGs (Sault, 2020), the

World Economic Forum highlights how technology is covered by three SDGs in particular:

SDG 8: Decent Work and Economic Growth. Achieving this goal requires boosting economic productivity through diversification, technological upgrades and innovation. Tech can help achieve other targets, too, like supporting job creation, entrepreneurship and the growth of micro, small- and medium-sized enterprises and expanding access to banking and financial services.

SDG 9: Industry, Innovation and Infrastructure. Targets include upgrading the technological capabilities of industrial sectors in all countries, supporting domestic technology R&D and innovation in developing countries and increasing access to information and communications technology, specifically universal and affordable internet access in LDCs by 2020.

SDG 12: Responsible Consumption and Production. Targets include reducing waste, making procurement more sustainable and strengthening scientific and technological capacities in developing countries to move towards more sustainable consumption and production. Tech can also play a role in helping companies adopt sustainable practices and report that information.

(Sault, 2020)

However, at the same time as technology is hailed as the key to a sustainable future, electronic waste—or e-waste—is, according to the United Nations University's Global E-waste Monitor, "the world's fastest-growing domestic waste stream fueled mainly by higher consumption rates of electric and electronic equipment, short life cycles, and few options for repair" (UN, 2020). The world produced as much as 53.6 million metric tonnes (Mt) in 2019, and is predicted to increase to 74 Mt in 2030. In fact, as little as 17.4 percent of all e-waste produced in 2019 was recycled. As much as US $57 billion-worth of such recoverable material was destroyed, including gold, silver, copper, and platinum. The total global cost of wasted material is more than the gross domestic product of most nations. While Africa and Oceania produced the least amount of e-waste, with 2.9 Mt and 0.7 Mt respectively, Asia topped the list of e-waste-producing continents, with 24.9 Mt, the Americas 13.1 Mt, and Europe 12 Mt (UN, 2020).

E-waste represents a major challenge for most countries. There is a general lack of facilities and infrastructure to deal with toxic material and large-scale recycling of the growing amount of e-waste. Instead, e-waste becomes part of the general flow of waste, burned, becomes landfill, or is exported. Export happens for two main reasons: it is cheaper to export to parts of the world with less strict regulations, for example in Western Africa and parts of Asia, and there is a demand for cheap electronics in the countries that import such e-waste.

The imported e-waste is usually handled manually by people lacking protection, who try to find materials that can be sold, and much of the e-waste is burned in open air (TCO Certified, 2021).

"The greenest smartphone is the one you already own," Maxwell and Miller state in their book *How Green Is Your Smartphone?* (2020: 58). The point is that we purchase and replace personal technology devices far often than we actually need to:

> Smartphones can last well beyond their warranties. But most of us get rid of them after less than two years [...]. The reason is rarely to do with replacing a broken phone or one that can't run the latest software. Not even planned obsolescence is a clear culprit, because most phones are designed for a longer life than consumers allow. We choose newer models because we are promised slightly faster processing, better cameras or improved data security.
>
> (Maxwell and Miller, 2020: 58)

As discussed earlier, the recycling of e-waste material is extremely low globally, and at the other end, when we purchase a smartphone, we also increase carbon emission due to the electricity and petroleum needed to produce and move smartphones, tablets, and other electronic devices across the world, but this has also other human and planetary costs:

> Our penchant for buying new phones also sets in motion a chain of events that reaches across the planet to mines and factories where smartphones are made. The hazards and despair that characterizes workers' lives in those locations intensify whenever we place orders for the latest model. For all these reasons, the greenest smartphone is the one you already own.
>
> (Maxwell and Miller, 2020: 59)

Furthermore, electronic waste, or e-waste, is also a major health and environmental hazard, as it contains toxic and hazardous material and substances such as mercury that may cause damage to the brain and nerve system (UN, 2020).

The major media tech companies are scrambling to announce sustainability and climate-friendly initiatives. Google announced it was "the first major company to reach carbon neutrality, and we're the largest corporate purchaser of renewable energy" (Google UK, 2020). By 2030, the company aims to fuel all its data centers and offices using carbon-free energy. So far, Google's carbon offsets are achieved mainly by capturing natural gas from pig farms and landfill sites, which does not itself solve the company's actual carbon emission. Microsoft aims to become "carbon negative" by 2030. Apple aims to achieve carbon neutrality across all its businesses and manufacturing supply chains by the same year. Amazon plans to reduce its carbon footprint to zero by 2040 (Harrabin, 2020). Furthermore, Google, for example, has announced a number of initiatives, from including carbon emission for some flights in Google Flights, carbon-neutral shipping in Google Shopping, and letting Google Maps provide more sustainable transport options, such as walking, biking, and public transportation, to providing data that can help improve the sustainability and the climate action plans of cities (Google, 2021).

Still—as consumption is considered a key reason for global carbon emission, pollution, waste, and the draining of the world's resources—Google, Facebook, and Amazon, despite becoming carbon neutral and launching new related initiatives, have major and fundamental challenges on their hands, which go to the core of their business models. Google and Facebook are two of the world's major generators of advertising, which at the end of the day promotes consumption, and Amazon is one of the world's major retailers, selling and distributing consumer products worldwide.

Search Engines, Social Media, and Digital Advertising

The development of internet search engines can be split in three key phases (van Couvering, 2008). While the first phase (1994–7) is characterized by entrepreneurship and development within academic and not-for profit settings, the second phase (1997–2001) is characterized by portals such as AOL and Excite@ Home that had "built-in" search functions, but with the aim to keep users within the portal through "walled gardens." The third phase (2002–) is characterized by consolidation and integration, as established media and communications companies decided to stop investing in search development, and the rapid growth of Google (van Couvering, 2008; Hillis et al., 2013; Laffey, 2007).

In fact, the largest media and communications players' resurging interest in Internet entities in the mid-2000s is ascribed to the rise of particularly Google. Google's idea of selling advertising linked to web searches was key to legitimizing the Internet as a medium for attracting advertising on a large scale. Google's advertising revenue increased dramatically in a very short time—from around $70 million in 2001 to around $1.4 billion in 2003 (Google, 2009). The global Internet search engine went public in August 2004. Only a few months after the public launch, the market value of Google surpassed that of News Corp.—one of the world's largest media conglomerates, and the year after the Google enterprise was considered more valuable than the media giants Walt

Disney and Time Warner (La Monica, 2009). The rapid escalation of the value of internet entities, fronted by Google, mirrored the late 1990s, but the increasingly viable advertising business models and large number of existing users could now more easily justify the valuation of these companies (Croteau and Hoynes, 2006; Schifferes, 2006). The increased possibilities for monetization along with a growing infrastructure and increasing number of internet users, legitimized online corporate expansion and fueled expectations. At the time, in 2005, there were already close to 1 billion internet users worldwide (ITU, 2021).

The same year that Google was listed on Nasdaq, the term Web 2.0 appeared in public. This was to become the buzzword epitomizing the revival of the Internet in the wake of the dotcom bust. Web 2.0, generally claimed to have first appeared at the Web 2.0 Conference, organized by O'Reilly Media in San Francisco, US, in 2004, was partly launched in an attempt to revive business and financial interest in the web (Web 2.0 Conference, 2004; O'Reilly, 2005). The emergence of Google and its technological characteristics did not go unnoticed by Tim O'Reilly. In his Web 2.0 manifesto, *What is Web 2.0?* (2005), O'Reilly pointed explicitly to how Google signified the new era of the web, and the web browser Netscape represented the old: "If Netscape was the standard bearer for Web 1.0, Google is most certainly the standard bearer for Web 2.0." O'Reilly attached the term Web 2.0 to one of the most significant internet technology-related inventions to date. The Google phenomenon certainly served the interest of both technological, financial, and political stakeholders—strengthening belief in the internet after the dotcom crisis (Mjøs et al., 2014).

At the time of the skyrocketing of Google and the launch of the Web 2.0 term, Rupert Murdoch, the powerful chairman of News Corp, along with several competing media conglomerates, signaled a return to Internet investments:

> It was clear, three or four years ago, that there was a lot happening on the internet, and revenues were going there. So we thought we'd better get in there pretty fast and look for opportunities. So we looked around at a lot of things and rejected most of them as too expensive or limited in their capacity to expand. And then we found MySpace.
>
> (*Esquire*, 2008)

The rise of Google, Yahoo!, and other popular advertising-based internet companies based on promising new technology were therefore key in restoring the belief in the financial potential of the internet (Schifferes, 2006; La Monica, 2009). The major media conglomerates plunged into costly new Internet ventures, rushing to acquire certain Internet properties. Services like MySpace, Facebook, and YouTube, or websites that facilitated the building of online communities, were particularly attractive as investors hoped to be able to "translate potential captive audiences into advertising revenue" (Wasko and Erickson, 2009: 378).

As such, Google's dramatic growth from 2001 and News Corp's willingness to pay $580 million for MySpace in 2005 were considered by many as representing a major corporate response to the ongoing changes within the sector and was part of the resurgent commercial belief in the Internet. Since the mid-2000s, a number of online-based, high profile, companies became popular and valuable, strengthening belief in the financial potential of the online environment. This helped reignite corporate investment that had more or less vanished since the dotcom bubble burst at the turn of the millennium, not least among traditional media and communications companies, seeking to position themselves to commercially exploit the online milieu. In the second half of the 2000s, the social media companies were particularly popular and were acquired at major cost (see Table 3.5).

In 2005, News Corp's acquisition of MySpace for $580 million dollars represented the first of several major social media acquisitions. In the run-up to the acquisition, Viacom and its MTV Networks were also interested in MySpace. Viacom and its global media youth brand saw the social media as a potentially vital part of their digital strategy, but eventually lost out to News Corp in a bidding war (Angwin, 2009). On 9 October 2006, Google announced its acquisition of YouTube. The deal was worth $1.65 billion. Internet users viewed around 100 million videos on YouTube per day, and this motivated Google's acquisition (Wasko and Erickson, 2009: 378). In 2007, Disney acquired Club Penguin, a virtual world for children with nearly a million paying users, for up to $700 million. Facebook, with roughly 15 million monthly visitors in

Table 3.5 Major Acquisitions and Investments in Social Media Companies

Year of Acquisition	Social Media	Acquiring Company	Price (in millions)
2005	MySpace	News Corp	$580 (est.)
2006	YouTube	Google	$1,650
2007	Facebook	Microsoft	$240 (1.6 percent)
2008	Bebo	AOL/Time Warner	$850
2012	Instagram	Facebook	$1,000
2013	Tumblr	Yahoo	$1,100
2014	WhatsApp	Facebook	$19,000

Source: Google, 2006; Stone, 2007a; Sabbagh, 2008; Angwin, 2009; Segall, 2012; O'Donnell, 2013; BBC, 2014.

mid-2006, generated interest—and offers—from both Viacom and Yahoo! that year, but Facebook declined both (Wasko and Erickson, 2009: 377). Still, in 2007, Microsoft paid $240 million for 1.6 percent ownership of Facebook—an investment valuing Facebook at $15 billion (Stone, 2007a). The year after, Time Warner paid $850 million in cash for Bebo, the third largest social internet network in the United States, with more than 40 million users worldwide (Olson, 2008; Sabbagh, 2008). The interest in social media companies continued to escalate in the following years. When Facebook went public in 2012, the valuation of the company was $104.2 billion, compared to Google's valuation of $26.4 billion in 2004 (Geron, 2012). In 2012, Facebook acquired Instagram for $1 billion, and in 2013, Yahoo! bought Tumblr for $1.1 billion (Segall, 2012; O'Donnell, 2013), and Facebook bought WhatsApp for $19 billion the year after (BBC, 2014).

Digital Advertising

In the 1990s, niche agencies focusing on the digital environment emerged. Traditional advertising agencies responded by either acquiring or spinning off such specialist agencies. Importantly, these agencies did not only focus on traditional advertising in a new, digital environment, but also on "database marketing" and "managing interactivity":

> Where advertising had been based on one-directional communication, they now had to address and develop opportunities for multi-pathway communication and track people's engagement with advertising. Initially, the digital sector was represented by interactive agencies, which originally meant working with the web. Boundaries, however, have become blurred. As digital becomes more mainstream it is growing increasingly difficult to say that one agency is digital whereas the other is traditional.
>
> (McStay, 2016: 17)

In 2020, advertising spending related to the internet accounted for over 50 percent of total global advertising for the first time. That year, advertising spending on television had a global market share of 28.35 percent, followed by newspaper advertising with around 6 percent (see Table 3.6).

While the global advertising market shrank by 7.5 percent in 2020 due to the Covid-19 pandemic, global advertising agency Zenith Media points out how digitization has accelerated due to social distancing and new consumer and user behaviors, and as a consequence, "Digital transformation is rapidly shifting budgets to digital advertising" (Zenith Media, 2021). Jonathan Barnard, Zenith's

Table 3.6 Global Distribution of Advertising
Spending Worldwide in 2020, by Medium (%)

Internet	51.04
Television	28.35
Newspaper	6.04
Outdoor	5.31
Radio	5.37
Magazines	3.47
Cinema	0.41

Source: Adapted from Guttmann, 2021.

head of forecasting, predicts major growth in digital advertising: "The coronavirus forced brands to embrace digital advertising even faster than expected and made digital transformation of businesses more urgent than ever [...]. This year will be the first in which digital advertising will attract more than half of total global adspend, a milestone we previously expected in 2021" (Zenith Media, 2020).

Digital advertising is expected to continue its rapid growth post-pandemic, while advertising spent on traditional media is not expected to return to pre-pandemic market shares: "Digital ad budgets were cut quickly in the crisis' first phase, given generally easier to cut without penalty. But as time progressed, brands allocated more budget into digital channels to take advantage of their flexibility and ability to optimize performance, particularly important qualities in an uncertain time" (Zenith Media, 2021).

In fact, by 2023, the share of global digital advertising is predicted to reach as much as 58 percent, with advertising spending on traditional media declining or showing weak growth (Zenith Media, 2021).

The most popular forms of digital advertising are search advertising, display advertising, and classified advertising. These forms are tightly linked with the dominating online services and platforms and will be examined in the next part of the chapter.

Social Media and Digital Advertising

In 2005, the number of unique visitors to the social media MySpace grew fast. In January 2005, MySpace had 5.8 million unique visitors, and by May the same year, the site attracted 15.6 million unique visitors (Angwin, 2009: 140). Still, millions of users do not create revenue automatically. To set up a social media service such as YouTube, or take control of a service like MySpace and develop it further, requires major investments. This can only be justified if the owner of the IP address can "prove the site or platform will attract the right kind of audience and attention" (Lister et al., 2009: 172). The approximately 100 million videos viewed daily on YouTube were a key reason for Google's acquisition of the video-sharing site (Wasko and Erickson, 2009), but in the case of MySpace, it was not only the large numbers of users that caught the conglomerates' attention. MySpace's ability to attract specifically young people proved attractive for investors. MySpace's young users, many aged between 16 and 24, were very attractive to advertisers (Cohn, 2005; Siklos, 2005; Naughton, 2006; La Monica, 2009).

MySpace's popularity among young people and potential as a vehicle for advertising were of great interest to News Corp, but as pointed out, also the Viacom-owned MTV Network that was developing a digital strategy. MTV saw MySpace as an attractive online asset, but eventually lost out to News Corp (Angwin, 2009). Throughout the second half of the 2000s, both MySpace and Facebook have attempted to turn themselves into profit-generating entities by launching a range of monetization initiatives either on their own or in collaboration with online industry giants such as Google and Microsoft. The social media services were, some argue, "probably the most hyped online advertising and marketing vehicle in 2007" (McStay, 2010: 61). While these services can be used as conventional advertising-carrying channels, the commercial worth of social media such as MySpace lies in the fact that these services can be utilized "as market research platforms," according to Spurgeon, who points out that "many accounts of the early history of MySpace suggest that it was established as a new kind of advertising medium: one where consumers were conceived as advertisers, and where advertisers would be invited into the quasi-private worlds of young consumers" (2008: 110). Facebook, too, may easily be described in such a way. The owners of web communities, such as global social media, have increasingly come to engage in a process of attracting, recruiting, and keeping users, while at the same time attempting to capitalize on them:

> Community management has become the starting point for web marketing—web media invite the user to join, to create a profile, to post blogs or their announcements, to make links, to invite other friends and so on. This is not because the advertising and media industries just want us all to play nice and have lots of warm friendships. It is because they are seeking, in a crowded, transient marketplace characterized by a nomadic audience to create brand engagement.
>
> (Lister et al., 2009: 172, 173)

The potential and prospect of the idea of "community management" motivated major media and communications conglomerates to enter the social media environment. This created unease and skepticism from a user perspective, but also uncertainty from the corporate perspective:

> Underpinning anxieties about News Corporation's acquisition of MySpace were concerns that it would stifle the vibrant social network site and cause its nascent innovation culture to stagnate. The concern for MySpace participants was over the burden of exit costs they might face if changed terms and conditions of involvement created disincentives and obstacles to participation.
>
> (Spurgeon, 2008: 110)

News Corp's acquisition of MySpace in 2005, then, also represented uncertainty for the media conglomerate. While News Corp had high hopes and ambitious plans for MySpace, it did not have any experience with owning and running a globally expanding social media: "The business concern was whether the marketing potential of the site would be fully realized" (Spurgeon, 2008: 110).

Since then, the efforts of the social media giants' strategies have represented a move toward increased observation of media users and much more customized and individualized targeted marketing practices. Shortly after acquiring MySpace, News Corp made a deal with Google for advertising linked to searches and also started developing other systems for gathering data on its users for corporate purposes.

Fox Interactive Media, the part of News Corporation controlling MySpace, strongly believed that scanning, gathering, and processing the information the users provide on their profile were key for developing a model for generating advertising revenue. Adam Bain, EVP at Fox Interactive Media, explained optimistically: "For users, MySpace is a platform for public self expression. For advertisers, it's now a platform for understanding user behavior" (Kaplan, 2007). Peter Levinsohn, president of Fox Interactive Media, claimed, "We are blessed with a phenomenal amount of information about the likes, dislikes and life's passions of our users" (Levinsohn, quoted in Stone, 2007b). While MySpace executives' observations were correct, the pioneering social media did not find a way to capitalize on it. Some point to MySpace's inferior technological solutions, while others emphasize that Facebook's usability was superior. MySpace profiles did not have Facebook's facilities for visualizing interaction and communication between users that were far more static: "[MySpace's] format has remained relatively stable over time (as compared with Facebook, which more frequently adds features and shifts its architectural format)" (Davis, 2010: 1105). Facebook's extensive personalization and language localization made it extremely competitive in many parts of the world. As MySpace scaled back its operations and global presence to focus on the United States, only a few years after News Corporation acquired it, this had an effect on its ability to attract users and to generate advertising revenue (Garrahan, 2009). As Facebook's popularity increased its efforts to create systems to utilize user information for advertising generation intensified.

Some warned against this development: "This new economy of web advertising has spawned a whole new method of audience analysis in the dark art of user metrics—measuring user behaviour and engagements" (Lister et al., 2009: 172). Turow points out how "Firms that exchange the information often do ensure that the targets' names and postal addresses remain anonymous—but not before they add specific demographic data and lifestyle information" (Turow, 2011: 4).

While MySpace refrained from "behavioral targeted" advertising, Facebook decided to take a different approach than MySpace when attempting to turn itself into a commercial environment. The Beacon program was launched by Facebook in November 2007 and aimed to map Facebook users' actions on websites outside Facebook that had paid to be part of the Beacon program. Beacon registered when a Facebook user made a purchase from an online retailer participating in the program. *The New York Times* published an example of how a purchase at the website Fandango that sells movie tickets in the United States was registered and forwarded to a Facebook friend of the purchaser. The Beacon initiative met fierce criticism for distributing details about the activity of members without their permission. MoveOn.org Civic Action organized a protest, and more than 50,000 members of Facebook opposed the practice of distributing this information without peoples' full consent. Facebook later changed the Beacon system and no longer distributes information about purchases and websites visited without the user's agreement (Story and Stone, 2007). In response to the reactions, Facebook's founder, Mark Zuckerberg, wrote on his Facebook blog:

> [W]e missed the right balance. At first we tried to make it very lightweight so people wouldn't have to touch it for it to work. The problem with our initial approach of making it an opt-out system instead of opt-in was that if someone forgot to decline to share something, Beacon still went ahead and shared it with their friends. It took us too long after people started contacting us to change the product so that users had to explicitly approve what they wanted to share. Instead of acting quickly, we took too long to decide on the right solution. I'm not proud of the way we've handled this situation and I know we can do better.
>
> (Zuckerberg, 2007)

These early clashes signaled what was to come. With Facebook's rapid expansion into the dominant global social media and monetization platform, privacy issues and controversial incidents and developments have escalated.

By 2021, Facebook products consist of Facebook, Instagram, Messenger, and WhatsApp. Facebook is available in over 100 languages and the company has offices or data centers in more than thirty countries. While Facebook has billions of users across the world, its products cannot be used in some parts of the world for legal and regulatory reasons. Facebook and related products are generally not available in, for example, China (see Table 3.7; Facebook, 2021a).

Table 3.7 Facebook—Daily Active Users, December 31, 2020 (Millions)

United States and Canada	195
Europe	308
Asia-Pacific	744
Rest of the World	598

Source: Facebook, 2021a: 54.

Daily active users (DAU) are defined as Facebook or Messenger users that are registered Facebook users and logged in on a given day (Facebook, 2021a: 54).

Facebook has turned into a global user-data collector and advertising machine. Its fast-growing advertising revenue reflects the efficiency of Facebook's extensive information gathering and user-targeting operations. The company collects information posted and provided by users of the service, but also information on the activity of the users. This information is used by advertisers to target users with certain desired characteristics, traits, and interests, as well as geographical location (see Table 3.8 and Box 1).

Table 3.8 Facebook's Global Revenue ($ Million)

	Advertising	Other Revenue	Total
2020	84,169	1,796	85,965
2019	69,655	1,042	70,697
2018	55,013	825	55,838

Source: Facebook, 2021a: 66.

Box 1 Facebook's Data Policy

This policy describes the information we process to support Facebook, Instagram, Messenger and other products and features offered by Facebook (Facebook Products or Products). [...]

What kinds of information do we collect?
To provide the Facebook Products, we must process information about you. The types of information we collect depend on how you use our Products. You can learn how to access and delete information we collect by visiting the Facebook Settings and Instagram Settings.

Things that you and others do and provide.
- **Information and content you provide.** We collect the content, communications and other information you provide when you use our Products, including when you sign up for an account, create or share content, and message or communicate with others.[...]
    - Data with special protections: You can choose to provide information in your Facebook profile fields or Life Events about your religious views, political views, who you are "interested in," or your health. This and other information (such as racial or ethnic origin, philosophical beliefs or trade union membership) is subject to special protections under EU law.
- **Networks and connections.** We collect information about the people, Pages, accounts, hashtags and groups you are connected to and how you interact with them across our Products, such as people you communicate with the most or groups you are part of. [...]
- **Your usage.** We collect information about how you use our Products, such as the types of content you view or engage with; the features you use; the actions you take; the people or accounts you interact with; and the time, frequency and duration of your activities. [...]
- **Information about transactions made on our Products.** If you use our Products for purchase or other financial transactions (such as when you make a purchase in a game or make a donation), we collect information about the purchase or transaction. [...].
- **Things others do and information they provide about you.** We also receive and analyze content, communications and information that other people provide when they use our Products. This can include information about you, such as when others share or comment on a photo of you, send a message to you, or upload, sync or import your contact information.

(Facebook, 2021b)

Through Facebook Ad Manager, individual users and professional advertising agencies alike target users and monitor reach and responses to advertisements and adjust their campaigns accordingly (Facebook, 2021b). Facebook generates its advertising revenue by displaying advertising: "[O]n Facebook, Instagram, Messenger, and third-party affiliated website or mobile applications. Marketers pay for ad products either directly or through their relationships with advertising agencies or resellers, based on the number of impressions delivered or the number of actions, such as clicks, taken by our users" (Facebook, 2021a: 89).

However, the financial worth of each Facebook user throughout the world is not equal. The value of each user is calculated by dividing the revenue generated in a region by the number of users within this region. Therefore, a Facebook user in North America is eleven times more valued than a user in Asia-Pacific. This is due to the size and maturity of the North American market. Facebook users in Europe are of lesser value than the North American users, but higher than users both in Asia-Pacific and in the rest of the world (see Table 3.9).

Table 3.9 Facebook's Average Revenue per User (ARPU), December 2020 ($)

United States and Canada	53.56
Europe	16.87
Asia-Pacific	4.05
Rest of the World	2.77

Source: Facebook, 2021a: 56.

Facebook underlines that the revenue per user in a particular region is thus "based on our estimate of the geography in which ad impressions are delivered, virtual and digital goods are purchased, or consumers hardware devices are shipped" (Facebook, 2021a: 56). While there are fewer users in the United States and Canada than in Asia-Pacific, the value of a user in the former is much higher. This is reflected in the regional differences in total revenue (Tables 3.9 and 3.10).

Table 3.10 Facebook's Revenue by Geography, 2018–20 ($ Million)

	2018	2019	2020
United States and Canada	25,727	32,206	38,433
Europe*	13,631	16,826	20,349
Asia-Pacific	11,733	15,406	19,848
Rest of the world	4,747	6,259	7,335
Total revenue	55,838	70,697	85,965

*Europe includes Russia and Turkey. Rest of the world includes Africa, Latin America, and the Middle East.
Source: Facebook, 2021a: 96.

Through Facebook, advertising may be bought directly by individuals, organizations, or companies, or may be placed by advertising agencies and other third-party advertising specialists. This means, for example, that if "an advertiser is promoting an airline sale to Hawaii, they might want to show their ad to people who recently visited websites related to traveling to Hawaii. We work with an advertising company to help that advertiser show the airline sale ad to those people" (Facebook, 2015). *The Wall Street Journal* points out how "third party" cookies that "can be used by ad-tracking or analytics services, are designed to follow users across the internet to learn their browsing habits. Those insights can be valuable to advertisers but have generated consumer privacy concerns for years" (Tweh and Patel, 2020).

Advertising agencies offer a vast range of services that aim to help advertisers reach potential customers online. The competition and innovation within this field is stiff and unpredictable, and companies come and go; still, some things within this environment are stable:

> The logic propelling them and more established firms forward, though, is consistent: the future belongs to marketers and media firms – *publishers*, in current terminology – that learn how to find and keep the most valuable customers by surrounding them with the most persuasive media materials. Special online advertising exchanges, owned by Google, Yahoo!, Microsoft, Interpublic and other major players, allow publishers to auction and media agencies to "buy" individuals with particular characteristics, often in real time. That is, it is now possible to buy the right to deliver an ad to a person with specific characteristics at the precise moment that the person loads a Web page.
>
> (Turow, 2011: 5)

Similarly to early concerns around information technology and surveillance, global social media is subject to critique: "MySpace is not about creativity, it is about detecting related *activity*. Facebook does not want to link friends to friends, it is in the business of linking people to advertisers and products. Not content, but connections and profiled actions are the new commodities" (van Dijck and Nieborg, 2009: 866).

Such critique has intensified as ever new ways of surveillance, mapping, and targeting of users have emerged. Facebook has increasingly become a platform that third parties can exploit to map and target users secretly and even illegally (see Case Studies 3.3 and 6.1).

Case Study 3.3 The Facebook "Like" Button—More Revealing than You Think

Facebook is an advanced marketing machine, where you as a user are a commodity that is quickly resold. Powerful commercial operators map our internet use in various ways, often through methods we are not aware of. New ways of mapping are constantly emerging, and this affects how we will use the internet in the future, which we currently do not know the consequences of.

How is this monitoring and mapping possible? As a new Facebook user, we tick off quickly that we have read the written agreement we make with the company. Few of us read it, and even understand it fully. We give social media extensive powers to use our information when we create profiles—even though we have not really read what we have agreed to. It seems that we are not so concerned about the content of the agreement, as we choose to take part in the online service nearly billions of users.

A handful of technological inventions are crucial for the functioning of Facebook. The web browser Netscape, launched in 1994, made it easy for anyone to surf the internet, and the cookie was introduced in this browser. Cookies made it possible for websites or services to recognize users in various ways and store information about their internet use—for example, which sites are visited and what has been clicked on. This technology facilitated an increasing mapping of internet use and categorization of users, and thus new ways to target advertising and other messages and content. At the same time, it is precisely this technology that enables Facebook to recognize us and for our accounts to work when we log on. The technology facilitates e-commerce and makes online "shopping carts" work, and makes it possible to create personal Amazon versions based on past purchases and activity.

Myspace was launched in 2003 and was the first popular international social media. Myspace tried early to systematize information on the many millions of user profiles created by users themselves. Film enthusiasts were divided into 300 subcategories, and sports fans were divided by their interest: basketball, soccer, skiing, and so on. Facebook, launched in 2004 and made available to internet users worldwide from 2006, quickly took over Myspace's position, and developed more sophisticated mapping. The story of Facebook is characterized by a number of controversial attempts to use personal information and friend links for commercial purposes, and criticisms of the unclear consequences of sharing personal information. We often read about how Facebook's technology and new features can facilitate new forms of surveillance, but the company stresses that we use the service voluntarily, and that new features are intended to increase users' opportunities.

We tell the outside world something about ourselves when we click "like," but the sum of our clicks, taken in conjunction with other personal information, helps to predict and reveal information about sexual preferences, personality traits, the use of addictive substances, and intelligence that will probably surprise many. Facebook creates a new arena for personal communications and internet activity, but also helps to increase mapping of internet usage that has unpredictable consequences which many are skeptical of.

Researchers at the University of Cambridge pointed out how easy it is to collect data and the possible consequences of the use of the like button: "Facebook Likes [...] can be used to automatically and accurately predict a range of highly sensitive personal attributes including: sexual orientation, ethnicity, religious and political views, personality traits, intelligence, happiness, use of addictive substances, parental separation, age, and gender" (Kosinski et al., 2013: 5802). While the like button may reveal more about ourselves than we think, it is only one of many forms of digital records of our internet use: "This study demonstrates the degree to which relatively basic digital records of human behavior can be used to automatically and accurately estimate a wide range of personal attributes that people would typically assume to be private [...]. Likes represent a very generic class of digital records, similar to Web search queries, Web browsing histories, and credit card purchases" (Kosinski et al., 2013: 5802).

A range of interested parties may get access to sensitive personal information without the direct consent of individual users or without them noticing it, and even though the individual user does not want to share it. Such mapping can pose a threat to an individual in many ways, the researchers warn:

> Commercial companies, governmental institutions, or even one's Facebook friends could use software to infer attributes such as intelligence, sexual orientation, or political views that an individual may not have intended to share. One can imagine situations in which such predictions, even if incorrect, could pose a threat to an individual's well-being, freedom, or even life. Importantly, given the ever-increasing amount of digital traces people leave behind, it becomes difficult for individuals to control which of their attributes are being revealed. For example, merely avoiding explicitly homosexual content may be insufficient to prevent others from discovering one's sexual orientation.
>
> (Kosinski et al., 2013)

Technological developments increase the opportunities for mapping users, but often unknown to the users, and with unknown consequences for the users. For example, Facebook's mobile phone interface has increased the possibilities for identifying information about users, as the mobile phone's GPS system sends a constant stream of information about the user's movement back to Facebook's servers. Facebook develops ever more advanced user profiles through correlating and compiling social activity and relationships, purchases in shops, and restaurant visits, with movement.

Search Engines and Digital Advertising

The concept of "search advertising" emerged as a new business model within the online environment in the 2000s. As we have seen, Google's idea of selling advertising linked to internet searches was key to legitimizing the internet as a medium for attracting advertising on a large scale since the mid-2000s:

> The search engine's basic business model rests on its ability to offer and sell advertising, but not on any platform other than its own. Instead of attracting audience with the offer of information or entertainment content, as with traditional media, search engines attract users to the service itself. In both cases, the audience and users collected are then "sold" to advertisers, but in distinct ways. In particular, traditional media depend on large scale advertisers, who place their advertising via an advertising agency. Yet, on one hand, search advertising has in principle diminished the need for any intermediary, such as an advertising agency, at the same time as it has enabled the rapid rise to power of Google, by far the most successful search engine in the field.
>
> (Sinclair, 2012: 53)

Google's business model generated an increase in advertising revenue from around $70 million in 2001 to around $1.4 billion in 2003 (Google, 2009). This phenomenal growth in revenues was considered as highly influential in the traditional media companies' resurgent interest in internet companies in the mid-2000s. Google's fast growth continued and its position in the online landscape has strengthened year by year. In fact, by 2020, Google accounted for 52 percent of the $292 billion spent on all global digital advertising spending (Schechner and Hagey, 2021).

Google is divided in three segments: Google Services, Google Cloud, and Other Bets, of which Google Services generates advertising revenue, which is the company's main income stream.

- **Google Services** includes products and services such as ads, Android, Chrome, hardware, Google Maps, Google Play, Search, and YouTube. Google Services generates revenues primarily from advertising; sales of apps, in-app purchases, digital content products, and hardware; and fees received for subscription-based products such as YouTube Platinum and YouTube TV.
- **Google Cloud** includes Google's infrastructure and data analytics platforms, collaboration tools, and other services for enterprise customers. Google Cloud generates revenues primarily from fees received for Google Cloud

Platform (GCP) services and Google Workspace (formerly known as G Suite) collaboration tools.

- **Other Bets** is a combination of multiple operating segments that are not individually material. Revenues from Other Bets are derived primarily through the sale of internet services as well as licensing and R&D services.

(Alphabet, 2021: 33)

Google Services' advertising income makes up the vast majority of the total revenues of the three segments (see Table 3.11).

Google Service's Google Ads and Google AdSense are the two key advertising generating services. Through Google Ads, formerly known as Google AdWords and by far the company's largest revenue generator, advertisers bid to display advertisements to internet users, when they search, but also when browsing regular websites. Through Google AdSense, website owners that are part of Google Network can use Google's services to advertise on their websites (Alphabet, 2021: 6).

By 2021, around 40 percent of advertising spending "on the open internet—meaning digital advertising outside of closed systems such as Google Search, YouTube or Facebook—goes through Google's ad buying tools" (Schechner and Hagey, 2021). Google's global market share is remarkable, and the service dominates in most parts of the world. The main exceptions are the BRICS countries China and Russia, which have their own search engines (see Tables 3.12 and 3.13).

Table 3.11 Google Revenues ($ Million)

	2019	2020
Google Search and Other	98,115	104,062
YouTube Ads	15,149	19,772
Google Network Members' Properties	21,547	23,090
Google Advertising	134,811	146,924
Google Other	17,014	21,711
Google Services Total	151,825	168,635
Google Cloud	8,918	13,059
Other Bets	659	657
Hedging Gains	455	176
Total Revenues	161,857	182,527

Source: Alphabet, 2021: 33.

Table 3.12 Global Market Share of Search Engines
(Desktop Users in %)

	2021	Country of Origin
Google	85.86	United States
Bing	6.84	United States
Yahoo	2.76	United States
Baidu	0.55	China
Yandex	0.59	Russia

Source: Adapted from Johnson, 2021b.

Table 3.13 Share of Desktop Search Traffic Originating
from Google in Selected Countries as of October 2020 (%)

Brazil	92.58
India	95.47
Italy	91.7
Spain	91.18
Australia	89.71
Canada	86.73
Hong Kong	87.92
Germany	85.62
United Kingdom	84.98
France	85.23
South Korea	83.62
United States	81.99

Source: Adapted from Johnson, 2021a.

Google's global reach and operations are underlined by its revenue streams. By 2020, the majority of global revenues, 53 percent, comes from outside the United States (see Table 3.14).

Google points out that its growth in revenue is in large part due to users in developing countries accessing the internet, the general global shift to online, and the "advent of the multi-device world" (Alphabet, 2021: 30). However, like Facebook, as Google has expanded it has also been criticized for its tracking of users and concerns over user privacy. In response, in 2021, Google announced it will discontinue the sale of advertisements based on user activity across different

Table 3.14 Google's Revenues by Geography (Determined by Addresses of Customers, %)

	2019	2020
United States	46	47
EMEA	31	30
APAC	17	18
Other Americas	6	5

Source: Alphabet, 2021: 36.

websites (Schechner and Hagey, 2021). The year before, Google, revealed that it will phase out the use of third-party cookies in its own web browser, Chrome, by 2022 (Tweh and Patel, 2020).

In general, digital advertising has grown at a spectacular rate in recent years. In 2017, internet advertising made up 37 percent of total global advertising spending, and surpassed television (35 percent) for the first time, and mobile advertising was bigger than desktop (Zenith Media, 2017: 4). In 2020, internet advertising had grown to over 50 percent of the total global advertising spend for the first time, and is expected to reach 58 percent by 2023, while advertising spent on traditional media is growing marginally or decreasing (Zenith Media, 2021).

The importance for traditional media companies of expanding into online and digital platforms is clear when looking at the rapid growth in both global digital advertising spending and online users.

While there are many examples of collaboration and mergers between traditional media companies and internet-based services, the acquisition of social media signifies the strategy to create new, integrated forms of global media and communications players across previously separate industries as well as expansion and consolidation within sectors. Throughout the twenty-first century, four trends have been key in shaping the largest media companies and how they operate: ownership concentration, the distribution of different products over one platform and one product via different platforms, the customization and segmentation of audiences, and the exploitation of synergy (although not always successful). As media groups have become integrated in the internet industry, "The result of these variegated trends and their interaction is *the formation of a new global multimedia system*" (Castells, 2013: 73). However, there is considerable risk involved in this. The acquisitions of social media companies Myspace and Bebo by traditional media conglomerates were commercially unsuccessful. Both were soon sold for a fraction of their original purchase prices, and particularly in the case of Myspace, News Corp's high hopes for synergy was not fulfilled. In the next part of the chapter, we examine the role of localization when expanding globally—a strategy News Corp's Myspace also attempted to follow, but failed, in contrast to Facebook.

Localization—the Mantra of Global Media Expansion

As News Corp took over MySpace, Rupert Murdoch expressed global aspirations for MySpace. He wanted to create an online "global portal" for young people, according to Angwin (2009: 231). Such ambitions should not come as a surprise. News Corp is the only traditional media conglomerate that does not originate in the United States. It has therefore always had a more global outlook than other media conglomerates and is described as "one of the most developed examples of a global media strategy" (Croteau and Hoynes, 2006: 139, 140).

News Corp was no stranger to localization. The company acquired a controlling stake in Star Television group in 1993, and by 2005 its pan-Asian television network, STAR (Satellite Television Asian Region) had 330 million viewers for its then over 50 television services in seven languages across 53 Asian countries. In India, STAR's rapid popularity and reach were ascribed to localization strategies. The television network has "skillfully prioritized the local over the global" by incorporating local content, using Indian languages, and promoting the network's closeness to the Indian nation (Thussu, 2007: 596). Similar to STAR, MySpace decided to launch regional or country specific versions. Chris DeWolfe, co-founder of MySpace, expressed the need for such an approach soon after News Corp took over the service: "The idea behind internationalization is localization" (DeWolfe, quoted in Levine, 2006). While global television channels took decades to localize their services across large parts of the world, MySpace expanded at unprecedented speed. Within only a six-month period, between June 2006 and January 2007, MySpace launched services in the UK, Ireland, Australia, France, Germany, Japan, Spain, and Italy, and aimed to have a presence in 28 countries by 2008 (Barrett, 2007; News Corp, 2007; Angwin, 2009). As MySpace began to expand its services throughout the 2000s, Facebook also started to plan overseas expansion through localization. Facebook, allowing the wider public to join the service in 2006, was by 2007 the second largest social media in the United States after MySpace, but having become the most popular social media in other English-speaking countries including Canada, Facebook also began to translate its service into non-English languages.

Local differences in territories outside the United States and Europe posed other kinds of challenges for MySpace, according to the newspaper *The Wall Street Journal*. In India and parts of Latin America, the capacity of internet connections is often limited. Therefore, the MySpace versions in these territories had to be less technically advanced. Furthermore, a version of MySpace in Hebrew would need to take into account that the language is read from right to left (Vascellaro, 2008). The expansion into these territories may not be profitable in the short term, but at the time, the service was "placing strategic bets" for the long term, according to Travis Katz, international managing director of MySpace (Katz, quoted in Vascellaro, 2008).

Globally expanding media services attempt to expand by localizing their services in various ways. However, the choice of localization strategy varies. This helps to explain why Facebook and Twitter have been able to reach and tailor their services to so many different localities around the world and outperform both MySpace and national social media competitors.

By 2009, only three years after launching its overseas rollout, MySpace had localized its service in close to thirty territories in Europe, the Americas, and Asia-Pacific. Still, the service soon closed its international offices as part of a larger international or global strategy to focus on the nine countries that generated 95 percent of the advertising revenue, and where the service might become market leader (Wauters, 2008). While MySpace scaled back its original localization infrastructure and local presence, Facebook continued to expand at a dramatic pace. One of the main reasons for Facebook's and Twitter's popularity is their approach to localization that differs from MySpace. This helps to explain the explosive growth of Facebook and Twitter.

MySpace's approach had clear parallels with the traditional global television channels' localization that its owner, News Corp, had successfully implemented across the world for many years. The trade press pointed out: "[MySpace] tend[s] to put a team on the ground locally [...] and then build the site not only in the local language, but promote local artists and other popular culture as well." In contrast, Facebook chose a very different strategy by "tapping users to do all the hard work for them" (Arrington, 2008).

When Facebook localized the service into German, more than 2,000 German-speaking Facebook users contributed to translating the site from English. The translation process took less than two weeks (Facebook, 2008a). Facebook used the same approach when translating the site into Spanish. Close to 1,500 Spanish-speaking Facebook users were involved and helped translate the site in less than four weeks (Facebook, 2008b). As such, Facebook has exploited the "contribution of users" through crowdsourcing (Howe, 2006). At the time Twitter also decided to start to localize its service with the help of its users: "Following a lead from Facebook, Twitter announced that it was crowdsourcing the translations through Tweeter volunteer linguists" (Grunwald, 2010).

China and Global Media

By 2021, Facebook was available in over 100 languages, yet despite the extensive localization efforts, neither US global social media (e.g., Facebook, YouTube, Twitter) nor other major media companies (e.g., Netflix, Disney+, HBO) have been able to establish themselves in China. China's domestic media and communications services completely dominate its home market.

The enormous size of China's domestic internet market, with over a billion internet users and major domestic social media services, is reflected in the global overview of users of such services. While the five most popular social media globally are US companies, the following five services are Chinese (see Table 3.15).

Table 3.15 Global Social Networks Ranked by Number of Monthly Active Users, 2021 (Millions)

Facebook	2,740
YouTube	2,291
WhatsApp	2,000
Facebook Messenger	1,300
Instagram	1,221
Weixin/WeChat	1,213
TikTok	689
QQ	617
Douyin	600
Sina Weibo	511
Telegram	500
Snapchat	498
Kuaishou	481
Pinterest	442
Reddit	430

Source: Adapted from Tankovska, 2021.

The Chinese online environment is characterized by the extensive implementation of governmental control, regulation, and censorship measures. In 1999, democracy activist Lin Hai was imprisoned for political activity online, and the year after, Chinese authorities implemented regulations that aimed to tackle online activity that could "damage national unification" and "endanger social stability" (Hughes, 2010). Since then, the range of censorship measures and regulations has intensified.

One of these new measures was the introduction of "internet commentators" in 2004. These commentators were paid to "directly intervene in online discussions by writing responses to posts and joining the debates," with the aim of influencing public opinion according to the official doctrine (Yang, 2009: 49). Such practices have since increased:

> The Chinese government has long exerted tight control over Internet access on the mainland, deploying an extensive apparatus to regulate what its citizens can read and publish on the web. The Chinese authorities employed more than 2 million people in 2013 to monitor web activity on blogs and social media sites like the wildly popular social media site Weibo, and blocks access to topics it deems sensitive, like the Free Tibet movement, for instance, and democratic activism.
>
> (Frizell, 2014)

The use of Google, along with Facebook, YouTube, and Twitter, has been either completely or partially blocked by Chinese authorities. Facebook has been "blocked in China for years as it's viewed suspiciously as a place to freely disseminate ideas," while the domestic Weibo flourishes and is easier to monitor and censor (Frizell, 2014). The Chinese measures are often referred to as the "Great Firewall," the term first mentioned in *Wired* magazine in 1997, which prevents access to international internet services and websites, as well as state control of the domestic Chinese internet (Thussu, 2018).

The China-based Google operations launched in 2006. The company did agree to a certain level of censorship to be able to conduct business in the country, yet there have been numerous disputes with Chinese authorities (Jin, 2015). In 2010, Google decided not to continue its partly censored service and threatened to close its operation in China, redirecting searches to google.cn to google.com.hk. Then, in 2014, Chinese authorities blocked practically all of Google's services in China (Sheenan, 2018). Still, since then, Google has worked in various ways with the aim to increase its presence in China. In 2018, British and US media reported that Google was developing a Chinese search engine conforming to the country's censorship laws, called Dragonfly (BBC, 2018; Hern and agencies, 2018). Google did not comment on this project until a US Senate hearing in 2019 when Karan Bhatia, Vice President of Public Policy at Google, acknowledged this work, but stated that it had ended: "We have terminated Project Dragonfly" (Bhatia quoted in Su, 2019).

Despite the intensified censorship and surveillance, since 2010 the Chinese internet sector has boomed, as new products and companies proliferated: "Chinese engineers and entrepreneurs returning from Silicon Valley, including many former Googlers, were crucial to this dynamism, bringing world-class technical and entrepreneurial chops to markets insulated from their former employers in the United States. Older companies like Baidu and Alibaba also grew quickly during these years" (Sheenan, 2018).

In fact, as China has focused on developing a high level of "cyber-sovereignty" in terms of economics, technology, and politics, it is the only country that has been able to create a controlled, domestic online sphere:

> [China is] creating and sustaining the world's largest online market for a global Sino-sphere, establishing domestic cyber properties and protecting them from competition from global digital giants by introducing and implementing strict regulatory regimes, and globalizing of Chinese digital corporations. China is the only country with its own version of Google, Facebook, Amazon, Twitter, WhatsApp and many other essentially US-based digital properties.
>
> (Thussu, 2018: 26)

While the global online media landscape is dominated by Facebook, Amazon, Netflix, and Google (FANG), the most prominent companies in the Chinese online market are Baidu, Alibaba, and Tencent (BAT). Baidu owns iQIYI, the most popular platform for content distribution online. Baidu also owns the main Chinese search engine, which is branded Baidu. The YouKu Tudou service, owned by Alibaba, offers a mix of professional and user-generated content. YouKu offers the video search engine Souko. Tencent has formed partnerships with US companies including HBO, Time Warner, and Paramount, to develop a major entertainment ecosystem. Bytedance is one of the more recent major Chinese newcomers, which has made its mark particularly through its service TikTok, which has become highly successful outside China, including in the United States (Zhu and Keane, 2021).

Platformization: The United States and China

The rise and dominance of Google, Facebook, WeChat, and Sina Weibo are part of the "platformization" of global media and communications and the world society. Digital platforms are increasingly seen as "the driver of economic progress and technological innovations." Individuals, companies, and organizations use these services for personal and professional communication, entertainment, and purchases and trade. These activities can in many ways avoid state regulations and corporate and public intermediaries (van Dijck et al., 2018: 1). Platformization can be seen as a global shift that combines personalization and concentration of corporate influence over a growing number of activities that are moved online, or are developed online, with unforeseen consequences: "[Platformization is] the penetration of infrastructures, economic processes and governmental frameworks of digital platforms in different economic sectors and spheres of life, as well as the reorganisation of cultural practices and imaginations around these platforms" (Poell et al., 2019: 1). Although the infrastructural platforms of Facebook, Amazon, Google, Apple, and Microsoft (the "Big Five") welcome new companies and services, there is "very little room for competitors to penetrate the *core* of the US-based ecosystem" (Poell et al., 2019: 1). Instead, other services, or even platforms, rely on the Big Five's services.

The global cloud industry and infrastructure exemplifies the extent of the platformization phenomena. For example, the online rental giant AirBnB uses Google Maps as well as other services from Google and Facebook, the music-streaming service Spotify uses Google Cloud, and online streaming service Netflix uses Amazon Web Services cloud (van Dijck et al., 2018: 25), and so do its competitors, HBO and Disney+. Apple pays Amazon Web Services a reported $30 million per month for cloud services, and its over 1.5 billion devices rely on this service. By 2020, the top five global cloud services were American and Chinese (see Table 3.16).

In 2006, Amazon was the first of the tech giants to move into cloud services, followed by Microsoft Azure, and then Google Cloud. In the first quarter of 2020, Amazon Web services' $10.2 billion represented over 13 percent of Amazons revenues, compared with Google Cloud's $2.78 billion. Google Cloud increased its revenue from Q1 2019 to Q1 2020 by 52 percent, and in the same period Microsoft Azures' revenue increased by 59 percent (Kaur Dang, 2020).

Table 3.16 Top Cloud Services Global Market Share (%)

1. Amazon Web Services	32
2. Microsoft Azure	20
3. Google Cloud Platform	9
4. Alibaba Cloud	6
5. IBM	5

Source: Dignan, 2021; Richter, 2021.

Digitization and the expansion of the internet and ICT technologies in emerging economies, such as Brazil and India, are accelerating the ICT take-up and industry, including the need for cloud services. Since early 2020, the Covid-19 pandemic contributed to furthering this development dramatically. Social distancing, working from home, and video conferences have increased the use of cloud services. Tools such as Microsoft Teams and Google Meet depend on cloud services, and the popular video conference service Zoom relies on Amazon Web Services (Dignan, 2021).

In many ways, platformization may be considered as "modern-day equivalents of the railroad, telephone, and electric utility monopolies of the late 19th and the 20th centuries" (Plantin et al., 2018: 307, cited in Poell et al., 2019: 4). The "Big Five" are constantly expanding their platforms with new services and applications and moving into new areas and spheres globally.

The disputes between governments and Facebook and Google highlight the power of the latter two. Since 2017, the EU has fined Google a total of nearly $10 billion for violating the EU's competition law through anticompetitive behavior and, for the latest fine, for over a decade (2006–16) of abusive practices in its dealing with online advertisements for other online services including newspapers and blogs. During this time, Google has had over 85 percent market share. Following the latest fine, the publication *Wired* made this point in the piece "The EU hits Google with a third billion dollar fine. So what?" (Tiku, 2019), as Google's dominant position remains and its enormous revenue stream continues to increase. In fact, one European judge, commenting on the latest fine, said that the sum of $2.6 billion is "a small amount of cash" for the company (White and Bodoni, 2020).

Google and Facebook's major share of digital advertising across the world is key to their platform power. For example, in Australia, over 80 percent of advertising spending goes to Google and Facebook. At the same time, Facebook is used as a distributor of news content, but as in other parts of the world, the social media company does not pay the news producers. The Australian government responded to this situation by proposing a law which would force Facebook and Google to pay for news content on their services and platforms. In response, Facebook decided to block its Australian users from sharing or viewing news on the service. Facebook users outside Australia was also denied access to Australian news sites via the service. The government reacted by stating that Facebook's actions clearly showed the "immense market power of these digital social giants." In contrast to Facebook, Google soon after signed deals with Australian publishers to pay for content (BBC, 2021).

China is the only world region and domestic market that has been able to create digital platforms of a scale that mirrors the US platforms. As such, it is Chinese and US companies that drive platformization globally: "In geopolitical terms, the power of the infrastructural core of the platforms ecosystem" is dominated by the US Big Five companies, which are "counterbalanced" by the major Chinese companies, and Tencent, Alibaba, and Baidu in particular (van Dijck et al., 2018: 26). While there may be variations across the globe in how platformization takes shape, and China is the powerful exception, the platformization process and platform economy is mainly driven by these US companies (de Kloet et al., 2019; Poell et al., 2019: 2).

References

Alphabet (2021) Form 10-K. US Securities and Exchange CommissionForm. https://abc.xyz/investor/static/pdf/20210203_alphabet_10K.pdf?cache=b44182d (accessed May 9, 2022).

Andersson, P. (2000) *Stenbeck. En reportage om det virtuella bruket.* Stockholm: Norsteds.

Angwin, J. (2009) *Stealing MySpace: The Battle to Control the Most Popular Website in America.* New York: Random House.

Arrington, M. (2008) Facebook taps users to create translated versions of site. Spanish, French and German available. TechCrunch, January 21. http://techcrunch.com/2008/01/21/facebook-taps-users-to-create-translated-versions-of-site/ (accessed March 5, 2010).

Barrett, M. (2007) It's WHAT'S NEXT. Paper presented at Accenture Global Leadership Conference, April 11.

BBC (2012) Samsung overtakes Nokia in mobile shipments. *BBC News*, April 27. http://www.bbc.co.uk/news/business-17865117 (accessed October 31, 2013).

BBC (2014) Facebook's $19bn WhatsApp deal explained in 60 seconds. *BBC News*, February 20. https://www.bbc.com/news/av/technology-26278217 (accessed March 16, 2021).

BBC (2016) Microsoft sells Nokia feature phones business. *BBC News*, May 18. https://www.bbc.com/news/technology-36320329 (accessed May 26, 2022).

BBC (2018) Google in China: Internet giant "plans censored search engine." *BBC News*, August 2. https://www.bbc.com/news/technology-45041671 (accessed August 11, 2022).

BBC (2021) Facebook blocks Australian users from viewing or sharing news. *BBC News*, February 8. https://www.bbc.com/news/world-australia-56099523 (accessed June 1, 2021).

Castells, M. (2013) *Communication Power.* Oxford: Oxford University Press.

Cohn, D. (2005) Bands embrace social networking. *Wired*, May 18. https://www.wired.com/2005/05/bands-embrace-social-networking/ (accessed June 21, 2022).

Croteau, D. and Hoynes, W. (2006) *The Business of Media: Corporate Media and the Public Interest*. Thousand Oaks, CA: Pine Forge Press.

Davis, J. (2010) Architecture of the personal interactive homepage: Constructing the self through MySpace. *New Media & Society*, 12, 7: 1103–19.

Dignan, L. (2021) Top cloud providers: AWS, Microsoft Azure, and Google Cloud, hybrid, SaaS players. January 11. https://www.zdnet.com/article/the-top-cloud-providers-of-2021-aws-microsoft-azure-google-cloud-hybrid-saas/ (accessed June 21, 2022).

Eadicicco, L. (2014) Microsoft has officially cut Nokia's brand from its most popular smartphone line. Insider, October 24. https://www.businessinsider.in/microsoft-has-officially-cut-nokias-brand-from-its-most-popular-smartphone-line/articleshow/44925672.cms (accessed June 21, 2022).

Esquire (2008) Rupert Murdoch has potential. September 11. https://www.esquire.com/news-politics/a4971/rupert-murdoch-1008/ (accessed June 21, 2022).

Facebook (2008a) Facebook releases site in German. March 2. https://about.fb.com/news/2008/03/facebook-releases-site-in-german/ (accessed June 21, 2022).

Facebook (2008b) Facebook releases site in Spanish; German and French to follow. February 7. https://about.fb.com/news/2008/02/facebook-releases-site-in-spanish-german-and-french-to-follow/ (accessed June 21, 2022).

Facebook (2015) Terms of Service. https://en-gb.facebook.com/terms.php (accessed March 5, 2015).

Facebook (2021a) Form 10-K. Facebook Inc. http://d18rn0p25nwr6d.cloudfront.net/CIK-0001326801/4dd7fa7f-1a51-4ed9-b9df-7f42cc3321eb.pdf (accessed May 11, 2021).

Facebook (2021b) Data policy. What kinds of data do we collect? https://www.facebook.com/about/privacy/update (accessed March 17, 2021).

Forbes (2014) Microsoft-Nokia eye bigger share in smartphone industry with new launches at year end. *Forbes*, September 11. https://www.forbes.com/sites/greatspeculations/2014/09/11/microsoft-nokia-eye-bigger-share-in-smartphone-industry-with-new-launches-at-year-end/ (accessed June 21, 2022).

Frizell, S. (2014) Here are 6 huge websites China is censoring. Time, June 4. https://time.com/2820452/china-censor-web/ (accessed June 21, 2022).

Garrahan, M. (2009) The rise and fall of MySpace. *Financial Times*, December 4. https://www.ft.com/content/fd9ffd9c-dee5-11de-adff-00144feab49a (accessed June 21, 2022).

Gartner (2014) *Gartner Says Annual Smartphone Sales Surpassed Sales of Feature Phones for the First Time in 2013*. Press release, February 13. https://www.gartner.com/en/newsroom/press-releases/2014-02-13-gartner-says-annual-smartphone-sales-surpassed-sales-of-feature-phones-for-the-first-time-in-2013 (accessed June 21, 2022).

Gartner (2021a) *Gartner Says Worldwide Smartphone Sales Declined 5% in Fourth Quarter of 2020*. Press release, February 22. https://www.gartner.com/en/newsroom/press-releases/2021-02-22-4q20-smartphone-market-share-release (accessed June 21, 2022).

Gartner (2021b) Gartner Says Worldwide Smartphone Sales Grew 26% in First Quarter of 2021. Press release, June 7. https://www.gartner.com/en/newsroom/press-releases/2021-06-07-1q21-smartphone-market-share (accessed August 4, 2022).

Gartner (2021c) Gartner Says Worldwide Smartphone Sales Grew 10.8% in Second Quarter of 2021. Press release, September 1. https://www.gartner.com/en/newsroom/press-releases/2021-09-01-2q21-smartphone-market-share (accessed August 4, 2022).

Gartner (2021d) Gartner Forecasts Worldwide Network Infrastructure Revenue to Grow 39% in 2021. Press release, August 4. https://www.gartner.com/en/newsroom/press-releases/2021-08-04-gartner-forecasts-worldwide-5g-network-infrastrucutre-revenue-to-grow-39pc-in-2021 (accessed August 4, 2022).

Geron, T. (2012) Facebook prices third-largest IPO ever, valued at $104 billion. *Forbes*, May 17. https://www.forbes.com/sites/tomiogeron/2012/05/17/facebook-prices-ipo-at-38-per-share/?sh=29dc9b66728a (accessed June 21, 2022).

Google (2006) Google to acquire YouTube for $1.65 billion in stock. October 9. http://googlepress.blogspot.com/2006/10/google-to-acquire-youtube-for-165_09.html (accessed June 21, 2022).

Google (2009) Investor relations. http://investor.google.com/fin_data2003.html (accessed April 5, 2009).

Google (2021) We must help build a more sustainable future for everyone. https://sustainability.google/commitments/#enabling-everyone (accessed May 9, 2022).

Google UK (2020) *We were the first major company to reach carbon neutrality, and we're the largest corporate purchaser of renewable energy* (Tweet, September 14). https://twitter.com/GoogleUK/status/1305462336585695232?ref_src=twsrc%5Etfw (accessed May 27, 2022).

Grunwald, D. (2010) Lost in translation? Twitter language crowdsourcing project. January 26. http://blog.gts-translation.com/2010/01/26/lost-in-translation-twitter-language-crowdsourcing-project (accessed October 31, 2010).

Guttmann, A. (2021) Global ad spend distribution 2020, by medium. Statista.com https://www.statista.com/statistics/376260/global-ad-spend-distribution-by-medium (accessed March 5, 2021).

Harrabin, R. (2020) Google says its carbon footprint is now zero. *BBC News*, September 14. https://www.bbc.com/news/technology-54141899 (accessed May 25, 2021).

Hern, A. and agencies (2018) Google "working on censored search engine" for China. *The Guardian*, August 2. https://www.theguardian.com/world/2018/aug/02/google-working-on-censored-search-engine-for-china (accessed August 11, 2022).

Hillis, K., Petit, M., and Jarrett, K. (2013) *Google and the Culture of Search*. London: Routledge.

HMD Global (2022) About us. https://www.hmdglobal.com/consumer-who-we-are (accessed May 26, 2022).

Howe, J. (2006) The rise of crowdsourcing. *Wired*, June 1. http://www.wired.com/wired/archive/14.06/crowds.html (accessed November 1, 2010).

Hughes, C. R. (2010) Google and the great firewall. *Survival: Global Politics and Strategy*, 52, 2: 19–26.

International Telecommunication Union (2014) *ITU Releases Annual Global ITC Data and ICT Development Index Country Rankings*. Press release, November 24. https://www.itu.int/net/pressoffice/press_releases/2014/68.aspx (accessed May 26, 2022).

International Telecommunication Union (2020a) *Measuring Digital Development: Facts and Figures 2020*. https://www.itu.int/en/ITU-D/Statistics/Documents/facts/FactsFigures2020.pdf (accessed May 9, 2022).

International Telecommunication Union (2020b) *Household Internet Access in Urban Areas Twice as High as in Rural Areas*. Press release. https://www.itu.int/en/mediacentre/pages/pr27-2020-facts-figures-urban-areas-higher-internet-access-than-rural.aspx (accessed May 9, 2022).

International Telecommunication Union (2021a) *Measuring Digital Development: Facts and Figures 2021*. https://www.itu.int/en/ITU-D/Statistics/Documents/facts/FactsFigures2021.pdf (accessed May 26, 2022).

International Telecommunication Union (2021b) *Mobile network coverage*. https://www.itu.int/itu-d/reports/statistics/2021/11/15/mobile-network-coverage/ (accessed August 7, 2022).

Iosifidis, P. (2011) *Global Media and Communication Policy*. London: Palgrave MacMillan.

Jin, D. Y. (2015) *Digital Platforms, Imperialism and Political Culture*. London: Routledge.

Johnson, J. (2021a) Share of desktop search traffic originating from Google in selected countries as of October 2021. Statista, May 11. https://www.statista.com/statistics/220534/googles-share-of-search-market-in-selected-countries (accessed June 3, 2022).

Johnson, J. (2021b) Global market share of search engines 2010–2021. Statista, March 12. https://www.statista.com/statistics/216573/worldwide-market-share-of-search-engines (accessed June 3, 2021).

Kaplan, D. (2007) MySpace ramps up ad targeting initiatives. November 4. http://paidcontent.org/article/419-myspace-ramps-up-ad-targeting-initiatives (accessed July 22, 2011).

Kaur Dang, T. (2020) Is Apple planning to enter cloud computing space? *Forbes*, May 31. https://www.forbes.com/sites/taarinikaurdang/2020/05/31/is-apple-planning-to-enter-cloud-computing-space (accessed March 21, 2021).

de Kloet, J., Poell, T., Zeng, G., and Chow, Y. F. (2019) The platformization of Chinese society: Infrastructure, governance, and practice. *Chinese Journal of Communication*, 12, 3: 249–56.

Kosinski, M., Stillwell, D., and Graepel Kosinski, M. (2013) Private traits and attributes are predictable from digital records of human behavior. *PNAS*, 110, 15: 5802–5. https://www.pnas.org/doi/epdf/10.1073/pnas.1218772110

La Monica, P. R. (2009) *Inside Rupert's Brain*. London: Penguin.

Laffey, D. (2007) Paid search: The innovation that changed the web. *Business Horizons*, 50, 3: 211–18.

Lapowsky, I. (2015) Microsoft finally gets that it won't win the smartphone war. *Wired*, June 17. http://www.wired.com/2015/06/microsoft-stephen-elop (accessed June 18, 2015).

Lee, D. (2013) Nokia: The rise and fall of a mobile giant. *BBC News*, September 3. https://www.bbc.com/news/technology-23947212 (accessed May 9, 2022).

Levine, R. (2006) MySpace aims for a global audience, and finds some stiff competition. *New York Times*, November 7. https://www.nytimes.com/2006/11/07/technology/07myspace.html (accessed May 28, 2022).

Lister, M., Dovey, J., Giddins, S., Grant, I., and Kelly, K. (2009) *New Media: A Critical Introduction*. Second edition. London: Routledge.

McStay, A. (2010) *Digital Advertising*. London: Palgrave.

McStay, A. (2016) *Digital Advertising*. Second edition. London: Palgrave.

Maxwell, R. and Miller, T. (2020) *How Green is Your Smartphone?* Cambridge, UK: Polity.

Mjøs, O. J., Moe, H., and Sundet, V. S. (2014) The functions of buzzwords: A comparison of "Web 2.0" and "telematics." *First Monday*, 19, 12. https://doi.org/10.5210/fm.v19i12.4896

Monaghan, A. (2013) Nokia: The rise and fall of a mobile phone giant. *The Guardian*, September 3. https://www.theguardian.com/technology/2013/sep/03/nokia-rise-fall-mobile-phone-giant (accessed June 21, 2022).

Naughton, J. (2006) MySpace or his space? Does Rupert get the problem? *The Observer*, September 17. http://www.guardian.co.uk/technology/2006/sep/17/comment.media (accessed April 8, 2009).

News Corporation (2007) NBC Universal and News Corp. announce deal with internet leaders AOL, MSN, MySpace and Yahoo! to create a premium online video site with unprecedented reach. http://www.newscorp.com/news/news_329.html (accessed April 8, 2009).

O'Donnell, C. (2013) Yahoo's $1.1 billion acqui-hire of David Karp. *Fortune*, May 20. http://fortune.com/2013/05/20/yahoos-1-1-billion-acqui-hire-of-david-karp (accessed February 23, 2014).

Olson, P. (2008) Time Warner bags Bebo. *Forbes*, March 13. https://www.forbes.com/2008/03/13/bebo-time-warner-markets-equity-cx_po_0312markets10.html?sh=19847a36685d (accessed June 21, 2022).

O'Reilly, T. (2005) What is Web 2.0? Design patterns and business models for the next generation of software. O'Reilly Network. https://www.oreilly.com/pub/a/web2/archive/what-is-web-20.html (accessed June 4, 2022).

Peters, T. J. (1992) *Liberation Management: Necessary Disorganization for the Nanosecond Nineties*. New York: Knopf.

Plantin, J.-C., Lagoze, C., Edwards, P. N., and Sandvig, C. (2018) Infrastructure studies meet platform studies in the age of Google and Facebook. *New Media & Society*, 20, 1: 293–310.

Poell, T., Nieborg, D., and van Dijck, J. (2019) Platformisation. *Internet Policy Review*, 8, 4. https://doi.org/10.14763/2019.4.1425

Ramnarayan, A. (2009) Nokia fights back for share of smartphone market. *The Guardian*, September 2. https://www.theguardian.com/business/2009/sep/02/nokia-smartphones-apple-iphone-music-mobiles (accessed May 26, 2022).

Richter, F. (2021) Amazon leads $130-billion cloud market. *Statista*, February 4. https://www.statista.com/chart/18819/worldwide-market-share-of-leading-cloud-infrastructure-service-providers (accessed March 21, 2021).

Sabbagh, D. (2008) AOL pays $850 in cash for Bebo as cornerstone of international strategy. *The Times*, 14 March. https://www.thetimes.co.uk/article/aol-pays-dollar850m-in-cash-for-bebo-as-cornerstone-of-international-strategy-7hxfsqlfsdf (accessed June 21, 2022).

Sault, S. (2020) Tech for Good: What are the challenges in making technology and digitization more sustainable? World Economic Forum. https://www.weforum.org/agenda/2020/09/what-are-the-challenges-in-making-new-technology-more-sustainable (accessed May 25, 2021).

Schechner, S. and Hagey, K. (2021) Google to stop selling ads based on your specific web browsing. *Wall Street Journal*, March 3. https://www.wsj.com/articles/google-to-stop-selling-ads-based-on-your-specific-web-browsing-11614780021?mod=djemalertNEWS (accessed March 17, 2021).

Schifferes, S. (2006) Has the dotcom boom returned? *BBC News*, October 10. http://news.bbc.co.uk/1/hi/business/6036337.stm (accessed 2 April 2009).

Segall, L. (2012) Facebook acquires Instagram for $1 billion. CNN, April 9. http://money.cnn.com/2012/04/09/technology/facebook_acquires_instagram/index.htm (accessed February 23, 2015).

Sheenan, M. (2018) How Google took on China—and lost. MIT Technology Review, December 19. https://www.technologyreview.com/2018/12/19/138307/how-google-took-on-china-and-lost (accessed May 28, 2022).

Siklos, R. (2005) News Corp. to acquire owner of MySpace.com. *New York Times*, July 18. http://www.nytimes.com/2005/07/18/business/18cnd-newscorp.html (accessed April 2, 2009).

Sinclair, J. (2012) *Advertising, the Media and Globalization: A World in Motion*. London: Routledge.

Spurgeon, C. (2008) *Advertising and New Media*. London: Routledge.

Stone, B. (2007a) Microsoft buys stake in Facebook. *New York Times*, October 25. http://www.nytimes.com/2007/10/25/technology/25facebook.html?_r=1 (accessed March 5, 2010).

Stone, B. (2007b) MySpace to discuss effort to customize ads. *New York Times*, September 18. http://www.nytimes.com/2007/09/18/technology/18myspace.html (accessed September 22, 2008).

Story, L. and Stone, B. (2007) Facebook retreats on online tracking. *New York Times*, November 30. https://www.nytimes.com/2007/11/30/technology/30face.html (accessed June 21, 2022).

Su, J. (2019) Confirmed: Google Terminated Project Dragonfly, Its Censored Chinese Search Engine. *Forbes*, June 19. https://www.forbes.com/sites/jeanbaptiste/2019/07/19/confirmed-google-terminated-project-dragonfly-its-censored-chinese-search-engine/ (accessed August 11, 2022).

Syvertsen, T., Enli, G., Mjøs, O. J., and Moe, H. (2014) *The Media Welfare State: Nordic Media in the Digital Era*. Ann Arbor, MI: University of Michigan Press.

Tankovska, H. (2021) Global social networks ranked by number of users 2021. Statista, February 9. https://www.statista.com/statistics/272014/global-social-networks-ranked-by-number-of-users (accessed March 18, 2021).

TCO Certified (2021) E-waste—a toxic waste stream where valuable finite resources are lost. https://tcocertified.com/e-waste (accessed May 9, 2022).

Thussu, D. K. (2007) The "Murdochization" of news? The case of Star TV in India. *Media, Culture & Society*, 29, 4: 593–611.

Thussu, D. K. (2010) Introduction, pp. 1–10 in D. K. Thussu (ed.) *International Communication: A Reader*. London: Routledge.

Thussu, D. K. (2018) The Globalization of Chinese Media: The Global Context, pp. 17–33 in D. K. Thussu, H. de Burgh, and A. Shi (eds.) *China's Media Go Global*. New York: Routledge.

Thussu, D. K. and Nordenstreng, K. (eds.) (2021) *BRICS Media: Reshaping the Global Communication Order?* Abingdon, UK: Routledge.

Tiku, N. (2019) The EU hits Google with a third billion dollar fine. So what? *Wired*, March 20. https://www.wired.com/story/eu-hits-google-third-billion-dollar-fine-so-what (accessed May 27, 2021).

Turow, J. (2011) *The Daily You: How the New Advertising Industry is Defining Your Identity and Your Worth*. New Haven, CT: Yale University Press.

Tweh, B. and Patel, S. (2020) Google Chrome to phase out third-party cookies in effort to boost privacy. *Wall Street Journal*, January 14. https://www.wsj.com/articles/google-chrome-to-phase-out-third-party-cookies-in-effort-to-boost-privacy-11579026834?mod=article_inline (accessed March 17, 2021).

UN (2020) The Global E-waste Monitor 2020—Quantities, Flows, and the Circular Economy Potential. https://ewastemonitor.info/gem-2020 (accessed May 28, 2022).

UN (2021) SDG Media Compact. https://www.un.org/sustainabledevelopment/wp-content/uploads/2019/12/Overview_for-members_2020.pdf (accessed May 27, 2021).

Van Couvering, E. (2008) The History of the Internet Search Engine: Navigational Media and the Traffic Commodity, pp. 177–206 in A. Spink and M. Zimmer (eds.) *Web Search: Multidisciplinary Perspectives*. Berlin: Springer-Verlag.

Van Dijck, J. and Nieborg, D. (2009) Wikinomics and its discontents: A critical analysis of Web 2.0 business manifestoes. *New Media & Society*, 11, 4: 855–74.

Van Dijck, J., Poell, T., and De Waal, M. (2018) *The Platform Society: Public Values in a Connective World*. Oxford: Oxford University Press.

Vascellaro, J. E. (2008) MySpace aims for trickier markets. *Wall Street Journal*, December 13. http://online.wsj.com/article/SB119749126310624423.html?mod=dist_smartbrief (accessed April 6, 2009).

Wasko, J. and Erickson, M. (2009) The Political Economy of YouTube, pp. 372–87 in P. Snickars and P. Vonderau (eds.) *The YouTube Reader*. Stockholm: National Library of Sweden.

Wauters, R. (2008) Myspace gives up on the Netherlands. *Techcrunch*, October 26. http://www.techcrunch.com/2008/10/26/myspace-gives-up-on-the-nether-lands/ (accessed April 6, 2009).

Web 2.0 Conference (2004) 5–7 October, San Francisco. https://web.archive.org/web/20050312204307/http://www.web2con.com/web2con/ (accessed June 21, 2022).

White, A. and Bodoni, S. (2020) Google's $2.6 billion fine is like loose change, judge says. Bloomberg, February 14. https://www.bloomberg.com/news/articles/2020-02-14/google-s-2-6-billion-fine-is-like-loose-change-judge-says (accessed May 27, 2021).

World Economic Forum (2020) *Accelerating Digital Inclusion in the New Normal*. World Economic Forum. http://www3.weforum.org/docs/WEF_Accelerating_Digital_Inclusion_in_the_New_Normal_Report_2020.pdf (accessed May 25, 2021).

World Trade Organization (2008) *WTO DG Lamy Celebrates Benefits of Opening Trade in Telecoms*. Press release, February 20. https://www.wto.org/english/news_e/pres08_e/pr517_e.htm (accessed May 26, 2022).

Yang, G. (2009) *The Power of the Internet in China: Citizen Activism Online*. New York: Columbia University Press.

Zenith Media (2017) Mobile internet advertising to overtake desktop in 2017. https://www.zenithmedia.com/mobile-internet-advertising/ (accessed August 2, 2022).

Zenith Media (2020) Coronavirus crisis accelerates shift to digital advertising. https://www.zenithmedia.com/coronavirus-crisis-accelerates-shift-to-digital-advertising (accessed May 10, 2022).

Zenith Media (2021) Ecommerce and video fuel faster-than-expected recovery in global adspend. https://www.zenithmedia.com/ecommerce-and-video-fuel-faster-than-expected-recovery-in-global-adspend (accessed March 9, 2021).

Zhu, Y. and Keane, M. (2021) China's Cultural Power Reconnects with the World, pp. 209–22 in D. Thussu and K. Nordenstreng (eds.) *BRICS Media: Reshaping the Global Communication Order?* Abingdon, UK: Routledge.

Zuckerberg, M. (2007) Thoughts on Beacon. December 5. https://m.facebook.com/nt/screen/?params=%7B%22note_id%22%3A349480096129541%7D&path=%2Fnotes%2Fnote%2F&refsrc=deprecated&_rdr (accessed June 21, 2022).

Media Companies, Content, and Branding in the Global Digital Age

Platforms, Distribution, and Production

This chapter focuses on media companies in a global digital context as digitization, convergence, and the worldwide popularization of the internet have had a major impact on this part of the industry. It explores the global media players, how audiovisual content is produced and distributed, and the role of marketing and branding. While the traditional export of television, film, and media content to national media outlets continues to grow, the emergence of globally expanding legal and illegal streaming services, and the arrival of new players from outside the media sector, along with geopolitical shifts and regional developments, represent drivers of change. New global online media content players are making inroads into national audiences across the world and thereby represent fierce competition for traditional national media and broadcasters, who seek to adapt. As the number of media content providers proliferates and media content is distributed cross-nationally at unprecedented scale and on different platforms and devices, branding and marketing have become of increased significance and value. This chapter also looks at how such practices are employed in relation to media companies, services, and content.

Global Media Content and Distribution Companies: Traditional and New Players

In the first decade of the twenty-first century, critics pointed out how "the centre of gravity" of the major global media companies in the world was in the developed world, more precisely, the United States (Sparks, 2007: 144). While the United States remains the most important market for the large US media companies in terms of revenue, this is beginning to change. This is particularly due to the global expansion of internet-based media companies, or media companies exploiting the internet, through streaming services.

Facebook's international revenue was over 50 percent in the last quarter of 2020. Alphabet's (including Google) revenue in 2017 was equally split between the United States and overseas. Netflix's revenue streams further underline the significance of overseas revenue for an internet-based company, yet with a more conventional business model based on subscriptions and the distribution of media content. In 2020, over 50 percent of the company's revenue was generated outside of the United States and Canada (see Table 4.1).

Walt Disney Company exemplifies the continuing significance of US revenue for the largest media companies. In 2019, over 65 percent of the global revenues of nearly $70 billion came from this region. However, the launch of Disney+ in 2019 and the rapid overseas expansion of this streaming service signals an increased focus on consumers outside the United States. Reaching 100 million subscribers worldwide by early 2021, Disney+ has in a short time become the company's main strategic priority (Walt Disney Company, 2020; 2021).

The online streaming phenomenon was key for media companies to enable them to exploit the internet for global distribution of film and television content, and with digitization and convergence, technology companies soon also began to insert themselves into the media sector value chain (Chalaby and Plunkett, 2020). In fact, already in 2005, Google indicated that it had also become a media company: "We began as a technology company and have evolved into a software, technology, Internet, advertising and media company all rolled into one" (Google, 2005: 13). In 2006, Google moved into the media content and distribution industry through its acquisition of YouTube, and later by launching Google Chromecast and Google TV. Amazon's streaming service, Amazon Prime Video, launched as Amazon Unbox in 2006, and since then the company has become a major media content investor. Apple introduced its digital media player device, AppleTV, in 2007, and launched the streaming service AppleTV+ in 2019, also

Table 4.1 Netflix Global Revenue by Region, 2020 ($ Thousand)

United States and Canada	11,455,396
Europe, Middle East and Africa	7,772,252
Latin America	3,156,727
Asia-Pacific	2,372,300

Source: Netflix, 2020.

with original content. Google, Apple, and Amazon entering into the handheld device market with their own smartphones and tablets, key devices for media distribution and consumption, further emphasizes how technology companies have inserted themselves into the media industry, or even turned themselves into media companies as well. The technology giants' role as cloud service providers for media companies and streaming services further underlines their increasingly central role in the media industry. Netflix uses Amazon Web Services' cloud (van Dijck et al., 2018: 25), and so do its competitors, HBO, Disney+, and Apple.

Streaming services such as Netflix, Disney+, Amazon Video Prime, and AppleTV+ are owned by technology companies, but rely on media content from traditional media companies. To succeed, they have acquired media companies, merged and created production alliances, and become major commissioners and producers of content themselves, and they have achieved strong positions across the global media and communications landscape over the past decade (see Table 4.2).

The global incumbents, the traditional major media and entertainment companies, "keep scrambling in an era of streaming media and cord-cutting," as the trade press put it (Bond and Szalai, 2019). The major consolidations taking place between media content companies and content and distribution companies is a key response to this development (Table 4.3).

In 2021, shortly before Amazon's acquisition of MGM Studio, AT&T and Discovery Coms. decided to combine their media content divisions (Warner Media and Discovery) into a new company to create one of the world's largest content and streaming operations (Kovach and Meredith, 2021).

Table 4.2 The Major Streaming Services' Programming Budget, 2020

Netflix	$16 billion
Amazon Video Prime	$7 billion
AppleTV+	$6 billion
Hulu	$3 billion
Disney+	$1.75 billion
HBO Max	$1.5 billion
Quibi	$1 billion
Peacock	$800 million

Source: Klebnikov, 2020.

Table 4.3 Major Acquisitions of Media Companies in 2018–21

Year	Acquiring Company	Acquired Company	Acquisition Costs
2018	AT&T	Time Warner	$85 billion
2018	Discovery Coms.	Scripps Network	$14 billion
2019	Disney	21st Century Fox	$71 billion
2019	Comcast	Sky	$39 billion
2019	CBS	Viacom	$12 billion
2021	Univision	Grupo Televisa	$4.8 billion
2021	Amazon	MGM Studios	$8.45 billion

Source: BBC, 2021; Bridge, 2019; Hayes, 2021; Lancefield, 2019.

These major takeovers and mergers clearly signal that "when faced with uncertainty, media giants strive to integrate content and production capabilities with large (and international) distribution networks" (Chalaby, 2020: 381). Such major mergers and acquisitions can have cost-reducing benefits, but importantly, also secure intellectual property rights, allowing for the expansion and wider distribution of both proprietary advertising and media content through, particularly, online streaming services (Lancefield, 2019). Disney's launch of Disney+ in 2019, the same year as its acquisition of 21st Century Fox, and HBO Max's launch in 2020 in the United States—after AT&T's acquisition of Time Warner—are examples of this approach. The Covid-19 pandemic has contributed to the intensification of the digital shift and the drive to move media outlets online, as new streaming services have launched and media consumption increased and, importantly, as spending on digital advertising has increased rapidly. Digital advertising's share of the total global advertising spending has increased from 48 percent in 2019 to 52 percent in 2020, and is expected to reach 58 percent in 2023 (Zenith Media, 2021).

The critique of the use of the term "global," both owing to the traditional US skew of revenue as well as limited reach, subscribers, and audience (see, e.g., Hafez, 2007; Sparks, 2007), is still relevant in some ways. Even Netflix, one of the companies most often referred to as "global," still has just over 220 million subscribers worldwide, and national broadcasters and media outlets continue to attract large shares of audiences. While the term "global" may refer to scale, for example to a media company with a presence in over 100 territories, it can also refer to the media value chains that stretch across the world and create "interdependence" between them: "A value chain is said to be global not merely because it is international but because it involves firms that interact with one another across borders and depend on one another to design, manufacture, transport, and market a product" (Chalaby, 2016b: 36). Therefore, "global" can refer to the way that media production and distribution is increasingly organized across the world: "A handful of global firms and products do not make a system global. What does are the GVCs [global value chains] that bind together national markets and connect interdependent businesses, institutions, places and networks" (Chalaby, 2020: 382).

The global value chains for television content emerge as the production and distribution of programming becomes more and more demanding. As single companies cannot have all the required expertise in-house, they have to collaborate. The scale of such collaboration is significant, as major media conglomerates can work with hundreds of firms and suppliers (Chalaby, 2019; 2020). The point is that the "global" in "global media system" can refer to the organization of such television content value chains that are spread across the world and involves the coordination of firms and national media markets (Chalaby, 2016b; 2020).

Internet distribution of video content has accelerated the internationalization and global expansion of production and suppliers. The majority of suppliers expand within a certain selected segment through international or global growth. This is seen across all production segments. The emergence of television production majors is a key example; in the facilities sector, for example, the film and television studio Pinewood Studios offers filming locations worldwide. International scale benefits all parts of production and contributes to maximizing funds for production and commissioning (Chalaby, 2020: 381). Netflix's worldwide presence and subscriber base has allowed for budgets of as much as $16 billion in 2020, and $17 billion in 2021. This is more than major media conglomerates spend. Amazon follows, with its programming budget for 2020 of $7 billion, and AppleTV+ with $6 billion (Klebnikov, 2020). These companies exploit the possibilities for cross-national production, online distribution, and rapid expansion and growth in subscribers to achieve economies of scale: "While the markets of broadcasters used to be delineated by national borders, it is far less the case with entertainment platforms. Access can be blocked, notably in China and Russia, progress in certain markets can be slow, but OTT platforms are essentially global and often reach 100+ territories within a few years of existence" (Chalaby, 2020: 382). In other words, international and global scale and presence are not just an advantage for media companies, "but a necessity that often makes the difference between success and failure" (Chalaby,

2020: 381). This is also the case in the trade in media products. While trade is still dominated by the Western part of the industry, companies from the "Global South" have increased their international reach. This growth is the result of increased "South–South" trade, while substantial "South–North" trade has still yet to materialize substantially: "Many of these firms have global activities but they have yet to make solid inroads into Western markets: Bollywood movies, telenovelas and South Korean formats are yet to be widely distributed in the West" (Chalaby, 2020: 376).

However, although the United States and Western countries dominate "the global communication space" both in terms of hardware and software, the distribution of media content from, for example, the BRICS countries has increased. This includes Russian- and Chinese-produced television news (RT and CGTN respectively) in English and other languages, and entertainment from India, Brazil, and South Africa. The flow of media content, particularly from China and India, is likely to increase substantially and become more visible across the world (Thussu and Nordenstreng, 2021: 7).

While the majority of programming distributed across the world is traditional, "canned" programming, the arrival of the global television format revolutionized the television industry and programming market throughout the twenty-first century. The global television format could be tailored for each country by changing the actual content within a copyrighted set of rules and restrictions. This represented a programming form that was cost-efficient and perfectly suited for global distribution (see Case Study 4.1).

Case Study 4.1 Global Television Formats

The global trade in television programming has mainly consisted of programming that has already been made—often referred to "canned" television productions—and mostly produced in Hollywood. The genre of television formats has been part of this trade since the 1950s, but "the format revolution came with the new millennium," and "transformed a small commerce that was lying at the fringe of the TV industry into a global business" (Chalaby, 2016a: 8). In the 1990s, the need for programming across the world increased as commercial television evolved in Central and Eastern Europe, the Middle East, Asia, and Latin America. The television format genre proved to be highly attractive for both broadcasters and their audiences as the latter preferred local content, yet traditional programs were more expensive to produce than the cost-efficient, pre-established production methods and guidelines already tested in other markets (Chalaby, 2020: 375). This genre stands out as it increases the amount and flows of media content across borders. However, in contrast to traditional programming content formats it articulates "both local and global dimensions": "A format (or part of it) can be called global, not because it travels to every single country, but because its IP definers—structure and brand attributes—will be replicated everywhere it goes" (Chalaby and Esser, 2017: 4).

While the global television channels and imported television programs are dubbed or subtitled into different languages, the popularity of global television formats represents a far more extensive form of linguistic and cultural adaptation to local and national contexts, and a television programming form with an unprecedented ability to travel across the world and appeal to television audiences worldwide. Large numbers of television formats are sold across the world, and the total value of income from production and distribution fees is estimated to be several billion dollars annually (Chalaby, 2016a: 1).

In the late 1990s, four television formats—or "super formats"—in particular were key to increasing the popularity of these concepts: *Who Wants to Be a Millionaire?*, *Survivor*, *Big Brother*, and *Idols*, both in terms of their worldwide distribution and, importantly, also by showing the potential for formats (Chalaby, 2012). The increase in numbers of commercial broadcasters and television channels increased the demand for programming, many "lacked the expertise to create what audiences always prefer," and formats were easy to produce and adapt (Chalaby, 2012: 37).

Formats are usually developed by a broadcaster or a producer in one country and then licensed to media outlets across the world. In contrast to traditional television programming, a format is tailored to specific television markets according to a set of format rules, directions and detailed guiding, as well as information and data on audience ratings that can contribute to making the format successful in different television markets: "The commodity known as the format package includes not only a licensing agreement but also a wealth of documentation (known in the trade as the 'Bible') of its previous local iterations, production notes and history—often including graphic design elements, character notations, musical theme and cues, staging information and other production detail—and information about ratings and target audiences" (Oren and Shahaf, 2012: 2). For example, by 2010, the global television format *Come Dine With Me* (ITV Studios, UK), had been exported to twenty countries with over 4,000 episodes produced. "It is a little like McDonald's or Starbucks," according to Tobi de Graaff, director of global TV distribution at the format producer ITV Studios: "Take what's successful about the show but don't ignore that you are dealing with different cultures and make the right twists to make it feel extremely home-grown and natural" (de Graaf, quoted in Brook, 2010).

Another reason that formats are attractive for broadcasters and producers is that they are considered as national domestic programs, and are popular among the national television audiences: "they fuel local and in-house production and contribute to domestic production quotas" (Colwell and Price, 2005). This means that a television format adapted to a national territory contributes to the national production quotas, set by media authorities and common across the world. In fact, they have become "part of business strategies to bypass local programming quotas" across the world (Waisbord, 2004: 363).

Yet, in a global context, views on the extent to which television formats change the power structures of the television market differ. On the one hand, many emphasize how the television format phenomenon represents an altering force in the power structures of the global television programming market "as players in previously hopelessly marginalized markets now successfully compete in this ever expanding market. The ability to come up with innovative broadcasting ideas on a shoestring budget—a skill every marginalized, underfinanced and scrappy television industry refined for sheer survival—is now the winning asset in the new format-dominated global television industry" (Oren and Shahaf, 2013: 3). On the other hand, the origins and "key principles of the format industry were established by the early 1950s," and "the first format license were adaptations of US shows acquired by British broadcasters" (Chalaby, 2016a). As within the global television programming market, the Anglo-American skew is also significant within television format sales, according to the Format Recognition and Protection Association (FRAPA). The UK became the leading country for format development and export in the 1990s. Between 2006 and 2008, the UK was by far the leading exporter, and one of the countries that had the least imports, and was followed by the United States and Netherlands. Argentina was the fourth largest exporter, as it had become "the format powerhouse of Latin America" (FRAPA, 2009: 3). During this period, 445 formats led to 1,262 versions across fifty-seven television markets (2009: 11, referred to in Chalaby, 2012). Still, the rise of the TV format has clearly contributed to the globalization of the production and distribution of media content and the diversity of genres, as well as the expansion of production companies. While TV formats used to include the game show and reality TV genres, today's formats also include drama and comedy genres. TV formats have enabled production companies to expand rapidly as these productions require far less investment than traditional television programming, and also generate license fees for the rights holders. This has resulted in the emergence of the global TV content production majors, such as Endemol Shine (Chalaby, 2020: 376–7).

Globalizing Streaming Video On-Demand Services

While several pioneering online distributors of audiovisual media content emerged in the United States in the late 1990s, such as CinemaNow and Intertainer, these lacked capital and size, and neither the technology nor the media audience were prepared for these new services. They either went out of business or were acquired. It was not until 2001 that the major Hollywood studios began to move into online distribution, and not with much success. That year, Sony, Paramount, Universal, MGM-UA, and Warner launched the video-on-demand service Movielink, and Disney started Moviebeam. In the mid-2000s, a third wave of major online media content distributors—the most prominent being Netflix, Hulu, Amazon, and iTunes—emerged and, together with HBO, these have become dominant players within this market segment (Cunningham and Silver, 2013: 3–4). Apple+ was launched later, and have rapidly become part of the dominant US online media content services.

While streaming has been used since at least the 1980s for data traffic and network distribution, it is over the past decade that the phenomenon has become mainstream and situated at the heart of popular media distribution and consumption (Spilker and Colbjørnsen, 2020).

Hulu represented the most significant early response by traditional studios and companies involved in media content production and distribution. Launched in 2006, the service's ownership structure is characterized by "near constant change" (Sanson and Steirer, 2019). In 2021, the online streaming video-on-demand service is a joint venture between Disney, who owns 67 percent, and NBCUniversal, controlling 33 percent of the company. While Google, Amazon, and Yahoo! launched bids for the service early on, it was not sold (Cunningham and Silver, 2013: 91). In 2010, the service's chief executive, Jason Kilar, stated that "We won't be satisfied until this is a global service" (Kilar, quoted in Laughlin, 2010). While Hulu achieved a considerable market share in the United States, at the time, it was still the only one controlled by the traditional media companies. Instead, "the new King Kongs of the online world are, almost without exception, new to screen distribution when considered against a backdrop of more than a century's history of film and television distribution" (Cunningham and Silver, 2013: 31).

Then, in 2019, the global traditional media giant Disney launched Disney+. The subscription-based video streaming service offered around 11,700 episodes and 700 films from Disney's library, and an growing number of original series and movies produced by the company's studios: "[W]e set a target of 100+ new titles per year, and this includes Disney Animation, Disney Live Action, Marvel, Star Wars, and National Geographic," according to Disney CEO Bob Chapek (quoted in Walt Disney Company, 2021; see also Walt Disney Company, 2020).

In fact, as Disney+ reached 100 million subscribers worldwide in early 2021, it is predicted that the service will surpass Netflix in terms of global subscribers by 2026, with 294 million subscribers compared with 286 million respectively (Middleton, 2021).

With the launch of Disney+, Walt Disney Company signaled a shift from traditional media outlets, particularly television channels, to streaming. While Disney+ reached 100 million subscribers and expanded into over fifty-nine countries in just sixteen months, including Canada, Australia, New Zealand, and in Europe, Latin America, and South East Asia, the Disney Channel subsequently closed down in, among others, Italy, Australia, New Zealand, and the UK. The global television channel Disney XD shut down in Germany, France, Spain, the UK, Spain, India, France, and across Africa, and in territories in South East Asia and Scandinavia. Media content that had fueled these television channels and new productions now bolster the expansion and development of Disney+.

While talks of international expansion of Hulu have been ongoing since its launch, this has not materialized. In fact, CEO of Disney Bob Chapek stated, "Hulu has no brand awareness outside of the US" (Alexander, 2021). Despite being the main owner of Hulu, Disney instead launched Star, a fully Disney-owned general entertainment streaming platform, internationally in 2021.

A key reason for the rapid expansion of Netflix and other internet-distributed video services into national media territories is the fact that they "can enter into and compete in a large number of international markets without extensive in-country infrastructure" (Lobato, 2019: 115). In fact, when entering a new country or territory, Netflix has often just "switched on" the service, as most of the localization and expansion has been done from its headquarters in California. For example, when opening its office in France, the office consisted of only three people, and when launching in Australia only a single freelance publicist was employed in the country (Lobato, 2019: 116).

While Netflix do have offices around the world, its operations are centered in a few global hubs, and the headquarters in California continues to deal with programming and marketing for a number of territories. When expanding outside the United States, the company focuses on investments in technology and media content, and not on establishing a physical presence (Lobato, 2019: 116; see also Case Study 4.2).

By 2025, Netflix, Disney+, and Amazon Prime are expected to have around 50 percent of global SVOD (subscription video on demand) subscriptions. The same year, it is estimated that one-third of the world's households will have a least one SVOD subscription. In 2019, only one-quarter of households worldwide subscribed to such services. By 2025, United States is predicted to continue to be the largest market, yet its market share is expected to drop from 49 percent to 42 percent due to the growth in subscribers in Europe and Asia. China is expected to remain the second-largest SVOD market, followed by the UK, Germany, and France, in which the French streaming service Salto is expected to grow (see Table 4.4; Easton, 2020).

Table 4.4 SVOD Revenues by Top Five Countries ($ Million)

	2019	2020	2025 (projected)
United States	24.619	29.580	42.061
China	6.063	7.214	9.127
UK	2.235	2.919	4.476
Germany	1.594	2.186	3.755
France	1.254	1.938	3.645
Others	14.105	18.840	36.497

Source: Easton, 2020.

Case Study 4.2 Netflix and Global Streaming

Netflix has over 221 million subscribers across the world, of which more than 146 million are from countries outside of the United States and Canada (see Table 4.5; Netflix, 2021a, 2021b). However, the media company started out in 1997 as a DVD rental business and later expanded into streaming video-on-demand. The streaming service was first only available in the United States, before it began to expand overseas, and it moved from being a licensor of second-

Table 4.5 Netflix Global Subscriptions (Thousands)

2021	221,840
2020	203,663
2019	167,090
2018	139,259
2017	110,644

Source: Netflix, 2020; Netflix, 2021a.

window film and television programming to becoming one of the world's main investors in original productions across most genres (Netflix, 2021a).

Netflix's reported $4 billion–investment in programming licensing deals in 2011 signaled the intent of the company to become a global player. The remake of the original BBC miniseries *House of Cards*, released in early 2013, reportedly cost $100 million, and importantly, the production received much attention internationally (Fagerjord and Kueng, 2019).

Netflix began to expand in 2010; by late 2011 it had around 1.5 million overseas subscribers, and by 2021 over 146 million subscribers outside the United States and Canada (see Table 4.6).

The rapid expansion of Netflix was due to its first-mover status both in the United States and internationally, and access to a large content library consisting of both licensed and, increasingly, originally commissioned content, as well as the service's early accessibility for platforms and devices: smartphones, smart TVs, tablets, game consoles, and conventional laptops (Cunningham and Silver, 2013: 91). To expand, Netflix depend on licensing content from a number of suppliers in each market. The company competes for exclusive SVOD rights over several years, with cable and broadcasters as well as other online distributors (Fagerjord and Kueng, 2019). However, Netflix have focused on increasing the number of original productions, and expect to spend a total of $17 billion on content in 2021.

To strengthen its production capabilities across the world, Netflix is setting up production houses in key market such as the UK in 2019, France in 2020, and Italy 2020. In India, Netflix has spent $400 million on original and licensed programming. Localization of content is seen as key to increase subscriptions in more mature markets and to compete with local or national outlets across the world (Moyser, 2021). The company emphasizes that its local programming can have significant audiences around the world (see Table 4.7).

Although Netflix, as well as Amazon, emphasize an increase in local programming, such content only makes up a small part of its catalogue.

Table 4.6 Netflix Subscribers by Region, 2021 (Millions)

United States and Canada	75.22
Europe, Middle East and Africa	74.04
Latin America	39.96
Asia-Pacific	32.63

Source: Netflix, 2021b.

Table 4.7 Local Programming Standouts, Country of Origin, and Viewers in the First Four Weeks of Release, Q1 2021 (Millions)

Who Killed Sara?	Mexico	55
Below Zero	Spain	47
Squared Love	Poland	31
Space Sweepers	Korea	26

Source: Netflix, 2021.

In fact, in most markets and regions, only around 10 percent of Netflix's catalogue is local content. In certain markets, regulations require quotas of local content for foreign OTT (over-the-top) platforms and SVODs, and these policies are de facto driving the localization of these services. Still, by 2020, as much as 50 percent of Netflix's in-production programming was planned to be produced in markets other than the United States (Thomson, 2020). A study of Netflix's content offerings and investments in the four EU countries Belgium, Romania, Spain, and Sweden showed a clear US dominance, but an increasing diversity in the catalogues. However, the amount invested depends on the size of the markets, favoring the largest and most mature markets, such as UK, France, Spain, and Germany, which are all rather well represented in all catalogues (Iordache, 2021). This mirrors the strategy of US cable and satellite channels such as Discovery, MTV, and Disney Channel as they expanded into Europe in the 1990s. The larger the market, the larger the amount invested in programming, and some of the largest European markets, such as the UK and Germany, could financially justify dedicated national television channels (Mjøs, 2010).

To attract and retain subscribers, Netflix focuses on improving the user experience through interface design, personalized recommendation systems, and individual access for household members to watch simultaneously and on multiple devices, and, importantly, attractive and suitable content offering in line with the taste of subscribers (Fagerjord and Kueng, 2019). The collection and exploitation of user data has been key for the company from early on, with the aim to optimize the user service, according to Ted Sarandos, Co-CEO of Netflix: "During the early days of the Internet, when everybody else was spending big money on Super Bowl, we were investing instead in technology, on taste-based algorithms, to make sure every single user had a personalized, highly effective matching tool to use when they visited our site" (Sarandos, quoted in Curtin et al., 2014: 135). The data is used to improve the recommendation feature in particular, but also to try to determine more accurately what content to invest in and produce; according to Netflix's Chief product officer, Neil Hunt:

> We take a proposal for an original production or for a piece of content we're going to buy and we plug in all the data we can about it into our models. We're able to predict reach and hours for that piece of content even before it exists with reasonable precision in a way that helps us to say, "this is worth funding" or 'that's not worth funding".

(Hunt, quoted in Kuburas, 2014)

While television channels and networks usually require producers to create a pilot or episode of a proposed television series or show, according to the UK newspaper *The Guardian*, Netflix commissioned *House of Cards* without one as "their data indicated there was a big audience who would appreciate a new political drama and the investment was a risk grounded in fact" (Datoo, 2014). The focus on data collection and analysis of user data is key for its expansion: "Whenever possible, Netflix prefers to invest in its technical infrastructures rather than spending money on foreign offices and staff. It mines its greatest assets—its cast stores of customer data—to identify trends that help it understand what kind of programming current and potential Netflix subscribers in international markets might want" (Lobato, 2019: 116).

In fact, digital technology and a growing global subscriber base enable Netflix to target "transnational clusters" of subscribers with its programming. While broadcasters "aggregate a nation-bound audience that can be sold to advertisers who conceive of audiences aggregated in national clumps," Netflix target subscribers' "tastes and sensibilities that fail to become significant when aggregated within a nation and can thus provide for different program tastes than services that scope their audience through a national lens" (Lodz, 2020).

The Response from National Incumbents on the Global SVODs

In 2020, many globally expanding SVODs, including Netflix, experienced an unusual increase in popularity. As media audiences were forced to spend more time at home due to the Covid-19 pandemic, Netflix's subscriber base, as an example, increased by 25 million in the first half of 2020. Disney+ reached its five-year subscriber growth plan in less than a year since launching in 2019 (Zenith Media, 2021). Even without the pandemic, it is clear that "Netflix and other transnational online video streaming services are disrupting long-established arrangements in national television systems around the world" (D'Arma et al., 2021; see also Case Studies 4.3 and 4.4).

Europe has so far been the key overseas market for the expanding US SVODs. In fact, today these services dominate the European SVOD market completely, changing the traditional legacy media landscape dramatically. The EU agency European Audiovisual Observatory (EAO) points out, "With the shift to direct-to-consumer SVOD streaming services, and the entry of global tech, US studios and entertainment players into EU national markets, the old market equilibrium is changing and new entrants dominate the EU SVOD market" (EAO, 2021; see Table 4.8). To address the dominance of the US services, in terms of both market share and origin of content in their catalogues, the 2018 revision of the EU's Audiovisual Media Service Directive demands on-demand audiovisual services to include, among others, a 30 percent quota of European content (Iordache, 2021).

Table 4.8 Top Three OTT SVOD Services in European Countries, 2020

Country	1st Rank	2nd Rank	3rd Rank	Total SVOD Subscribers (Thousands)	Market Share
Austria	Amazon	Netflix	Disney+	2,378	87%
Belgium	Netflix	Amazon	Streamz	3,152	81%
Bulgaria	Netflix	AppleTV+	Amazon	440	89%
Czech Rep.	Netflix	AppleTV+	Amazon	876	98%
Denmark	Netflix	Viaplay	TV2 Play	3,826	65%
Finland	Netflix	Viaplay	Ruutu+	2,536	58%
France	Netflix	Amazon	AppleTV+	15,453	92%
Germany	Amazon	Netflix	Disney+	33,333	82%
Ireland	Netflix	Amazon	AppleTV+	978	100%
Italy	Netflix	Amazon	TIM Vision	13,136	62%
Netherlands	Netflix	Amazon	Videoland	6.250	74%
Poland	Netflix	IPLA	Amazon	4,685	77%
Portugal	Netflix	AppleTV+	Amazon	1,473	81%
Romania	Netflix	Voyo	Amazon	1,160	99%
Spain	Netflix	Amazon	AppleTV+	10,824	79%
Sweden	Netflix	Viaplay	HBO Nordic	5,039	63%
UK	Netflix	Amazon	Disney+	31,791	86%

Source: Adapted from EAO, 2021.

How are European television broadcasters and channels responding? Public service media (PSM) are legacy media, many of which are strong national incumbents and part of the institutional establishment. In Italy, Flanders, and the UK, the public service media notably first responded with certain "complacency and resistance," but then responded through focused strategies that aimed "to differentiate PSM offerings, while also diversifying into activities, primarily across new platforms, that mimic SVoD approaches and probe production collaborations" (D'Arma, 2021). Still, the strategic responses of the European public service media are not always coherent and linear. In fact, a range of responses may coexist and contradict each other. While the public service media "exhibit some degree of resistance, usually through lobbying to protect their market position (e.g., on prominence, rights, quotas) they all simultaneously seek international sales and production collaborations with SVoD rivals" (D'Arma, 2021).

In the United States, "Netflix has catalyzed a paradigm shift" in the audiovisual sector through its rapid growth in subscribers, and indirectly through fostering "cord-cutting" and "cord-shaving" practices and other consumer behaviors among media users and audiences, with consequences for the business models of traditional film and television producers, broadcasters, and distributors (Jayakar and Park, 2020).

In face of these transformations and disruptions, a key industry response is the major consolidations between US global media companies and content and distribution companies (Lancefield, 2019; see Table 4.3). Such consolidations mirror those seen in Europe, yet this has resulted in the formation of new alliances and new forms of competition. For example, European broadcasters and media companies both compete with Netflix for revenue and audiences while at the same time act as suppliers of media content, and thereby rely on income from licensing and sales from the company. Similarly, the US incumbents' responses and relation to Netflix may contradict each other and thereby "create the scope for complex interactions" (Jayakar and Park, 2020; see also Case Study 4.3).

While expanding rapidly across world regions, Netflix has not succeeded in creating a presence in China: "We got turned down by the Chinese government several years ago. And we have not been spending any time on China in the last couple years" (Reed Hastings, CEO of Netflix, quoted in Stankiewicz, 2020). Netflix was blocked due to the Chinese internet regulations—the "Great Fire Wall"—which prevented foreign media entering the country. This exemplifies how national policies may be able to regulate their territories, and thereby protect their domestic incumbents. Still, even if Netflix could enter China, the service would face severe competition from incumbents. First, as in India, the subscription pricing of Netflix would have positioned it as a niche service. Netflix's global subscription fee is about four times the price of the Chinese online video service iQiyi. Second, China's streaming incumbents owned by the three BAT companies, Baidu, Alibaba, and Tencent, dominate this space. In contrast to Netflix's video-only service, the Chinese services are made up of diverse offerings. Such "multipurpose platforms" include, in addition to video, dating, shopping, and transport, among others (Lobato, 2019: 131–3).

Case Study 4.3 Popcorn Time and Online Video Piracy

In 2014, *Time Magazine* published a story titled "Popcorn Time is so good at movie piracy, it's scary," arguing that "Basically it's the version of Netflix that you've always wanted." While iTunes, Netflix, Amazon, and Hulu showed that one may "fight piracy by providing a better, easier service to paying customers," *Time Magazine* wrote, "What happens when piracy fights back with something just as convenient?" (Newman, 2014).

Popcorn Time appeared online in 2014 as a free streaming service and software. It did not host content, but found it through YTS, a website that indexes film and movie torrent files (Newman, 2014). Popcorn Time has been very popular since its launch, and users across the world can choose from hundreds of film and television program titles, many of them subtitled. The user interface is similar to that of Netflix and other film and television content streaming services, but the content has not been subject to copyright clearance, nor do producers of the content receive any payment (Lobato, 2020).

Prior to Popcorn Time, downloading and watching films and television programming illegally demanded a certain level of technical know-how. However, the creators of Popcorn Time wanted to improve the usability of such services to similar levels as legal services, but with a far larger library of content, and for free: "It was all too geeky. My mom couldn't use it. She couldn't just click and watch the movie she wanted. When I design something, she's my case study. If she can't use it, no one can use it," according to Federico Abad, designer and programmer based in Buenos Aires, Argentina and creator of the original Popcorn Time: "The whole idea was that you should be able to watch a movie by just clicking twice" (Abad, quoted in Kibar, 2015).

However, as with other file sharing and downloading services, Popcorn Time has been forced to close down several times. Following court orders in Canada and New Zealand to shut the service down, Chris Todd, CEO of Motion Picture Association of America (MPAA), stated that Popcorn Time "exist for one clear reason: to distribute stolen copies of the latest motion pictures and television shows without compensating the people who worked so hard to make them," and argued, "By shutting down these illegal commercial enterprises [Popcorn Time and YTS], which operate on a massive global scale, we are protecting not only our members' creative work and the hundreds of innovative, legal digital distribution platforms, but also the millions of people whose jobs depend on a vibrant motion picture and television industry" (MPAA, 2015). Still, Federico Abad, founder of Popcorn Time, argues that:

> I think the blocking of sites is damaging to Hollywood. [...] To combat piracy, they must have global premieres in all platforms. A good Netflix without country restrictions. But Hollywood only makes problems. Why should not I be able to watch a film shown in the cinema in the US? [...] Culture has no borders. Netflix' series are popular worldwide because they are released everywhere at once in high quality with subtitles.
>
> (Abad, quoted in Kibar, 2015)

However, Popcorn Time has since been relaunched by different groups of designers and programmers (Eriksen and Ingebrethsen, 2016; Greenberg, 2015), and shut down again. In 2021, Popcorn Time was sued by the film industry, yet at the same time was planning a comeback (Jensvoll, 2021). Just a year after it first launched, Abad pointed out why such services will continue to exist: "I am convinced that the Popcorn Time-killer is going to be a Netflix without borders. They should remove national restrictions for films, making them available in cinemas and in streaming services simultaneously everywhere, regardless of platform for phone, tablet and TV, wherever you want, with subtitles. Had they done so, it would kill Popcorn Time once and for all" (quoted in Kibar, 2015).

Since the mid- to late 2000s, online television piracy has developed from torrent trackers and services such as The Pirate Bay (Lobato, 2020: 479) to the global trend of online streaming, distribution, and consumption. Services such as the open-source media player Kodi and subscription-based pirate IPTV in particular are increasing in popularity (Lobato, 2020: 481; Spilker and Colbjørnsen, 2020). However, the pirate streaming landscape differs across the world: "the power balance among these systems will of course vary geographically according to local custom and infrastructure, so only general observations can be made" (Lobato, 2020: 481).

Popcorn Time exemplifies exactly how the piracy ecosystem is characterized by the take-up of ever new technologies, leading to fragmentation, while at the same time there are increasing connections and interdependence between these technologies. While Popcorn Time may look like Netflix, the service "uses a P2P client to download the content. This activates as soon as the user clicks on the desired title: users download content packets in sequential order, resulting in a near-on-demand experience" (Lobato, 2020: 481). Still, the general trend in pirate distribution is from conventional downloads to streaming, reflecting the legal television industry move to Netflix and similar SVOD services (Lobato, 2020: 480).

Digitization and new information communication technology have contributed to intensifying competition, as convergence and reduced restrictions of geographic borders have led to global, national, and, in many cases, local companies competing for the same audiences and in the same markets. Today, not only internationally operating firms, but also domestic firms are affected by competition from foreign companies (Kotabe and Helsen, 2009: 4). As a consequence, the need to be noticed by and appeal to potential audiences and create loyalty among media users is a key issue that cuts across the whole media and communications sector. For this reason, media companies and services, and producers and distributors of media content, consider media branding as increasingly important (Arvidsson, 2006; Chalaby, 2002; 2009; Sinclair, 2012). The importance of branding is further emphasized, as it is increasingly considered to have an economic function (Arvidsson, 2006: 6). There is a growing preoccupation with the financial value of brands, and it is commonly accepted that they contribute to the overall value of companies, and that this value can be measured.

Global Media Branding

Branding is considered as a key means for enterprises and organizations to achieve their aims, whether this is profit, support, loyalty, or recognition. The practice of branding attempts to manage the relationship between an organization, products, or services and the environment in which the organization operates. It serves to create ties and bonds with individuals, consumers, groups, or other organizations. Although a brand may be a product, the brand "adds other dimensions that differentiates it in some way from other products designed to satisfy the same need. These differences may be rational and tangible—related to product performance of the brand—or more symbolic, emotional and intangible—related to what the brand represents," according to marketing scholar Keller (Keller, 2003: 50). Or, as Kornberger (2010: 16) argues, "Branding turns a commodity into a cultural entity. In that sense, the brand is the meaning of a commodity. A bar of soap remains a commodity unless a symbolic or cultural dimension (purity) is added."

A product or commodity is turned into a brand through advertising, packaging, design, words, and messages, and in this process is transformed into "personal and emotional goods" (Kornberger, 2010: 13). These objects become "social and cultural markers"—used by consumers to signal, who they are or want to be, and belonging and difference to other groups and individuals in society (2010: 13). As such, brands have become vital parts of "the social fabric": "Brands now became something of an omnipresent tool by means which identity, social relations and shared experiences (like spending a night in bed talking about Apple products) could be constructed. They were spun into the social fabric as a ubiquitous medium for the construction of a common social world" (Arvidsson, 2006: 3).

The significance of branding of media and communications companies and outlets intensified within the US television landscape as deregulation heightened competition for media audiences. Cable, broadcasting, telephony and satellites—often considered as separate businesses—increasingly became competitors in the same market (Bellamy and Chabin, 1999: 213, 216). Many of today's well-known cable and satellite television emerged in the United States in the last decades of the 20th century. HBO launched in the early 1970s, the sports television channel ESPN launched in 1979, and the first cable television channel for children, Nickelodeon, started the same year. These were followed by CNN (1980), MTV (1981), Disney Channel (1983) and A&E (1984) (Papathanassopoulos, 2002: 228; Kalagian, 2007: 150). While the traditional broadcaster networks had targeted a general, mainstream audience though a mixed programing fare, the new cable entrants focused on more specific topics and program genres, such as news, sports, and music: "focused on the interests of demographically specific niche audiences" (Croteau and Hoynes, 2006: 131). In a media environment in which the number of media outlets was increasing, it was important to have a robust "brand image" (Kung-Shankleman, 2000: 109).

Having established branded television outlets in the United States, many cable and television channels replicated it globally, using the same logo and brand name, yet addressing national preferences in the form of language, advertising, and a varying degree of programing content. While they target national and local audience segments, these television channels are centered around: "a core broadcasting philosophy" (Chalaby, 2005: 56), and "a well-defined television concept and the selling of a clear proposition to the audience" (Chalaby, 2009: 59), manifested in a common global brand.

The global cable and satellite television channels pioneered a double function in relation to branding and marketing. Although the networks create a brand of themselves, they also facilitate the same opportunities for their advertisers, allowing them to create brands across the world (Chalaby, 2005b: 52; Chalaby, 2002). In general, for advertisers, the opening up of national media markets and the proliferation of new distribution and communications hardware: "have made possible a commercial media culture capable of reaching into, appropriating and recycling styles and influences from areas that used to lie beyond the frontiers of consumer culture, such as China, Africa, India and the countries of the former Eastern Bloc" (Arvidsson, 2006: 3).

Although the concept of branding has traditionally referred to the branding of products, the concept has increasingly come to involve the company and organization behind the product (Balmer and Grey, 2003; Lury, 2004: 25, 33). The branding of a company or an organization—the corporate brand—extends to both corporate activities and relations with the aim to create "deep" relationships with stakeholders (Grainge, 2008: 29). The corporate brand opens for a branding strategy described by marketing scholar Aaker as a "branded house strategy" (Aaker, 2004). Diversification within the television and media industry has relied on the lending of branding approaches from marketing strategies within retail (Chris, 2002: 8).

Disney has created a corporate brand that is central when extending its brand into consumer products, feature-length films and television series, television channels, cruises, and theme parks, and most recently the launch of the global streaming service Disney+. Launched in 2019, Disney+ is a branded portal for Disney, Pixar, Marvel, Star Wars, and National Geographic branded content (Littelton, 2021). Similarly, Google, Facebook, and Baidu, the dominating Chinese search engine, all adopt a corporate brand strategy when expanding into new services and products:

> [Google's] business depends on strong brands, and failing to maintain and
> enhance our brands would hurt our ability to expand our base of users, advertisers,
> customers, content providers, and other partners. [...] Our brands may be
> negatively affected by a number of factors, including, among others, reputational

issues, third-party content shared on our platforms, data privacy and security issues and developments, and product or technical performance failures."

(Alphabet, 2021)

Google's approach to corporate branding is of particular interest due to its dominant position globally and its use of the corporate slogan "Don't be evil" in its original Code of Conduct. This exemplifies the risk of damaging the brand, as in the branding process it attempts to interlink services and products provided by the company, and the corporate practices and culture:

> "Don't be evil." Googlers generally apply those words to how we serve our users. But "Don't be evil" is much more than that. Yes, it's about providing our users unbiased access to information, focusing on their needs and giving them the best products and services that we can. But it's also about doing the right thing more generally – following the law, acting honorably and treating each other with respect.
>
> The Google Code of Conduct is one of the ways we put "Don't be evil" into practice. It's built around the recognition that everything we do in connection with our work at Google will be, and should be, measured against the highest possible standards of ethical business conduct. We set the bar that high for practical as well as aspirational reasons: Our commitment to the highest standards helps us hire great people, build great products, and attract loyal users. Trust and mutual respect among employees and users are the foundation of our success, and they are something we need to earn every day.
>
> Our users value Google not only because we deliver great products and services, but because we hold ourselves to a higher standard in how we treat users and operate more generally.

(Google, 2015)

However, in 2018, the high-profile and much referred to slogan "Don't be evil" was toned down and was mentioned only once, toward the end of Google's revised Code of Conduct: "And remember ... don't be evil, and if you see something that you think isn't right—speak up!" (Cuthbertson, 2018). The reason for this sudden change, according to the UK newspaper *The Independent*, was the resignation of a dozen employees and calls from researchers for Google to end its work on AI technology for the US military. The concerned parties argued that this work was very much in conflict with the "Don't be evil" slogan (Cuthbertson, 2018).

The global expansion and diversification of enterprises and the increased preoccupation with branding has led to an increased interest in the financial valuation of brands. Throughout the 1990s and 2000s, the brand has been increasingly considered "as a commercial asset" (Grainge, 2008: 30), and thereby having an economic function (Arvidsson, 2006: 6). There is a growing preoccupation with the financial value of brands, and it is accepted that they contribute to the overall value of companies: "it is increasingly possible for companies to treat the brand as they do any other form of valuable asset" (Lury, 2004: 121). The global brand consultancy Interbrand has for many years promoted the concept of brand value as measurable:

> Having coined the term "branding", Interbrand pioneered brand valuation more than thirty years ago, changing the way the world thought about brands – from trade marks to valuable business assets. Soundly based on modern business valuation principles, the foundations of our valuation technique remain unchanged. Our methodology was the first to be awarded the International Brand Valuation standard ISO 10668 Certification and our uniquely holistic approach involves strategists, designers and economists.
>
> (Interbrand, 2020)

The company also publishes annual rankings of the most valuable global brands. Media, technology, and electronics companies are considered the most valuable brands across all sectors (see Table 4.9).

A key reason for the high valuation of brands is because of the "tremendous difficulty and expense of creating similar brands from scratch" (Kotler and Keller, 2006: 275). Even if the "weight" of brands compared to other assets may differ from industry to industry, "there is no doubt that brand equity represents very substantial values of today's financial markets" (Arvidsson, 2006: 6).

The way the global media tech companies at the very top of Interbrand's list of best global brands are very consciously communicating their awareness and initiatives related to sustainability and climate actions is of course also a strategy to position their brands accordingly: for example, Google ("the first major company to reach carbon neutrality"), Microsoft ("carbon negative" in 2030), and Apple ("carbon neutrality" across the entire supply chain by 2030) (Harrabin, 2020).

Although the concept of branding is increasingly embraced and valued, the practice has long been subjected to critique by scholars and activists alike. Sociologist Celia Lury argues that brands may "allow markets to be controlled more effectively" as the dominant position of successful brands such as Microsoft, Coca-Cola, and Heinz lead to "long-standing monopolies or dominance of certain markets and afford protection of long term investment against risk" (Lury, 2004: 71). Naomi Klein, author of the book *No Logo* (1999) that fiercely criticized corporate branding which became a worldwide bestseller at the turn

Table 4.9 Media and Technology Companies in the
Top 100 Best Global Brands, 2020

Company	Brand Value ($ Millions)
1. Apple	322,999
2. Amazon	200,667
3. Microsoft	166,001
4. Google	165,444
5. Samsung	62,289
6. Huawei	6,301
10. Disney	40,773
12. Intel	36,971
13. Facebook	35,178
14. IBM	34,885
19. Instagram	26,060
30. YouTube	17,328
41. Netflix	12,665
51. Sony	12,010
53. Philips	11,671
65. HP	9,740
70. Spotify	8,389
71. Canon	8,057
76. Nintendo	7,296
85. Panasonic	5,844
90. LinkedIn	5,210
100. Zoom	4,481

Source: Adapted from Interbrand, 2020.

of the millennium, points out how the corporate brands of global companies are homogenous, with little room for adaptation to local conditions:

> [The brand identity] may be tailored to accommodate local language and cultural preferences (like McDonald's serving pasta in Italy), but its core features—aesthetic, message, logo—remain unchanged. This consistency is what brand managers like to call "the promise" of a brand: it's a pledge that wherever you go in the world, your experience at Wal-Mart, Holiday Inn, or a Disney theme park, will be comfortable and familiar. Anything that threatens this homogeneity dilutes a company's overall strength.
>
> (Klein, 2002)

This critique also extends to the protection of the brand identity through copyright laws. The brand identity is seen as a "rigorously controlled one-way message" which is "hermetically sealed off," limiting the possibility of changing "that corporate monologue into a social dialogue" (Klein, 2002). From a corporate perspective, such control is key, as registered trademarks protect a brand name and the intellectual property rights provide the necessary security needed for a company to invest in a brand (Kotler and Keller, 2006: 274).

As such, the concept of branding is powerful and brands may dominate and exert hegemonic power. In fact, some argue that branding has become so widespread that "even phenomena such as Naomi Klein's No Logo movement, Adbusters sub-vertising or Banksy's brandalism use the tools of branding to fight branding" (Kornberger, 2010: 267).

Some point out how media brands "exploit" their "fan community" (Lopera-Mármol et al., 2021: 165–6), as "brand managers have recognized the usefulness of fans and are seeking to exploit fan labor" (Guschwan, 2012). The term "brandom" aims to "describe the pseudo-fan culture engineered by brand managers eager to cultivate consumer labor and loyalty while preempting the possibility of resistance that participatory fan culture promises," as brand management aims "to optimize the relationship between the brand and brand-centered consumer communities" (Guschwan, 2012).

It is clear how Disney, Facebook, Google, and Baidu, to name a few, are all fiercely utilizing corporate branding in their global expansion, exploiting the fact that "The global, vertical integration of the industry facilitates the delivery of brands through multiple channels that reinforce each other." As such, the global media and entertainment industry has been a forerunner and fostered "branded consumerism"—the spending on and use of branded media content, services, and products (Castells, 2013: 121).

References

Aaker, D. A. (2004) *Brand Portfolio Strategy: Creating Relevance, Differentiation, Energy, Leverage, and Clarity.* New York: Free Press.

Alexander, J. (2021) Disney is launching a new Star-branded streaming service internationally. *The Verge.* https://www.theverge.com/2020/8/4/21354712/disney-star-streaming-service-international-expansion-hulu-plus-abc-fx-fox (accessed April 23, 2021).

Alphabet (2021) Form10-K. US Securities and Exchange CommissionForm. https://abc.xyz/investor/static/pdf/20210203_alphabet_10K.pdf?cache=b44182d (accessed April 28, 2021).

Arvidsson, A. (2006) *Brands: Meaning and Value in Media Culture*. New York: Routledge.

Balmer, J. M. T. and Grey, E. R. (2003) Corporate brands: What are they? What of them? *European Journal of Marketing*, 37, 7/8: 972–97.

BBC (2021) Amazon buys Hollywood studio MGM for $8.45bn. *BBC News*, May 26. https://www.bbc.com/news/business-57249849 (accessed May 26, 2021).

Bellamy, R. and Chabin, J. B. (1999) Global Promotion and Marketing of Television, pp. 211–32 in S. T. Eastman, D. A. Ferguson, and R. A. Klein (eds.) *Promotion and Marketing for Broadcasting and Cable*. Third edition. Boston: Focal Press.

Bond, P. and Szalai, G. (2019) Will M&A be the big entertainment story in 2019? *Hollywood Reporter*, January 8. https://www.hollywoodreporter.com/news/will-m-a-be-big-entertainment-story-2019-1171030 (accessed April 29, 2021).

Bridge, G. (2019) Top 19 media trends of 2019: Mega mergers. Variety, December 12. https://variety.com/2019/biz/opinion/top-19-media-trends-of-2019-mega-mergers-1203434577 (accessed April 29, 2021).

Brook, S. (2010) Britain leads the way in selling global TV formats. *The Guardian*, April 5. https://www.theguardian.com/media/2010/apr/05/britain-tv-formats-sales (accessed May 29, 2022).

Castells, M. (2013) *Communication Power*. Oxford: Oxford University Press.

Chalaby, J. K. (2002) Transnational television in Europe—the role of pan-European channels. *European Journal of Communication*, 17, 2: 183–203.

Chalaby, J. K. (2005) The Quiet Invention of a New Medium: Twenty Years Of Transnational Television in Europe, pp. 43–65 in J. K. Chalaby (ed.) *Transnational Television Worldwide: Towards a New Media Order*. London: I. B. Tauris.

Chalaby, J. K. (2009) *Transnational Television in Europe: Reconfiguring Global Communications Networks*. London: I. B. Tauris.

Chalaby, J. K. (2012) At the origin of a global industry: The TV format trade as an Anglo-American invention. *Media, Culture & Society*, 34, 1: 36–52.

Chalaby, J. K. (2016a) *The Format Age: Television's Entertainment Revolution*. Cambridge, UK: Polity.

Chalaby, J. K. (2016b) Television and globalization: The TV content global value chain. *Journal of Communication*, 66, 1: 35–59.

Chalaby, J. K. (2019) Outsourcing in the UK television industry: A global value chain analysis. *Communication Theory*, 29, 2: 169–90.

Chalaby, J. K. (2020) Understanding Media Globalization: A Global Value Chain Analysis, pp. 373–84 in S. Shimpach (ed.) *The Routledge Companion to Global Television*. New York: Routledge.

Chalaby, J. and Esser, A. (2017) The TV format trade and the world media system: Change and continuity. *International Journal of Digital Television*, 8, 1: 3–7.

Chalaby, J. K. and Plunkett, S. (2020) Standing on the shoulders of tech giants: Media delivery, streaming television and the rise of global suppliers. *New Media & Society*. https://doi.org/10.1177/1461444820946681

Chris, C. (2002) All documentary, all the time? Discovery Communications, Inc. and trends in cable television. *Television and New Media*, 3, 1: 7–27.

Colwell, T. and Price, D. (2005) *Rights of Passage: British Television in the Global Market*. London: British Television Distributors' Association.

Croteau, D. and Hoynes, W. (2006) *The Business of Media: Corporate Media and the Public Interest*. Thousand Oaks, CA: Pine Forge Press.

Cunningham, S. and Silver, J. (2013) *Screen Distribution and the New King Kongs of the Online World*. Basingstoke, UK: Palgrave Pivot.

Curtin, M., Holt, J., and Sanson, K. (2014) Ted Sarandos, Chief Content Officer, Netflix, pp. 132–45 in M. Curtin, J. Holt, and K. Sanson (eds.) *Distribution Revolution: Conversations About the Digital Future of Film and Television*. Berkeley, CA: University of California Press.

Cuthbertson, A. (2018) Google quietly removes "don't be evil" from code of conduct. *Independent*, May 21. https://www.independent.co.uk/life-style/gadgets-and-tech/news/google-dont-be-evil-code-conduct-removed-alphabet-a8361276.html (accessed April 27, 2021).

D'Arma, A., Raats, T., and Steemers, J. (2021) Public service media in the age of SVoDs: A comparative study of PSM strategic responses in Flanders, Italy and the UK. *Media, Culture & Society*. https://doi.org/10.1177/0163443720972909

Datoo, S. (2014) How Netflix uses your data to work out what you want it to commission. *The Guardian*, March 7. https://www.theguardian.com/media-network/media-network-blog/2014/mar/07/netflix-data-house-cards (accessed May 29, 2022).

EAO (2021) European VOD revenues increased 30-fold over the last ten years. February 9. https://www.obs.coe.int/en/web/observatoire/home/-/asset_publisher/wy5m8bRgOygg/content/european-vod-revenues-increased-30-fold-over-the-last-ten-years (accessed April 22, 2021).

Easton, J. (2020) US$100 billion in SVOD revenues by 2025. *Digital TV Europe*, September 28. https://www.digitaltveurope.com/2020/09/28/us100-billion-in-svod-revenues-by-2025 (accessed May 29, 2022).

Eriksen, D. and Ingebrethsen, C. (2016) Popcorn Time tilbake med ny tjeneste. *NRK*, February 4. https://www.nrk.no/kultur/popcorn-time-tilbake-med-ny-tjeneste-1.12787690 (accessed May 11, 2022).

Fagerjord, A. and Kueng, L. (2019) Mapping the core actors and flows in streaming video services: What Netflix can tell us about these new media networks. *Journal of Media Business Studies*, 16, 3: 166–81. https://www.tandfonline.com/doi/full/10.1080/16522354.2019.1684717 (accessed May 11, 2022).

FRAPA (2009) The FRAPA Report 2009: TV Formats to the World. Cologne: FRAPA.

Google (2005) Form 10-K. US Securities and Exchange Commission Form. https://www.sec.gov/Archives/edgar/data/1288776/000119312506056598/d10k.htm (accessed April 29, 2021).

Google (2015) Code of Conduct. https://investor.google.com/corporate/code-of-conduct.html (accessed February 20, 2015).

Grainge, P. (2008) *Brand Hollywood: Selling Entertainment in a Global Media Age.* London: Routledge.

Greenberg, A. (2015) Inside Popcorn Time, the piracy party Hollywood can't stop. *Wired.*, March 18. https://www.wired.com/2015/03/inside-popcorn-time-piracy-party-hollywood-cant-stop (accessed May 11, 2022).

Guschwan, M. (2012) Fandom, brandom and the limits of participatory culture. *Journal of Consumer Culture*, 12, 1: 19–40.

Hafez, K. (2007) *The Myth of Media Globalization.* Cambridge, UK: Polity Press.

Harrabin, R. (2020) Google says its carbon footprint is now zero. *BBC News*, September 14. https://www.bbc.com/news/technology-54141899 (accessed May 25, 2021).

Hayes, D. (2021) Univision acquires Grupo Televisa assets for $4.8 billion; merger deal creates global Spanish-language media entity. *Deadline*, April 13. https://deadline.com/2021/04/univision-acquires-grupo-televisa-merger-4-8-billion-spanish-language-company-1234733829 (accessed April 29, 2021).

Iordache, C. (2021) Netflix in Europe: Four markets, four platforms? A comparative analysis of audio-visual offerings and investments strategies in four EU states. *Television & New Media*, May 8. https://doi.org/10.1177/15274764211014580

Interbrand (2020) *Best Global Brands 2020: A New Decade of Possibility.* https://learn.interbrand.com/hubfs/INTERBRAND/Interbrand_Best_Global_Brands%202020.pdf (accessed June 21, 2022).

Jayakar, K. and Park, E.-A (2020) Emergence of OTT video and the production expenditures of established audiovisual producers. *Journal of Broadcasting & Electronic Media*, 64, 5: 836–57. https://doi.org/10.1080/08838151.2020.1842688

Jensvoll, A. (2021) Popcorn Time planlegger comeback. iTavisen, April 26. https://itavisen.no/2021/04/26/et-liv-etter-doden-for-popcorn-time (accessed April 27, 2021).

Kalagian, T. (2007) Programming Children's Television: The Cable Model, pp. 147–64 in J. A. Bryant (ed.) *The Children's Television Community.* Mahwah, NJ: Lawrence Erlbaum.

Keller, K. L. (2003) *Strategic Brand Management: Building, Measuring, and Managing Brand Equity.* Second edition. Upper Saddle River, NJ: Prentice Hall.

Kibar, O. (2015) Inside Popcorn Time—the world's fastest growing piracy site. DNMagasinet, September 7. https://www.dn.no/magasinet/popcorn-time/spotify/federico-abad/pirate-bay/inside-popcorn-time-the-worlds-fastest-growing-piracy-site/1-1-5453911 (accessed April 27, 2021).

Klebnikov, S. (2020) Streaming wars continue: Here's how much Netflix, Amazon, Disney+ and their rivals are spending on new content. *Forbes*, May 22. https://www.forbes.com/sites/sergeiklebnikov/2020/05/22/streaming-wars-continue-heres-how-much-netflix-amazon-disney-and-their-rivals-are-spending-on-new-content/?sh=733b9b80623b (accessed June 21, 2022).

Klein, N. (2002) Brand USA America's attempt to market itself abroad using advertising principles is destined to fail. *Los Angles Times*, March 10.

Kornberger, M. (2010) *Brand Society: How Brands Transform Management and Lifestyle.* Cambridge, UK: Cambridge University Press.

Kotabe, M. and Helsen, K. (2009) Theoretical Paradigms, Issues, and Debates, pp. 3–12 in M. Kotabe and K. Helsen (eds.) *The SAGE Handbook of International Marketing.* Los Angeles: SAGE.

Kotler, P. and Keller, K. L. (2006) *Marketing Management.* Twelfth edition. Upper Saddle River, NJ: Prentice Hall.

Kovach, S. and Meredith, S. (2021) AT&T announces $43 billion deal to merge WarnerMedia with Discovery. *CNBC*, May 17. https://www.cnbc.com/2021/05/17/att-to-combine-warnermedia-and-discovery-assets-to-create-a-new-standalone-company.html (accessed May 21, 2021).

Kuburas, M. (2014) Netflix's data engine worth $500M a year. October 14, https://playbackonline.ca/2014/10/10/netflixs-data-engine-worth-500m-a-year (accessed May 29, 2022).

Kung-Shankleman, L. (2000) *Inside the BBC and CNN: Managing Media Organisations.* London: Routledge.

Lancefield, D. (2019) Transforming TV by going back to the future. Strategy+Business, August 29. https://www.strategy-business.com/article/Transforming-TV-by-going-back-to-the-future (accessed May 11, 2022).

Laughlin, A. (2010) Hulu "puts UK launch back on agenda." DigitalSpy, July 9. https://www.digitalspy.com/tech/a240992/hulu-puts-uk-launch-back-on-agenda (accessed May 29, 2022).

Littleton, C. (2021) Disney Plus tops 100 million subscribers. Variety, March 9. https://variety.com/2021/tv/news/disney-plus-100-million-subscribers-worldwide-1234925654 (accessed May 29, 2022).

Lobato, R. (2019) *Netflix Nations: The Geography of Digital Distribution.* New York: New York Press.

Lobato, R. (2020) Evolving Practices of Informal Distribution in Internet Television, pp. 479–87 in S. Shimpach (ed.) *The Routledge Companion to Global Television.* New York: Routledge.

Lodz, A. (2020) In between the global and the local: Mapping the geographies of Netflix as a multinational service. *International Journal of Cultural Studies*, 24, 2: 195–215.

Lopera-Mármol, M., Jiménez-Morales, M., and Bourdaa, M. (2021) Televertising Strategies in the Age of Non-advertising TV, pp. 154–88 in L. Mas-Manchón (ed.) *Innovation in Advertising and Branding Communication.* New York: Routledge.

Lury, C. (2004) *Brands: The Logos of the Global Economy.* London: Routledge.

Middleton, R. (2021) Disney+ "to surpass Netflix within five years", with 300m subs predicted. *TBI*, February 15. https://tbivision.com/2021/02/15/disney-to-surpass-netflix-within-five-years-with-almost-300m-subs (accessed April 22, 2021).

Mjøs, O. J. (2010) *Media Globalization and the Discovery Channel Networks.* London: Routledge.

Moyser, R. (2021) TBI Tech & Analysis: How Netflix can thrive in the 2020s. TBI, January 25. https://tbivision.com/2021/01/25/tbi-tech-analysis-how-netflix-can-thrive-in-the-2020s (accessed April 29, 2021).

MPAA (2015) Major piracy sites shut down: Closure of both Popcorn and YTS strengthens marketplace for legal online commerce. Motion Picture Association, November 3. https://www.motionpictures.org/press/major-piracy-sites-shut-down (accessed May 11, 2022).

Netflix (2020) Form 10-K. Annual Report 2020. https://s22.q4cdn.com/959853165/files/doc_financials/2020/ar/8f311d9b-787d-45db-a6ea-38335ede9d47.pdf (accessed April 23, 2021).

Netflix (2021a) Shareholder letter. https://s22.q4cdn.com/959853165/files/doc_financials/2021/q1/FINAL-Q1-21-Shareholder-Letter.pdf (accessed May 11, 2022).

Netflix (2021b) Annual Report 2021, December 31. https://s22.q4cdn.com/959853165/files/doc_financials/2021/q4/da27d24b-9358-4b5c-a424-6da061d91836.pdf (accessed August 4, 2022).

Newman, J. (2014) Popcorn Time is so good at movie piracy, it's scary. *Time*, March 10. http://time.com/18867/popcorn-time-is-so-good-at-movie-piracy-its-scary (accessed May 12, 2022).

Oren, T. and Shahaf, S. (eds.) (2012) *Global Television Formats: Understanding Television Across Borders*. New York: Routledge.

Papathanassopoulos, S. (2002) *European Television in the Digital Age: Issues, Dynamics and Realities*. Cambridge, UK: Polity.

Sanson, K. and Steirer, G. (2019) Hulu, streaming, and the contemporary television ecosystem. *Media, Culture & Society*, 41, 8: 1210–17.

Sinclair, J. (2012) *Advertising, the Media and Globalization: A World in Motion*. London: Routledge.

Sparks, C. (2007) What's wrong with globalization? *Global Media & Communication*, 3, 2: 133–55.

Spilker, H. S. and Colbjørnsen, T. (2020) The dimensions of streaming: Toward a typology of an evolving concept. *Media, Culture & Society*, 42, 7–8: 1210–25.

Stankiewicz, K. (2020) Netflix's Reed Hastings: "We have not been spending any time" trying to get into China. *CNBC*, September 9. https://www.cnbc.com/2020/09/09/reed-hastings-on-why-netflix-has-not-focused-lately-on-entering-china.html (accessed April 26, 2021).

Thomson, S. (2020) Ampere: Netflix and Amazon going local but facing more competition. Digital TV Europe, May 5. https://www.digitaltveurope.com/2020/05/05/ampere-netflix-and-amazon-going-local-but-facing-more-competition (accessed April 30, 2021).

Thussu, D. K. and Nordenstreng, K. (2021) Introduction, pp. 1–19 in D. K. Thussu and K. Nordenstreng (eds.) *BRICS Media: Reshaping the Global Communication Order?* Abingdon, UK: Routledge.

Van Dijck, J., Poell, T., and De Waal, M. (2018) *The Platform Society: Public Values in a Connective World*. Oxford: Oxford University Press.

Waisbord, S. (2004) McTV: Understanding the global popularity of television formats. *Television & New Media*, 5, 4: 359–83.

Walt Disney Company (2020) Form 10-K. Walt Disney Co, Annual Report, November 25. https://sec.report/Document/0001744489-20-000197/dis-20201003.htm (accessed April 12, 2021).

Walt Disney Company (2021) Disney+ tops 100 million global paid subscriber milestone, March 9. https://thewaltdisneycompany.com/disney-tops-100-million-global-paid-subscriber-milestone (accessed April 14, 2021).

Zenith Media (2021) Ecommerce and video fuel faster-than-expected recovery in global adspend. https://www.zenithmedia.com/ecommerce-and-video-fuel-faster-than-expected-recovery-in-global-adspend (accessed March 9, 2021).

Part Two

Key Theoretical Traditions: The Continuity of Themes and Concerns

5

The Role of Media and Communications in Development

Modernization, Progress, and Social Change

Throughout the twenty-first century, public, private, and civic stakeholders increasingly agree on ICT and digital media and communications as among the most significant factors for achieving development and social change in the world. This chapter discusses how scholars, policy makers, and practitioners have for decades explored and debated how media, communication, and technology can contribute to development. The chapter details key theoretical concepts and perspectives that have shaped this tradition within global media, often broadly referred to as "development communication." Beginning with the early influential "top-down" modernization theory tradition (e.g., Lerner, [1958] 1962; Schramm, 1964), the chapter moves on to the emergence of the more "bottom-up," participatory approach in development communication which followed as a reaction (e.g., Beltran, 1975; Freire, [1970] 2000). The technology-focused approach called "telecommunication for development" then emerged, which was a forerunner to the current, highly influential "information communication technologies (ICT) for development" paradigm. Scholars, politicians, and organizations emphasize how ICT and digital media and communications clearly play a significant role in development (e.g., International Telecommunication Union [ITU], 2003; Thussu and Nordenstreng, 2021; World Bank, 2016; 2021; World Economic Forum, 2020). However, many also emphasize that there remain major, global digital divides and gaps in connectivity in the world, and, importantly, a number of factors other than ICT access are crucial for successfully closing the digital divide and achieving development (e.g., van Dijk, 2005; 2020; ITU, 2018; 2020a; Norris, 2001; Ragnedda and Muschert, 2013; Wessels, 2013). Critics also draw attention to how the world's largest ICT companies originate in the West, and then mostly from the United States, or developed and industrialized Eastern countries such as Japan, Korea, and, increasingly, China. These global technology companies and digital media and communications companies (e.g., Apple, Huawei, Samsung, Google, and Facebook) have enormous market power and can be accused of seeing development as mainly market opportunities. In fact, some argue that it is companies of the developed world and governments that benefit from the development of ICT (Mosco, 2009; Unwin, 2017). The rise of China has created geopolitical tension and competition for influence with Western countries, the United States particular, as Chinese authorities have launched a number of major technology and digital infrastructure initiatives and partnerships with developing countries across the world (Hillman, 2021; Lisinge, 2020; Thussu, 2018a; Thussu and Nordenstreng, 2021).

Modernization Theory

The theme of development became an important issue in the early 1960s, following the newfound independence of former European colonies (Sreberny, 2000: 94). Daniel Lerner's book *The Passing of Traditional Society* ([1958] 1962) and Wilbur Schramm's *Mass Media and National Development* (1964) promoted the idea that communications and media have a central role in the modernization and development of these societies, both from an academic and practical perspective (Sparks, 2007; Sreberny, 2000: 94). Based on a study of several countries in the Middle East, Lerner introduced a theoretical perspective that was founded on the idea that traditional values and norms hindered the development of traditional societies into modern societies. There was a lack of motivation for change within the broader part of the population of these societies, while the elite was more willing and open to change (Lerner, [1958] 1962; Sparks, 2007). Sparks points out how Lerner identified two "types of mental structures" among the inhabitants. A large part of the population were "essentially illiterate, and was fixed and oriented towards stability and the past," and this created obstacles for development. In contrast, "the modern personality" was characterized by being "literate, fluid, and open to change" and "was capable of 'empathy'." "Empathy", Lerner argued, "meant that it could imagine itself in different circumstances, so it had a future orientation that was unavailable to the traditional personality" (Sparks, 2007: 22 referring to Lerner, 1958). Lerner argued that by mobilizing the latter part of the population, the former would be influenced and motivated to change. Media was key in this process:

> The media teach people participation of this sort by depicting for them new and strange situations and by familiarizing them with a range of opinions among which they can choose. Some people learn better than others, the variation reflecting their differential skill is empathy. For empathy, in the several aspects illustrated throughout this book, is the basic communication skill required of modern men. Empathy endows a person with the capacity to imagine himself as proprietor of a bigger grocery store in a city, to wear nicer clothes and live in a nice house, to be interested in "what is going on in the world" and to "get out of this hole."

(Lerner, [1958] 1962: 412)

However, Lerner's perspectives and theories were criticized for many reasons. The very foundations of the theory and the way the communications process was understood were questioned (Sparks, 2007: 38). Some emphasize how "the now mostly discredited modernization theory" should be seen in connection with the US politics on foreign aid in the 1950s and 1960s (Miller, 2009: 12). Others point out that modernization theories emerged within the context of the Cold War. Modernization theories represented a response and counterpoise to state socialism, and national media "were similarly expected to emulate Western patterns of behavior and contribute to the construction of democracy" (O'Neil, 1998: 3, quoted in Miller, 2009). Modernization theories were criticized for being ethnocentric and ahistorical (Sreberny, 2000: 95). In fact, by the mid-1970s, the whole modernization theory perspective was rejected also by the most vigorous advocates (Sparks, 2007: 38). Still, even though it was rejected, in retrospect, Thompson (1995: 190) argues, "while in many ways being dated," Lerner's research drew attention to "a number of points which remain relevant today." First, Lerner pointed out "the fact that the media play a crucial role in the cultural transformations associated with the rise of modern societies" Thompson (1995: 190). The problem was that Lerner considered the role of media as "too overdetermined by a theory of modernization oriented towards a particular goal." Second, Lerner's "key idea that the media enable individuals to acquire experience across space and time, through forms of interaction that are not face-to-face in character, is surely correct and is only accentuated by the advent of television" (Thompson, 1995: 191).

Participatory Development

It was the emerging framework of participatory development that was to replace modernization theory. Instead of the top-down approach to development, this new framework emphasized a more bottom-up method. A major contributor to this turn was the early critique of the modernization theory paradigm by, in particular, Latin American scholars in the 1970s. Freire ([1970] 2000) pointed to a parallel between teachers' use of traditional forms of pedagogy and the approach to development and modernization taken by development practitioners:

> Whatever the specialty that brings them into contact with the people, they are almost unshakably convinced that it is their mission to "give" the latter their knowledge and techniques. They see themselves as "promotors" of the people. Their programs of action (which might have been prescribed by any good theorist of oppressive action) include their own objectives, their own convictions, and their own preoccupations. They do not listen to the people, but instead plan to teach them how to "cast off the laziness which creates underdevelopment."
>
> (Freire, [1970] 2000: 155–6)

Instead, one should listen to and include people in the development processes, and reject Lerner's preoccupation with the measuring of development according to changes in countries' economic performances (e.g., GDP):

> In order to determine whether or not a society is developing, one must go beyond criteria based on indices of "per capita" income (which, expressed in statistical form, are misleading) as well as those which concentrate on the study of gross income. The basic, elementary criterion is whether or not the society is a "being for itself." If it is not, the other criteria indicate modernization rather than development.
>
> (Freire, [1970] 2000): 162)

On a more theoretical and conceptual level, Beltran's critique of the modernization paradigm drew attention to the fact that Latin American communication scholars had imported and adopted theories and methodology from the United States and Europe: "The areas most directly influenced by a North American orientation are diffusion of agricultural innovations; structure and functions of print and electronic mass media; experiments with instructional television; special formats of radio education; and audiovisual education in group communication situations" (Beltran, 1975: 187). The US and European approaches were dominant in Latin America due to several factors. Among them were "a lack of a conceptual framework of its own" and "an uncritical adoption" of such methodologies (Beltran, 1975: 187).

In the 1970s and 1980s, the United Nations Educational, Scientific and Cultural Organization (UNESCO) addressed the inequality and unevenness in access to communication technologies and information internationally through the international forum New World Information Communication Order (NWICO). One of UNESCO's key initiatives was the formation of the International Commission for the Study of Communication Problems, led by Sean MacBride and consisting of member states. In its report *Many Voices, One World*, the Commission documented the differences and asymmetry in access to information, means of communication and opportunities to participate between the North and the South, the developed and the developing world. The report suggested a range of measures to narrow this gap in favor of the developing world:

> [U]tmost importance should be given to eliminating imbalances and disparities in communication and its structures, and particularly in information flows. Developing countries need to reduce their dependence, and claim a new, more just and more equitable order in the field of communication. This issue has been fully debated in various settings; the time has now come to move from principles to substantive reforms and concrete action.
>
> (MacBride Report, 1980)

Political disagreement among the UNESCO members followed. As a result, the United States and the UK, under US president Reagan and the UK prime minster Thatcher respectively, left the organization in 1984. The former rejoined in 2003, and the latter in 1997 (Frau-Mengs et al., 2012; MacBride Report, 1980; Miller, 2009). While the NWICO, as described in the Commission's report, had, according to some, "at best only a marginal impact on the restructuring of international communications relations" and the asymmetry between the North and the West, it served as a "moral platform" for the improvement and adjustment of the asymmetry of the distribution of information across the world. As such, "[t]he elevation of concerns in communications to a global agenda remains the most significant achievement of the NWICO" (Thomas, 1997: 165).

While the "top-down" or "North to South" approach of the modernization theory to achieve development through the practical application of "diffusion of innovations" and "two-step flow" models, the emphasis of "participatory communication" was to focus on participation. While there are different understandings of—and varieties of methods—within this approach or model, a key point is "It stresses the importance of cultural identity of local communities and of *democratization and participation at all levels*—international, national, local and individual. It points to a strategy, not merely inclusive of, but largely emanating from, the traditional 'receivers'" (Servaes, 2008: 21). The participation model, favoring grassroots activity and mobilization, has been popular among scholars and practitioners alike. Throughout the 1980s and 1990s, the modernization theory approach "completely disappears," and in its place, "the most frequently used theoretical framework is participatory development," which is "almost the polar opposite of Lerner who viewed mass communication as playing a top-down role in social change" (Fair and Shah, 1997: 10, quoted in Servaes, 2008: 16).

Yet, critics question its feasibility and effect. While the approach represented a move away from the top-down methodology, critics argue that "the structure of elite domination was not disturbed as the participation that was expected was often directed by the sources and change agents. Although the people were induced to participate in self-help activities, the basic solutions to local problems had already been selected by the external development agencies"(Melkote, 2010: 113). In fact, Melkote argues, "the outcome in most cases has not been true empowerment of the people, but the attainment of some indicator of development as articulated in the modernization paradigm" (2010: 113).

While "almost nobody would dare to make the optimistic claims of the early years any longer," Servaes point out how the implied and unspoken conventions "on which the so-called dominant modernization paradigm is built do still linger on" (2008: 17). These norms and traditions "continue to influence the policy and planning-making discourse of major actors in the field of communication for development, both at theoretical and applied levels" (2008: 17).

Information Communication Technologies for Development

In the 1970s and 1980s, a new strand of international development research emerged: "tele-communications for development." Agencies such as the ITU, the World Bank, and the Organisation for Economic Co-operation and Development (OECD) in particular argued that "telecommunication can significantly contribute to economic growth, social service delivery, and a more equitable distribution of economic benefits" (Shields and Samarajiva, 1990: 197). This approach was preoccupied with participation, but also on structural developments. The approach focused on the potential for "interactive telecommunications network" and "interactive communication media rather than one-way media" to contribute to economic, political, and social development, integration and participation (McDowell, 2003; Samarajiva and Shields, 1990:87; Shields and Samarajiva, 1990). "Telecommunication for development" was easy to understand and support for policy makers and researchers alike: "Developed countries saw ways in which they could provide official development assistance that would also benefit their own national groups, such as telecommunications firms. Less developed countries also saw new sources of development assistance and the possibility of the transfer of high technology and related expertise" (McDowell, 2003: 11).

The logic of connecting technology and development signaled what was to come, namely "information and communications technologies (ICTs) for development." Throughout the 1990s, the growth in ICTs and, not least, the development of the internet was by many considered a backbone in international development: "Assuring equitable access to digital technology and bringing the 'new economy' to developing countries are now widely recognized to be among the most significant challenges of the new century" (Jussawalla, 2003: 5). In fact, some argued that "Developing countries have an advantage over developed countries" as they do not have to replace older communications hardware, and can move straight to the newest technology: "Instead of digging out copper wire to install fiber-optic cable, they can connect remote areas with wireless networks through mobile systems" (Jussawalla, 2003: 5).

The UN's NWICO initiative's failed impact in the late 1980s and early 1990s was largely due to the United States (and the UK) withdrawing its UNESCO membership and thereby funding. The United States considered NWICO as an obstacle to the free market ideology, and put pressure on to steer media and communications policy in this direction to the benefit of the commercial sector. In addition, the emergence of the internet meant that UNESCO's political and social ethos became less significant compared with economic and private motives, which increasingly came to the fore in debates on technological advancement (Iosifidis, 2011: 134–5).

Following the extensive growth of ICTs and the rapid adoption of such technologies, major UN-backed international initiatives were launched to discuss the potential and role of such technologies in sociocultural development and how to best govern them. A range of stakeholders took part in the World Summit on the Information Society (WSIS), held in 2003 and 2005, including governments and, in contrast to the NWICO debates, representatives from the private sector and also "a large number of NGOs pursuing political and sociocultural agendas" (Iosifidis, 2011: 134). As NWICO, the WSIS 2003 Summit took a "socially conscious tone" (Chakravarthy and Sarikakis, 2006: 139) and stated a Declaration of Principles, which apparently contrasted with the profit motives of the private stakeholders, yet considered them as key:

> b) The commitment of the private sector is important in developing and diffusing information and communication technologies (ICTs), for infrastructure, content and applications. The private sector is not only a market player but also plays a role in a wider sustainable development context.
>
> c) The commitment and involvement of civil society is equally important increasing an equitable Information Society, and in implementing ICT-related initiatives for development.
>
> (Declaration of Principles, World Summit on the Information Society, 2003, quoted in Chakravarthy and Sarikakis, 2006: 139)

While the participation of the civil society is given major significance, some argue that "the role 'officially' recognized for civil society appears to be that of a secondary, assisting agent, behind the private sector upon which the whole Information Society rests" (Chakravarthy and Sarikakis, 2006: 139). In fact, some argue that "modernization theory influenced many of the debates" at WSIS in both 2003 and 2005 (Iosifidis, 2011: 95).

Still, similar to NWICO, WSIS contributed by putting "information and communication firmly on the global agenda." The WSIS process (the sum of official and unofficial activities) "identified the problematic issues in global communication, indicated the range of views on how to deal with them, provided various blueprints of what should and could be possible in the way of solutions, and gingerly explored ways of dealing with these questions in the future"(Raboy, 2004: 225, quoted in Iosifidis, 2011: 135).

Throughout the 2000s the position of—and belief in—ICTs for development became more and more prominent. Following the major WSIS events of 2003 and 2005, the WSIS Forums have been organized since 2006. These have extensive stakeholder participation, and emphasize how development is at the top of the agenda:

> The World Summit on the Information Society Forum 2020 represents the world's largest annual gathering of the "ICT for development" community. The WSIS Forum, co-organized by ITU, UNESCO, UNDP and UNCTAD, in close collaboration with all WSIS Action Line Facilitators/Co-Facilitators, has proven to be an efficient mechanism for coordination of multi-stakeholder implementation activities, information exchange, creation of knowledge, sharing of best practices and continues to provide assistance in developing multi-stakeholder and public/private partnerships to advance development goals. This

Forum will provide structured opportunities to network, learn and participate in multi-stakeholder discussions and consultations on WSIS implementation.

(WSIS, 2020)

Major organizations, agencies, and bodies, including the UN and World Economic Forum, also contributed to the promotion of the ICT for development agenda by producing indexes that compare and rank the role and impact of such technologies globally in a development context. The United Nations' specialized agency for information communications technologies, ITU, publishes annually the report *Measuring the Information Society*, which has included the key index ICT Development Index. Importantly, the report and index signal the preoccupation with ICT in development also as an enabler for other developmental goals, such as poverty reduction, improvements in education and health, and reduction in gender inequality (ITU, 2014: iii; 2018; 2020a).

Throughout the twenty-first century, the World Bank has continued to promote ICT for development. Both the reports *World Development Report 2016: Digital Dividends* and the *World Development Report 2021: Data for Better Lives* focused on ICT and data for development. The latter suggests that one should be "Advancing development objectives through data," particularly by "using data more effectively to improve development outcomes, particularly for poor people in poor countries" (World Bank, 2021: 3).

The overall growth in ICT-related products and their adoption have increased at a dramatic pace, and the current growth is taking place particularly in the developing regions (ITU, 2020a; 2020b). However, despite this expansion in the developing world regions, there are still huge differences in access to ICTs. Already in 1999, the UNDP's *Human Development Report 1999* warned against the escalating differences between the countries that are able to invest in ICT infrastructures and those that cannot (UNDP, 1999).

The ICT Development Index

Since 2009, the ITU has published the ICT Development Index. The index has been a major effort to map and compare the state of ICT development across the world and between countries (ITU, 2017b; see Table 5.1). The "IDI value" in the index is calculated using three groupings of ICT indicators that measure infrastructure, use, and skills within each country. The first group includes infrastructure and access indicators: fixed and mobile telephone subscriptions per 100 inhabitants, internet bandwidth per internet user, and percentage of households with a computer and internet access. The second, ICT usage indicators, includes percentage of individuals using the internet, and fixed-broadband subscriptions and active mobile-broadband subscriptions per 100 inhabitants. The third, ICT skills indicators, includes mean years of schooling, and gross school enrolment at secondary and tertiary level (ITU, 2017a; see Table 5.1, ITU, 2017b).

Table 5.1 ICT Development Index (IDI) 2017: The Twenty Top and Bottom Countries

Economy	IDI 2017 Value
1 Iceland	8.98
2 Korea (Rep.)	8.85
3 Switzerland	8.74
4 Denmark	8.71
5 United Kingdom	8.65
6 Hong Kong, China	8.61
7 Netherlands	8.49
8 Norway	8.47
9 Luxembourg	8.47
10 Japan	8.43
11 Sweden	8.41
12 Germany	8.39
13 New Zealand	8.33
14 Australia	8.24
15 France	8.18
16 United States	8.18
17 Estonia	8.14
18 Singapore	8.05
19 Monaco	8.05
20 Ireland	8.02
...	
157 Solomon Islands	2.11
158 Djibouti	1.98
159 Afghanistan	1.95
160 Angola	1.94

Economy	IDI 2017 Value
161 Benin	1.94
162 Burkina Faso	1.90
163 Equatorial Guinea	1.86
164 Comoros	1.82
165 Tanzania	1.81
166 Guinea	1.78
167 Malawi	1.74
168 Haiti	1.72
169 Madagascar	1.68
170 Ethiopia	1.65
171 Congo (Dem. Rep.)	1.55
172 Burundi	1.48
173 Guinea-Bissau	1.48
174 Chad	1.27
175 Central African Rep.	1.04
176 Eritrea	0.96

Source: Adapted from ITU, 2017b.

The ICT Development Index and its methodology show the complexity and nuances that need to be considered when discussing ICT and development globally. In fact, the ITU stopped publishing the index in 2017 due lack of quality data and also to disagreements as to which indicators should be used. The complexities are also clearly evident when discussing how ICTs actually impact on societies and economies. This is emphasized in the World Bank's *World Development Report 2016: The Internet and Development*:

> [T]he full benefits of the information and communications transformation will not be realized unless countries continue to improve their business climate, invest in people's education and health, and promote good governance. In countries where these fundamentals are weak, digital technologies have not boosted productivity or reduced inequality. Countries that complement technology investmentswith broader economic reforms reap digital dividends in the form of faster growth, more jobs, and better services.
>
> (World Bank, 2016: xiii)

As we can see, it is complicated to measure and assess the role and impact of ICTs within and between regions and countries. A key term in this discussion is the "digital divide."

The Global Digital Divide

Writing in 2001, Norris pointed out how the concept and term "digital divide" became "so popular as an instant sound-bite that it has entered everyday speech as shorthand for any and every disparity within the online community" (Norris, 2001: 4). While one may refer to it as simply the differences in access to the internet, Norris argued that the digital divide concerns much wider issues and is a "multidimensional phenomenon":

- The *global divide* refers to the divergence of Internet access between industrialized and developing societies.
- The *social divide* concerns the gap between information rich and poor in each nation.
- The *democratic divide* signifies the difference between those who do, and do not, use the panoply of digital resources to engage, mobilize, and participate in public life.

(Norris, 2001: 4)

Internet access alone is not adequate to explain the digital divide: "an understanding of digital inequality requires placing Internet access in a broader theoretical context" (DiMaggio et al., 2004, quoted in Meinrath et al., 2013: 310). As with Norris (2001), this points to a wider understanding of the concept, shared also by van Dijk (2005; 2020), as the digital divide is linked to social inequalities.

The complexity of understanding the digital divide is reflected by the fact that despite the growth in internet access and sales of mobile phones, there has been "little progress in bridging the gap between the world's most networked economies and the rest of the world," the World Economic Forum stated as late as 2014. According to the World Economic Forum's *Global Information Technology Report 2014*, the lack of "progress is worrisome for emerging and developing nations, which are at risk of missing out on many positive impacts information and communications technologies (ICT) bring, including increased innovation, economic competitiveness and greater social inclusion" (World Economic Forum, 2014).

Similarly, the UN's International Telecommunications Union agency, ITU, points out the complexity involved in reducing the digital divide:

> While the information society is growing worldwide, digital divides remain –
> and are even widening – in some segments. In particular, there is a significant
> and persistent urban-rural digital divide, whereby urban citizens enjoy

ubiquitous mobile network coverage, affordable high-speed Internet services and the higher levels of skills required to make effective use of online content and services, while the opposite is often the case in rural and remote areas of many developing countries.

(ITU, 2014: 1)

The multidimensional character of the digital divide has for several decades made it challenging to grasp, and raises several questions:

- What explains variations across countries in Internet use, in particular its levels of socioeconomic development, investments in human capital, the process of democratization, or something else?
- Does the Internet create new inequalities, or reinforce existing divisions evident for decades in the spread of old communication technologies? Attempts to move beyond speculative theorizing about these questions face major challenges. The World Wide Web remains in its adolescence; any examination of trends is limited to just one decade.

(Norris, 2001: 9)

The digital divide is made up of a range of dimensions in addition to differences in access to technology across the world; ethnicity, age, gender, education, socioeconomic status and background, and lack of cultural capital and knowledge to enable use of digital technologies are all aspects that shape and define the digital divide (Wessels, 2013: 18). We therefore need to take a critical approach and ask:

- [D]o the traditional inequalities simply replicate themselves in the digital sphere, or does the digital divide operate under its own dynamics?
- [Does] the digital divide simply [exacerbate] traditional inequalities, or [does] it also include counter-trends that might mitigate traditional inequalities, even while forming new forms of stratification?
- [Do the] inequalities in the digital world translate culturally, or [do] they manifest themselves in culturally-specific ways[?]

(Ragnedda and Muschert, 2013: 4)

The increase in mobile broadband access and number of individual internet users in the world has been rapid throughout the twenty-first century. In fact, by 2021, almost 88 percent of the global population have access to 4G networks, and over 95 percent have access to a mobile broadband network (see Table 3.1). However, in terms of mobile broadband access, considerable "connectivity gaps" endure. Over 97 percent of global households in urban areas have access to 4G, compared to 75 percent in the rural parts of the world. In the least developed countries, only 53 and 30 percent of the populations have access to 4G and 3G respectively, while 7 percent have access to only 2G and 10 percent does not have access to a mobile network (ITU, 2021). During the Covid-19 pandemic, as differences in access became particularly noticeable with travel restrictions, and people working and studying from home, Houlin Zhao, the Secretary-General of the UN organization, ITU, raised the question: "How much longer can we tolerate the significant gap in household connectivity between urban and rural areas [?]" (ITU, 2020b). In fact, some argue that the Covid-19 pandemic "exposed the digital divide like never before" (Broom, 2020). Even in developed countries access is perhaps more limited than expected: 6 percent of the US population and 13 percent of Australians do not have high-speed internet connection. This is of particular concern during the Covid-19 pandemic as health information does not reach the most vulnerable, and with over a billion school children staying away from schools during the pandemic, many were not able to follow online teaching (Broom, 2020).

The global digital divide persists throughout the twenty-first century, and a number of challenges remain and need to be resolved. The *Measuring Digital Development* report (ITU, 2018, 2020a) points out that gender disparities in terms of access exist in many parts of the world, and, importantly, lack of ICT skills prevents people taking part in the digital society:

- **There is an increased need for "soft" skills beyond technical and navigational skills.** A breadth of skills—including technical operational, information management, and social and content-creation skills—will be fundamental for achieving positive and avoiding negative outcomes. Furthermore, algorithms, the proliferation of bots, and a shift to the Internet of Things and artificial intelligence augment the need for critical information and advanced content-creation skills. With the increased complexity of ICT systems, and an exponential increase in the amount of data being collected, transferable digital skills and lifelong learning are indispensable.
- **ITU data and other cross-nationally comparative data sources show that there are considerable gaps across the board in the skills needed at all levels.** A third of individuals lack basic digital skills, such as copying files or folders or using copy and paste tools; a mere 41 percent have standard

skills, such as installing or configuring software or using basic formulas on spreadsheets; and only 4 percent are using specialist language to write computer programs.

- **Scarce data suggest developing countries are particularly disadvantaged when it comes to digital skills.** There is a lack of data collected on skills in developing regions, but the available data suggest that inequalities reflect other inequalities between the different regions of the world, particularly in relation to basic skills. The patterns for standard skills are less clear.
- **Within-country inequalities in basic and standard skills reflect historical patterns of inequality.** On average, those in employment were ten percentage points more likely to have a skill than the self-employed, who are in turn ten percentage points more likely than the unemployed to have a skill.
- **There are skill inequalities between children as much as there are between adults.** While little data are available on this outside of Europe, available data suggest that digital inequalities are not a generational thing and will persist into the future.

(Adapted from ITU, 2018: 22)

Over two decades ago, Norris argued that the often heated debate on the role of technology and the internet, in particular in development and in reducing the digital divide, is driven by the polarization and disagreement between "optimists envisaging the positive role of the Internet for transforming poverty in developing societies, skeptics who believe that new technologies alone will make little difference one way or another, and pessimists who emphasize that digital technologies will further exacerbate the existing North-South divide" (Norris, 2001: 9). Some critics of the ICT for development approach argue that the main beneficiaries are private media companies, particularly from the North, and that the aim is more to integrate developing countries in the global economy than for social development (McDowell, 2003). The WSIS Summit failed to deliver as many hoped, as its early emphasis was on social challenges such as the global digital divide, yet it "gradually metamorphosed into a technical dispute over Internet governance" and the dominant role of the US authorities and private corporations (Iosifidis, 2011: 135, referring to Pickard, 2007). In fact, some argue that ICT for development is just a variety of the process described by modernization theorists: "When massive media investment failed to promote development, modernization theorists went in search of revised models that include telecommunication and new computer technologies" (Mosco, 2009: 130).

Digitization and Technology in the Context of the UN's Sustainable Development Goals

The Covid-19 pandemic showed how important digital connectivity is in everyday life, as many countries implemented lockdown of societies. Those with sufficient digital infrastructure, access, and technology can uphold key activities through remote working, healthcare, and education, but the crisis also showed more clearly the gaps that prevail in terms of digital access and the severe consequences this has, as even those with broadband and coverage may not use the internet due to costs, skills, or content in local language (World Economic Forum, 2020). It is of key importance that this is addressed in a post-Covid-19 world, as the world seeks to achieve the UN's seventeen Sustainable Development Goals (SDGs).

Technology and digitization are seen by many as key to helping achieve the SDGs, and thereby reducing inequalities (see Case Study 3.2). Still, others are more skeptical and warn against possible negative consequences and disappointments. In fact, the more optimistic view holds that technology can speed up the progress of all SDGs—that includes fighting poverty, ending hunger, and improving health, and providing access to quality education, employment and decent work for all, and affordable clean energy, as well as fostering responsible consumption and production, and economic growth—according to the World Economic Forum organization:

- Technology can help level the playing field for even the smallest businesses in the least-developed countries, helping them reach new markets and access finance.
- It can make job training faster and more effective, providing workers with new skills needed for the jobs of the Fourth Industrial Revolution.
- It can allow more people to access education, pandemic or not.
- Blockchain can create greater transparency, security and efficiency in supply chains
- Artificial Intelligence (AI) and data analytics can help us better prepare for and respond to pandemics—and better screen for, diagnose and treat disease.

On the other hand, technology can also worsen inequalities:

- Responsible technology governance is needed to protect against discriminatory algorithms, unethical use of data and job displacement—especially in the midst of a global pandemic, when we're relying on technology more than ever to work, learn, buy food and necessities, even see the doctor.

- And with this increased dependency on the internet, cyberattacks are up – so cybersecurity is more important than ever, especially for companies handling private data.
- More work needs to be done to provide universal and affordable access to the internet and close the digital skills gap.

(Quoted and adapted from Sault, 2020)

Still, some are skeptical of the strong belief in information and communications technology's role in development and social change. Critics point out that it is companies of the developed world and governments that benefit from the expansion of such technologies, while the benefits for the poorest are far from clear and certain (Mosco, 2009; Unwin, 2017). While "the early modernization literature concentrated on the need to build the mass media infrastructure, including newspapers, radio, television, and cinema" (Mosco, 2009: 130), a revised form of the modernization theory argues that development will happen if an ICT infrastructure is created. This will enable business to operate in the developing world, and these businesses should lead the modernization process. This revised version is a continuation of the earlier modernization theory, according to critics, as:

> Its essence continues to include exporting Western technology, now with greater stress on telecommunication, and incorporating Western media models, if not specific Western programming. What differentiates this revisionist tendency is a greater reliance on local social structures and cultural practices to carry out the process. Departing from earlier strategies, based on the view that people had to incorporate Western values before they could industrialize, this view now calls for using local cultures as well as critical approaches to achieve the result.
>
> (Mosco, 2009: 131)

Such a critical perspective draws attention to how the world's largest ICT companies originate in the West or developed and industrialized Eastern nations such as Japan and Korea, and increasingly China.

Among the BRICS countries (Brazil, Russia, India, China, and South Africa), of which four of the five are considered developing countries, the impact of the internet on development in China and India has been particularly significant. The adoption of digital communication devices and services "has helped millions of farmers and micro-entrepreneurs to improve their health, education and livelihoods" (Thussu, 2021: 294). In fact, some argue that the rise of the BRICS countries may create a new global communication order, in which the position of the United States will be significantly weakened (Thussu and Nordenstreng, 2021; see also Case Study 5.1).

Case Study 5.1 The "Digital Silk Road" and the Chinese Belt and Road Initiative (BRI)

The "Digital Silk Road," launched by the Chinese government in 2015, aims to build digital infrastructure outside China. This is part of the larger Chinese Belt and Road Initiative (BRI), launched in 2013, with the aim to expand globally both physical and digital infrastructure, including ports, power plants, 5G networks, and fiber-optic cables. The initiative is "widely considered to be the centrepiece of China's new foreign policy and a reflection of its ascendancy in the global arena, economically, politically, and strategically" (Lisinge, 2020). Around 140 countries are part of the BRI initiative, of which 39 are in sub-Sahara, 34 in Europe (mainly Eastern) and Central Asia, 25 in East Asia and Pacific, 18 in Latin America and the Caribbean, and 17 in the Middle East and North Africa. While these countries are diverse (both high- and low-income countries), the countries that have decided not to join BRI are "generally more democratic, politically stable and economically developed" (Sacks, 2021). It is therefore clear that "For many developing countries that are involved in the BRI projects it opens-up huge potential for rapid access to modern amenities and infrastructure" (Thussu, 2018a). While a number of countries declined or banned the inclusion of Chinese technology, most notably from the company Huawei, when developing 5G networks, "overwhelmingly these countries are wealthy democracies" (Hillman, 2021). The list of countries outside this category "with varying levels of development and governance" is long, and here the "competition is set to intensify" between China and, particularly, the United States, as pointed out by the Center for Strategic and International Studies (CSIS):

> The Digital Silk Road is well-timed, dovetailing with powerful, longer-running trends. China is already the world's leading exporter of communications technology, and it is increasingly competitive in delivering advanced systems, such as subsea cables, that only the United States and its allies could provide just over a decade ago. Digital infrastructure is becoming even more essential to modern economies with the arrival of faster networks, cheaper sensors, and the proliferation of connected devices. The potential for growth in the developing world is vast. Asia and Africa, where demand for international bandwidth is growing fastest, are expected to account for 90 percent of global population growth through 2050.
>
> (Hillman, 2021)

According to *The Wall Street Journal*, one example of the US government's response to China's expanding ICT efforts in developing countries, fronted by the companies Huawei and ZTE, is to attempt to "persuade developing countries to shun Chinese telecommunications equipment, offering financial assistance to use alternatives that Washington says are safer and have fewer strings attached. The U.S. is ready to offer loans and other financing, potentially worth billions of dollars in total, to countries to buy hardware from suppliers in democratic countries rather than from China" (Woo, 2020).

Not only ICT hardware players such as mobile and telecommunications companies, but also the major online social media and search companies consider the developing world as key growth areas, and they rely on each other in their expansion. Their collaborative approach is evident in their involvement in ICT for development as Facebook and Google, but also non-Western players such as the former Chinese microblog Tencent Weibo, teamed up with the major mobile carriers and other telecommunications companies to increase uptake of their services and products in the developing world (see Case Study 5.2).

Case Study 5.2 Facebook, Google, and Development

The US services Facebook and Google first expanded in the West, and then rapidly across most of the world's regions. The Chinese market has developed its own internet-based services like WeChat and TikTok, with rapidly increasing take-up outside China. These globally expanding services have in many ways fronted the popularization, as well as the commercialization of the internet. However, these services are also part of the ICT for development tradition through a range of initiatives and collaborations.

Facebook's initiative Internet.org was launched in the mid-2010s, and aims to develop technology that will increase internet access and the delivery of data to underserved areas, increase the efficiency of data transfer, and contribute to the development of new business models. In addition to Facebook, the partners of Internet.org are some of the world's major ICT companies: Ericsson (communications technology and services), MediaTek Inc (producer of semiconductors), Opera Software, Samsung (technology), Nokia (mobile communication and products), and Qualcomm (wireless communication technologies) (Internet.org). Facebook points out how Internet.org has a clear ICT for development aim:

Last August, Facebook partnered with leading technology companies to launch Internet.org—a global effort to make affordable basic Internet services available to everyone in the world. Connecting the world is one of the fundamental challenges of our time. When people have access to the internet, they can not only connect with their friends, family and communities, but they can also gain access to the tools and information to help find jobs, start businesses, access healthcare, education and financial services, and have a greater say in their societies. They get to participate in the knowledge economy.

(Facebook, 2014)

In the mid-2010s, according to Facebook-funded research by the global consultancy Deloitte, internet access could create another 140 million jobs and contribute to reducing poverty for millions:

Expanded access to information, increased business and job opportunities, and ultimately higher incomes are all factors that can combine to eradicate extreme poverty. Deloitte estimates that extending internet access in developing economies to the level seen in developed countries can raise living standards and incomes by up to $600 per person a year, thus lifting 160 million people out of extreme poverty in the regions covered by this study.

(Deloitte, 2014: 4)

Facebook's Internet.org, and the related project Connectivity Lab, focuses on strengthening and inventing new distribution technologies: "[A] new generation of launch and satellite technology, plus new ideas about what constitutes a satellite, are transforming the sky above our heads into waypoints for data that could reach our mobile devices as quickly as from terrestrial networks, with the advantage of global coverage" (Mims, 2014).

In Facebook founder's Mark Zuckerberg's words, the company aimed to "beam internet to people from the sky" (Zuckerberg, quoted in Gibbs, 2014), and aimed to develop "Solar-powered drones the size of Boeing 747s" that "could someday compete with both satellites and balloons to deliver Internet access" (Mims, 2014). Similarly, Google aimed to increase internet distribution and access via the sky. The company's Project Loon was created to increase internet access through the use of adjusted weather balloons (Mims, 2014), but Google also used drones, and spent an estimated 1$ billion on 180 low-orbit satellites with the aim to provide internet access to world regions (Gibbs, 2014). As with Facebook, Google underlined the development aspects of their initiatives: "Internet connectivity significantly improves people's lives. Yet two-thirds of the world have no access at all. It's why we're so focused on new technologies that have the potential to bring hundreds of millions more people online in the coming years" (Google spokesman, quoted in Rushton, 2014). However, as critics pointed out, the initiatives of Facebook are not just philanthropic:

The push is rooted in altruism and global community, but may eventually serve to boost the businesses of all mobile companies. By enlarging the pie—getting more people online—everyone in the mobile business could benefit. That includes Facebook and the device manufacturers spearheading this project, but also the carriers, app developers, e-commerce companies, advertisers, and even artists who distribute their work via mobile.

(Constine, 2013)

Similarly, critics pointed out how Google's efforts have a commercial strategic motive: "It wants to increase their growth potential by unlocking an untapped market, and to position itself as the entry point to the internet as the populations in those developing regions are forming their online habits" (Rushton, 2014),

One of Facebook's key initiatives, predating the Internet.org initiative, has been the development and distribution of Facebook Zero in developing countries and regions in collaboration with mobile operators. Facebook Zero launched in 2010, in cooperation with fifty telecommunications operators in forty-five countries. This gave Facebook a boost in the number of users, nearly doubling its worldwide user base in the following two years, which raised the company's financial and investment appeal prior to its IPO (initial public offering) in 2012 (Bergen, 2014).

Facebook Zero was a basic, stripped-down phone version of the social media service that is offered free from mobile carriers, for which the social media service is reportedly subsidizing the distribution costs. Similarly, Google Zero and Twitter Access (Bergen, 2014) have been launched: "We partner with mobile operators around the world to offer a dynamic mobile web experience through Twitter to non or low data subscribers" (Twitter, 2015). Non-Western internet companies are also following this approach. The Chinese internet company Tencent subsidized its offering of its WeChat app in Nigeria (Bergen, 2014).

The internet giants' extensive initiatives in the developing world are clearly motivated by commercial strategies and growth demands, as critics point out: "The idea is that if Facebook can get low-tech mobile users hooked early, they'll stick with it and stay connected to their social graph as they move on to smartphones" (Constine, 2013). In fact, Zuckerberg describes how Internet.org also aims to provide basic internet services that are free to use: "a 911 for the internet" (Zuckerberg, quoted in Lunden, 2014). Such services could include Facebook, along with search services and messaging services, and represent an access point for internet users in the developing world, or in a critic's word: "a gateway drug of sorts" to these services (Lunden, 2014). As one critic pointed out, as Facebook Zero started to expand in the developing world:

> [T]he key to Facebook's strategy is that no matter where users start on the ladder of mobile technology, from the most basic device to the newest smartphone, Facebook becomes better and more fun to use as they upgrade. And this is also why carriers are so eager to partner with Facebook, because

the next billion to come onto the internet will do it through a mobile device, on which every megabyte that they use in connecting with their friends can be measured and billed.

(Mims, 2012)

In fact, Facebook's expansion into the developing world soon led to a misconception among users in these countries: that Facebook is the internet, as reported in the business news publication Quartz. While these surveys are limited in scale, of those surveyed in Nigeria, as many as 65 percent agreed with the following statement: "Facebook is the internet." Sixty-one percent of those surveyed in Indonesia, and 58 percent in India, agreed with the statement (Mirani, 2015). The head of localization and internationalization at Facebook, Iris Orriss, points out that "Awareness of the Internet in developing countries is very limited. In fact, for many users, Facebook is the internet, as it's often the only accessible application" (Orriss, quoted in Mirani, 2015). Internet.org's "showpiece" is an app with free access to only Facebook, Facebook Messenger, and a few other services (Mirani, 2015).

In India, the Internet.org expansion faced the most severe criticism. The activist group calling themselves Save the Internet argued that "Facebook was acting as a gatekeeper of the Internet by pre-selecting services available on Internet.org, without transparency and with a Western bias detrimental to local services and start-ups" (Nothias, 2020b: 333). Facebook responded by providing "a platform allowing any service that met Facebook's technical requirements to be included on Internet.org. Facebook also invested heavily in a nationwide, online, and offline advertisement campaign emphasizing Internet.org's 'philanthropic' mission" (Nothias, 2020b: 333).

While the brand and applications of Facebook's "Free Basics" initiative, which provides free access to a range of basic services, may change, it continues to expand and take root in the developing world. Google's Project Loon was shut down in 2021, and neither Facebook Zero nor Internet.org exists in its original form, but Facebook's initiative Facebook Connectivity points out how the company's:

Free Basics offers access to basic online services without data charges.

In collaboration with mobile operators, Free Basics allows people to experience the relevance and benefits of being online for free. Free Basics acts as an onramp to the broader internet, with services such as news, health information, local jobs, communications tools, education resources, and local government information. Any mobile operator can participate, and Free Basics is open to any service that meets the program's technical criteria, which are openly published.

(Facebook, 2021)

Critics argue that these services continue to influence ICT expansion worldwide: "zero-rating programs are pervasive across the Global South and thus shape the Internet experience of a tremendous number of people across the world" (Nothias, 2020b: 334). As companies like Facebook, Amazon, and Google invest in network infrastructures, these companies not only create "monopolistic platforms in terms of content," but may well be "also becoming almost like internet service providers—a form of vertical integration with far reaching consequences for network sovereignty and (un)democratic control of digital infrastructures" (Nothias, 2020a).

References

Beltran, L. R. (1975) Research ideologies in conflict. *Journal of Communication*, 25, 2: 187–93.

Bergen, M. (2014) The secret sauce for Twitter's global growth strategy: Subsidized data. Ad Age, July 7. http://adage.com/article/digital/twitter-facebook-rate-telecom-deals-abroad/293741 (accessed April 9, 2015).

Broom, D. (2020) Coronavirus has exposed the digital divide like never before. World Economic Forum, April 22. https://www.weforum.org/agenda/2020/04/coronavirus-covid-19-pandemic-digital-divide-internet-data-broadband-mobbile (accessed May 21, 2021).

Chakravarthy, P. and Sarikakis, K. (2006) *Media Policy and Globalization*. Edinburgh: Edinburgh University Press.

Constine, J. (2013) Facebook and 6 phone companies launch Internet.org to bring affordable access to everyone. TechCrunch, August 21. https://tinyurl.com/2pn2kxwn (accessed June 21, 2022).

Deloitte (2014) *Value of Connectivity: Economic and Social Benefits of Expanding Internet Access*. London: Deloitte. https://www2.deloitte.com/uk/en/pages/technology-media-and-telecommunications/articles/value-of-connectivity.html (accessed June 21, 2022).

DiMaggio, P., Hargittai, E., Celeste, C., and Shafer, S. (2004) From Unequal Access to Differentiated Use: A Literature Review and Agenda for Research on the Digital Divide, pp. 355–400 in K. Neckerman (ed.) *Social Inequality*. New York: Russell SAGE Foundation.

Facebook (2014) Connecting the World from the Sky. March 28. http://internet.org/press/connecting-the-world-from-the-sky (accessed August 2, 2022).

Facebook (2021) Free Basics. https://connectivity.fb.com/free-basics (accessed March 30, 2021).

Fair, J. E. and Shah, H. (1997) Continuities and discontinuities in communities in communication and development research since 1958. *Journal of International Communication*, 4, 2: 3–23.

Frau-Meigs, D., Nicey, J., Plamer, M., Pohle, J., and Tupper, P. (2012) Introduction, pp. 1–11 in D. Frau-Meigs, J. Nicey, M. Plamer, J. Pohle, and P. Tupper (eds.) *From NWICO to WSIS: 30 Years of Communication Geopolitics—Actors and Flows, Structures and Divides*. Bristol, UK: Intellect.

Freire, P. ([1970] 2000) *Pedagogy of the Oppressed*. Thirtieth Anniversary Edition. New York: Continuum.

Gibbs, S. (2014) Google to spend more than $1bn on satellite internet, reports indicate. *The Guardian*, June 2. http://www.theguardian.com/technology/2014/jun/02/google-to-spend-more-than-1bn-on-satellite-internet-reports-indicate (accessed April 9, 2015).

Hillman, J. (2021) Competing with China's Digital Silk Road. CSIS, February 9. https://www.csis.org/analysis/competing-chinas-digital-silk-road (accessed June 22, 2021).

Iosifidis, P. (2011) *Global Media and Communication Policy*. Basingstoke, UK: Palgrave.

Internet.org (2015) (accessed April 10, 2015).

International Telecommunication Union (2003) *Declaration of Principles. Building the Information Society: A Global Challenge in the New Millennium*. December 12. https://www.itu.int/net/wsis/docs/geneva/official/dop.html (accessed June 14, 2021).

International Telecommunication Union (2014) *Measuring the Information Society Report*. Geneva: International Telecommunication Union. https://www.itu.int/en/ITU-D/Statistics/Documents/publications/mis2014/MIS2014_without_Annex_4.pdf (accessed June 1, 2022).

International Telecommunication Union (2017a) *Measuring the Information Society Report 2017*, volume 1. https://www.itu.int/en/ITU-D/Statistics/Documents/publications/misr2017/MISR2017_Volume1.pdf (accessed April 8, 2021).

International Telecommunication Union (2017b) ICT Development Index 2017. https://www.itu.int/net4/ITU-D/idi/2017/index.html (accessed April 8, 2021).

International Telecommunication Union (2018) *Measuring the Information Society Report*. https://www.itu.int/pub/D-IND-ICTOI (accessed April 1, 2021).

International Telecommunication Union (2020a) *Measuring Digital Development. Facts and Figures: 2020*. https://www.itu.int/en/ITU-D/Statistics/Documents/facts/FactsFigures2020.pdf (accessed May 13, 2022).

International Telecommunication Union (2020b) *Household Internet Access in Urban Areas Twice as High as in Rural Areas*. Press release. https://www.itu.int/en/mediacentre/pages/pr27-2020-facts-figures-urban-areas-higher-internet-access-than-rural.aspx (accessed May 13, 2022).

International Telecommunication Union (2021) *Mobile Network Coverage*. https://www.itu.int/itu-d/reports/statistics/2021/11/15/mobile-network-coverage/ (accessed August 7, 2022).

Jussawalla, M. (2003) Bridging the "Global Digital Divide," pp. 3–24 in M. Jussawalla and R. D. Taylor (eds.) *Information Technology Parks of the Asia Pacific: Lessons for the Regional Digital Divide*. Armonk, NY: M. E. Sharpe.

Lerner ([1958] 1962) *The Passing of Traditional Society: Modernizing the Middle East.* New York: Free Press.

Lisinge, R. T. (2020) The Belt and Road Initiative and Africa's regional infrastructure development: Implications and lessons. *Transnational Corporations Review*, 12, 4: 425–38.

Lunden, I. (2014) WhatsApp is actually worth more than $19B, says Facebook's Zuckerberg, and it was Internet.org that sealed the deal. TechCrunch, February 24. http://techcrunch.com/2014/02/24/whatsapp-is-actually-worth-more-than-19b-says-facebooks-zuckerberg (accessed June 22, 2021).

MacBride Report (1980) *Communication and Society Today and Tomorrow, Many Voices One World, Towards a New More Just and More Efficient World Information and Communication Order.* International Commission for the Study of Communication Problems. New York: UNESCO.

McDowell, S. D. (2003) Theory and research in international communications: An historical and institutional account, pp. 5–18 in B. Mody (ed.) *International and Development Communication: A 21st-Century Perspective.* London: SAGE.

Meinrath, S. D., Losey, J., and Lennett, B. (2013) Afterword: Internet Freedom, Nuanced Digital Divides, and the Internet Craftsmen, pp. 309–15 in M. Ragnedda and G. W. Muschert (eds.) *The Digital Divide: The Internet and Social Inequality in International Perspective.* London: Routledge.

Melkote, S. R. (2010) Theories of Development Communication, pp. 105–21 in D. K. Thussu (ed.) *Internationalizing Media Studies.* London: Routledge.

Miller, J. (2009) NGOs and "modernization" and "democratization" of media: Situating media assistance. *Global Media and Communication*, 5, 1: 9–33.

Mims, C. (2014) The internet's future lies up in the skies. *Wall Street Journal*, December 14. http://www.wsj.com/articles/the-internets-future-lies-up-in-the-skies-1418603566 (accessed June 22, 2021).

Mims, C. (2012) Facebook's plan to find its next billion users: Convince them the internet and Facebook are the same. Quart, September 24. http://qz.com/5180/facebooks-plan-to-find-its-next-billion-users-convince-them-the-internet-and-facebook-are-the-same (accessed June 22, 2021).

Mirani, L. (2015) Millions of Facebook users have no idea they're using the internet. Quartz, February 9. http://qz.com/333313/milliions-of-facebook-users-have-no-idea-theyre-using-the-internet (accessed June 22, 2021).

Mosco, V. (2009) *Political Economy of Communication.* Second edition. London: SAGE.

Norris, P. (2001) *Digital Divide: Civic Engagement, Information Poverty, and the Internet Worldwide.* Cambridge, UK: Cambridge University Press.

Nothias, T. (2020a) The rise and fall ... and rise again of Facebook's Free Basics: Civil society and the challenge of resistance to corporate connectivity projects. Global Media Technologies & Cultures Lab, April 21. https://globalmedia.mit.edu/2020/04/21/the-rise-and-fall-and-rise-again-of-facebooks-free-basics-civil-and-the-challenge-of-resistance-to-corporate-connectivity-projects (accessed March 30, 2021).

Nothias, T. (2020b) Access granted: Facebook's free basics in Africa. *Media, Culture & Society*, 42, 3: 329–48.

O'Neil, P. H. (1998) Democratization and Mass Communication: What Is the Link?, pp. 1–20 in P. H. O'Neil (ed.) *Communicating Democracy: The Media and Political Transition*. Boulder, CO: Lynne Rienner.

Pickard, V. (2007) Neoliberal visions and revisions in global communications policy from NWICO to WSIS. *Journal of Communication Inquiry*, 31, 2: 118–39.

Raboy, M (2004) The World Summit on the Information Society and its legacy for global governance. *International Communication Gazette*, 66, 3–4: 225–32.

Ragnedda, M. and Muschert, G. W. (2013) Introduction, pp. 1–15 in M. Ragnedda and G. W. Muschert (eds.) *The Digital Divide: The Internet and Social Inequality in International Perspective*. London: Routledge.

Rushton, K. (2014) Google spending $1bn on internet in developing world. *The Telegraph*, June 2. http://www.telegraph.co.uk/finance/newsbysector/mediatechnologyandtelecoms/digital-media/10870369/Google-spending-1bn-on-internet-in-developing-world.html (accessed June 22, 2021).

Sacks, D. (2021) Countries in China's Belt and Road Initiative: Who's in and who's out? Council on Foreign Relations, March 24. https://www.cfr.org/blog/countries-chinas-belt-and-road-initiative-whos-and-whos-out (accessed June 22, 2021).

Samarajiva, R. and Shields, P. (1990) Integration, telecommunication, and development: Power in the paradigms. *Journal of Communication*, 40, 3: 84–105.

Sault, S. (2020) Tech for Good: What are the challenges in making technology and digitization more sustainable? World Economic Forum, September 20. https://www.weforum.org/agenda/2020/09/what-are-the-challenges-in-making-new-technology-more-sustainable (accessed May 25, 2021).

Schramm, W. (1964) *Mass Media and National Development: The Role of Information in the Developing Countries*. Stanford, CA: Stanford University Press.

Servaes, J. (2008) Introduction, pp. 14–30 in J. Servaes (ed.) *Communication for Development and Social Change*. London: SAGE.

Shields, P. and Samarajiva, R. (1990) Telecommunication, rural development and the Maitland report. *International Communication Gazette*, 46, 3: 197–217.

Sparks, C. (2007) *Globalization, Development, and Mass Media*. New York: SAGE.

Sreberny, A. (2000) The Global and the Local in International Communication, pp. 93–119 in J. Curran and M. Gurevitch (eds.) *Mass Media and Society*. London: Arnold.

Thomas, N. T. (1997) An Inclusive NWICO: Cultural Resilience and Popular Resistance, pp. 163–74 in P. Golding and P. Harris (eds.) *Beyond Cultural Imperialism: Globalization, Communication and the New International Order*. London: SAGE.

Thompson, J. B. (1995) *The Media and Modernity: A Social Theory of the Media*. Cambridge, UK: Polity.

Thussu, D. K. (2018a) BRI: Bridging or breaking BRICS? *Global Media and China*, 3, 2: 117–22.

Thussu, D. K. (2018b) Globalization of Chinese Media: The Global Context, pp. 17–33 in D. K. Thussu, H. de Burgh, and A. Shi (eds.) *China's Media Go Global*. New York: Routledge.

Thussu, D. K. (2021) BRICS De-Americanizing the Internet? pp. 280–301 in D. K. Thussu and K. Nordenstreng (eds.) *BRICS Media: Reshaping the Global Communication Order?* Abingdon, UK: Routledge.

Thussu, D. K. and Nordenstreng, K. (eds.) (2021) *BRICS Media: Reshaping the Global Communication Order?* Abingdon, UK: Routledge.

Twitter (2015) Twitter Access. https://about.twitter.com/products/partners (accessed April 9, 2015).

UNDP (1999) *Human Development Report*. New York: UNDP/Oxford University Press.

Unwin, T. (2017) *Reclaiming Information and Communication Technologies for Development*. Oxford: Oxford University Press.

Van Dijk, J. (2005) *The Deepening Divide: Inequality in the Information Society*. Thousand Oaks, CA: SAGE.

Van Dijk, J. (2020) *The Digital Divide*. Cambridge: Polity Press.

Wessels, B. (2013) The Reproduction and Reconfiguration of Inequality: Differentiation and Class, Status and Power in the Dynamics of Digital Divides, pp. 17–28 in M. Ragnedda and G. W. Muschert (eds.) *The Digital Divide: The Internet and Social Inequality in International Perspective*. London: Routledge.

Woo, S. (2020) US to offer loans to lure developing countries away from Chinese telecom gear. *Wall Street Journal*, October 18. https://www.wsj.com/articles/u-s-to-offer-loans-to-lure-developing-countries-away-from-chinese-telecom-gear-11603036800 (accessed June 22, 2021).

World Bank (2016) *World Development Report 2016: Digital Dividends*. Washington, DC: World Bank.

World Bank (2021) *World Development Report 2021: Data for Better Lives*. Washington, DC: World Bank.

World Economic Forum (2014) *The Global Information Technology Report 2014*. Thirteenth edition. https://www3.weforum.org/docs/WEF_GlobalInformationTechnology_Report_2014.pdf (accessed May 13, 2022).

World Economic Forum (2020) *Accelerating Digital Inclusion in the New Normal*. http://www3.weforum.org/docs/WEF_Accelerating_Digital_Inclusion_in_the_New_Normal_Report_2020.pdf (accessed May 25, 2021).

WSIS (2020) WSIS Forum 2020. Fostering digital transformation and global partnerships: WSIS Action Lines for achieving SDGs. https://www.itu.int/net4/wsis/forum/2020 (accessed May 13, 2022).

6

The Power of Media and Communications

Imperialism, Influence, and Dominance

The corporatization and commercialization of the global digital media and communications landscape and worldwide expansion of US companies, fronted by Google's and Facebook's dominant positions in search and social media markets and Netflix's and other streaming services' rapid growth worldwide, raise concerns among scholars, the public, policy makers, and regulators. There are concerns about dominance; competition for the national media audiences and advertising market; exploitation of user data; and reduced national autonomy in regard to regulation, privacy of citizens, and the public sphere. The rise of China also leads to geopolitical tensions and new competition for power and influence across the global media and communications landscape. However, several of these current concerns mirror those of the past. The distribution of US films, television programming, and cultural products and the parallel international growth of media companies triggered and motivated the emergence of a theoretical tradition concerned with the uneven structural power and asymmetry in influencing these processes and the consequences of this development. While the development for communication approaches viewed media and communications as a force for societal change and improvement, the new tradition was concerned with the harmful effects of imported media and foreign media companies' activity. In the 1960s, 1970s, and 1980s, several concepts and terms, such as "cultural imperialism" (Schiller, [1976] 2018), "media imperialism" (Boyd Barrett, 1977), and "cultural synchronization" (Hamelink, 1983), were introduced to support this argument, and became central in this tradition. Several of these terms achieved prominence in academia and were also adopted in politics and in public. This chapter first traces the emergence of this tradition and its concepts and discusses the presence of similar concerns today. The continuing preoccupation with, for example, the term "imperialism," through recent concepts such as "platform imperialism" (Jin, 2015) and "regional imperialism" (Boyd Barrett, 2015), along with terms such as "digital colonialism" (Kwet, 2019), "data colonialism" (Couldry and Mejias, 2019), "algorithmic injustice" (Birhane, 2021; Birhane and Cummins, 2019), and "micro-targeting propaganda" (Boyd Barrett, 2020), clearly shows that concerns of uneven power, exploitation, and dominance remains strong throughout the twenty-first century. This chapter will therefore trace the manifestations of such critical thinking and theories throughout the history of international communication and global media.

The Concept of Cultural Imperialism and Donald Duck

The critique of the United States's strong position within an internationalizing media and communications industry became particularly significant in the 1960s. The United States' political and economic self-interest, when leading the development of an international communications industry and systems at the cost of smaller states and cultures, was the target of the political economist Schiller's early critique in his books *Mass Communications and American Empire* (1971) and *Communication and Cultural Domination* ([1976] 2018). Through cultural domination, US media undermined and weakened indigenous and traditional culture. There was a major unevenness in center-periphery relations, Schiller pointed out, and referred to it as *cultural imperialism*: the "processes by which a society is brought into the modern world system and how its dominating stratum is attracted, pressured, forced, and sometimes bribed into shaping social institutions to correspond to, or even to promote, the values and structures of the dominant centre of the system" (Schiller, [1976] 2018: 9). Schiller argued that mass media "are the foremost example of operating enterprises that are used in this penetrative process." (Schiller, [1976] 2018: 9-10). The export of US media and cultural products, including television programming, were a key part of this process. The concept of "cultural imperialism" received considerable attention and was particularly influential in the 1970s. A key study on the concept was Dorfman and Mattelart's (1975) study of the influence and role of Disney products in South America.

Dorfman and Mattelart's highly critical book, *How to Read Donald Duck: Imperialist Ideology in the Disney Comic*, a study of Disney products in "dependent countries like Chile" in South America (1975: 95), aimed to show the "cultural imperialism" thesis in practice, arguing "power to Donald Duck means the promotion of underdevelopment" as the population of these countries considers comics: "as instruction in the way they are supposed to live and relate to the foreign power center" (Dorfman and Mattelart, 1975: 98):

> The daily agony of Third World peoples is served up as a spectacle for permanent enjoyment in the utopia of bourgeois liberty. The non-stop buffet of recreation and redemption offers all the wholesome exotica of underdevelopment: a balanced diet of the unbalanced world. The misery of the Third World is packaged and canned to liberate the masters who produce it and consume it. Then, it is thrown-up to the poor as the only food they know. Reading Disney is like having one's own exploited condition rammed with honey down one's throat.
>
> (Dorfman and Mattelart, 1975: 98)

The book received considerable attention and became a bestseller, as the cover of the second edition of the book (Dorfman and Mattelart, 1984) promoted: "New enlarged edition—Over 500,000 copies worldwide in 13 languages! Already the classic work on cultural imperialism + children's literature." The book focused on the uneven power between the United States and Chile. It argued that Disney represented a key cultural "weapon" for suppressing Chilean cultural identity: "*How to Read Donald Duck* was born in the heat of the struggle to free Chile from that dependency; and it has since become, with its eleven Latin American editions, a most potent instrument for the interpretation of bourgeois media in the Third World" (Kunzle, 1975: 11). The aim of the book, then, was to contribute to removing the "cultural imperialist":

> As long as he [Donald Duck] strolls with his smiling countenance so *innocently* about the streets of our country [Chile], as long as Donald is power and our collective representative, the bourgeoisie and imperialism can sleep in peace. Someday, that fantastic laugh and its echoes will fade away, leaving a mere grimace in its stead. But only when the formulae of daily life imposed upon us by our enemy ceases, and the culture medium which now shapes our social praxis is reshaped.
>
> (Dorfman and Mattelart, 1975: 99)

The impact of the concept of "cultural imperialism" was considerable and "endured to become part of the general intellectual currency of the second half of the twentieth century" (Tomlinson, 1991: 2). Concepts that supported the argument of the cultural imperialism thesis appeared and became part of the discourse. One such concept, *cultural synchronization*, implied that there was a center that dominated its surroundings and the periphery, and that US transnational media companies were driving this process:

> [T]he decisions regarding the cultural development in a given country are made in accordance with the interests and needs of a powerful central nation and imposed with subtle but devastating effectiveness without regard for the adaptive necessities of the dependent nation. The principal agents of cultural synchronization today are transnational corporations, largely based in the United States, which are developing a global investment and marketing strategy. The transnational corporations which are most directly involved with the cultural component of this global expansion are the international communications firms.
>
> (Hamelink, 1983: 22–3)

The Concept of Media Imperialism and News Agencies

Mirroring the concern of cultural domination, political economist and media scholar Boyd Barrett's (1977) concept of *media imperialism* drew attention to the uneven distribution of power between countries and the dominating role of the United States and primarily Western countries, specifically within the international media sphere (1977: 117). Boyd Barrett referred to the unevenness within the internationalization of the media landscape, and defined the concept of "media imperialism" as the "process whereby the ownership, structure, distribution or content of media in any one country are singly or together subject to substantial external pressures from media interests of any other country or countries without proportionate reciprocation of influence by the country so affected" (1977: 117). While the concept of "cultural imperialism" is concerned with ideological and cultural influence and power, "Media imperialism theory is somewhat less structural and Marxist in orientation and focuses more on imbalances of power and flows of media (Boyd Barrett, 1977; Lee, 1980)" (Straubhaar, 2007: 59). A key study of "media imperialism" is Boyd Barret's (1980) study of the asymmetry of news flows internationally and the role of news agencies within this dynamic. There was a "one-way" distribution news from the international news agencies Reuters, United Press International, Agence France Presse, and Associated Press, Boyd Barrett argued (Boyd Barrett, 1980).

In fact, well into the 2000s, within the news market the "classic manifestations of unidirectional, power-inflected media imperialism have persisted" as "the business of wholesale global news-gathering and distribution, mainstream media everywhere continue to be highly dependent on a narrow range of enterprises for print, electronic and video news whether general or specialized" (Boyd Barrett, 2015: 122). The current international news agency market is dominated by the Associated Press (AP) and Thomsen Reuters, and their respective video news companies APTN and Reuters Television, as well as Agence France Press (AFP) and their video news operation AFPTV, and Bloomberg, News Corporation's Dow Jones, and *The Wall Street Journal*. Boyd Barrett argues that within television news the major global organizations such as CNN and BBC Worldwide as well as, at the time, those originating in Qatar (e.g., Al Jazeera), and television operators in China, Russia, and Germany, are in various ways tied to state power, that is, soft power (Boyd Barrett, 2015: 122).

The analyses that came out of the imperialism perspectives "contributed in many ways to a wave of policy intervention against foreign investment in broadcasting and importation of foreign media products that was remarkably effective in many countries" (Straubhaar, 2007: 64). Although the cultural imperialism thesis and cultural synchronization argument focused on the US–Third World relationship, some warned against the consequences of the uneven cultural power between United States and Western Europe, particularly within television (Schiller, 1985: 11). A similar view was expressed from within the European Commission in the mid-1980s. American films and television programs dominated the European media space, creating "a certain uniformity" on television screens (European Commission, 1984: 47). This development was also observed at the turn of the century as "Fiction content is dominated by American films and home-made series." And this "tendency is especially perceived among the sharply increased number of commercial channels," and, despite political measures to level the competition between European and US television channels, "The European system of quotas has not been able to stem the 'Dallasification' of television content" (De Bens and de Smaele, 2001: 72). However, as the television industry changed, the unevenness associated with the original concept of media imperialism, has been altered:

> [T]here are considerably more television outlets in most countries; there is much higher consumption of television; television production costs have fallen, so that in most countries there has been a considerable increase in local productions – which are preferred by consumers, other things being equal – particularly in primetime hours. So a simple argument of US-based media imperialism that is founded on a criterion of the proportion of local programming imported from the USA for primetime viewing no longer has much meaning for most countries.
>
> (Boyd Barrett, 2015: 123)

In fact, Boyd Barrett acknowledged earlier that his original definition of the model of media imperialism "ignored the question of audience" (1998: 168), as it did not address the preferences of audiences or the consumption of cultural products. Yet, he emphasized, that the significance of the relation between audiences and media does not lie in "area of effects," as one should be careful not to presume a straightforward connection between the "colonization of communication space and the attitudes, beliefs and behaviours of audiences" (Boyd Barrett, 1998: 168). Instead, Boyd Barrett argued, one must address issues of inequalities in relation to the audience by asking, "Whose voices get to be heard, and which voices are excluded?" As the popularity of the Internet was increasing, Boyd-Barret pointed out that despite new technologies and the internet, access to such resources, and also the skills to use them and the ability to reach large audiences, are not equally distributed (1998: 168).

For example, within the children's media sector the issue of uneven power is clearly relevant. The US media have long dominated global expansion and export of television programming, films, and other content within children's media, and Disney is by far the largest children's media player globally.

Global Children's Media and Disney

This section looks at three key interrelated Disney brands and activities in its global media expansion: Disney Channel, the streaming service Disney+, and Disney's global licensing and merchandising operation. Disney Channel launched in 1983 and has spearheaded Disney throughout the world since then and into the twenty-first century. By 2019, Disney Channel was localized into forty-seven channels available in thirty-three languages. Disney+ launched in late 2019 and reached 100 million subscribers globally in early 2021. Disney+ is increasingly taking over from the Disney Channel, which is closing in key markets, and its content added to the Disney+ platform. Disney is the world's largest licensor of merchandising products.

The first dedicated children's television channel, Nickelodeon, was launched in 1979 (Papathanassopoulos, 2002: 228). In 1983, Disney Channel followed and attracted 500.000 subscribers in its first year of running. In late 1984, the number of US television households was around 85 million, but only 25 percent of the households could receive Nickelodeon, and the Disney Channel reached a mere 1 percent of households. While the achievements of the new cable television entrants were modest at first, de-regulation of business sectors, including the media sector, along with economic and technological development led to the rise of cable television. By the mid-1980s, cable television channels began to challenge the terrestrial broadcasters (Croteau and Hoynes, 2006). From having a share of 98 percent of the children's television audience in the 1980s, in 2006, the American terrestrial channels had only around 15 percent of this audience, while the cable channels drew 77 percent of this audience (Alexander and Owers, 2007: 59).

In Europe, throughout the 1980s and 1990s, national deregulation, privatization, and liberalization of cross-border activity and ownership rules were the dominating trends in the broadcasting industry (Mjøs, 2010a; Tunstall and Machin, 1999). Since the mid-1990s, all the major US cable and satellite television channels for children have expanded internationally (Papathanassopoulos, 2002: 228). Just like satellite and cable operators drove the fragmentation of the American children's television sector, they have played a similar role in Europe and in other parts of the world (Chalaby, 2009; 2005a; 2005b; Iosifidis *et al.*, 2005).

In 1993, Nickelodeon—owned by the media conglomerate Viacom— launched in the UK. Cartoon Network, controlled by Time Warner, started broadcasting in Latin America and Europe in the following year, and in Asia the year after. Disney Channel first launched in Europe and Taiwan in 1995 and has since rolled out globally (Table 6.1).

The US cable and satellite children's television operators spearheaded by Disney's tier of television channels, of which Disney Channel is the main television brand, have a major presence among television households across the world (see Table 6.2).

Table 6.1 Disney Channel: Global Expansion in Selected Countries

Territory	Launch/Year
Taiwan	1995
UK	1995
Australia	1996
Asia	1996
France	1997
Middle East	1997
Italy	1997
Spain	1998
Germany	1999
Latin America	2000
Brazil	2001
Portugal	2001

Territory	Launch/Year
Scandinavia	2003
Japan	2003
India	2004
South Africa	2006
Poland	2006
Turkey	2007
Malaysia	2008
Bulgaria	2009
Hungary	2009
Czech Republic	2009
Greece	2009
Israel	2009
Russia	2010
Belgium	2011
Netherlands	2011
South Korea	2011
Belgium	2012
Sri Lanka	2014
Canada	2015

Source: C21 Media, 2006; Clarke, 2015; Grant, 2007; Indian Television, 2004; JTA, 2009; Kirchdoerffer, 1998; Reuters, 2007; Smith and White, 2011.

Table 6.2 Disney Branded Children's Television Channels—Estimated Subscribers, September 2020 (Millions)*

	International	United States
Disney Channel	196	85
Disney Junior	166	66
Disney XD	105	66

*Unique subscribers with access to one or more of these Disney branded channels (Walt Disney Company, 2020: 17).

The streaming service Disney+ launched in the United States in November 2019 and expanded overseas fast. In less than a year and a half, the service achieved 100 million paying subscribers (see Table 6.3), which had increased to nearly 130 million by the end of 2021. Disney+ includes Disney, Pixar, Marvel, Star Wars, and National Geographic branded content, and is currently the company's "top priority," according to Disney CEO Bob Chapek (Littelton, 2021). At the

Table 6.3 Disney+ Global Subscribers, 2019–21

November	2019	10 million
December	2019	26.5 million
February	2020	28.6 million
March	2020	33.5 million
April	2020	50 million
May	2020	54.5 million
June	2020	57.5 million
August	2020	60.5 million
October	2020	73.7 million
December	2020	86.8 million
January	2021	94.9 million
March	2021	100 million

Source: Littleton, 2021.

same time, all the major children's television channels in the United States are experiencing a decline in viewership. In 2020, Disney Channel and Nickelodeon had 33 and 32 percent less viewers, respectively, and Disney Junior was 27 percent down (Schneider, 2020). This has major consequences for the Disney Channel and other Disney branded television channels.

The Walt Disney Company points out that the focus on Disney+ and other direct-to-consumer services (DTC) will have consequences for its television channels as "we shift the primary means of monetizing our film and television content from licensing of linear channels to use on our DTC services" (Walt Disney Company, 2020). As Disney+ expanded into over fifty-nine countries in just sixteen months—including Canada, Australia, and New Zealand, and in Europe, Latin America, and South East Asia—the Disney Channel has closed down in countries including Italy, Australia, New Zealand, and the UK (Walt Disney Company, 2021).

Disney's Global Licensing and Merchandising

Disney Channel and Disney+ both play a key role in the company's licensing and merchandising operations. The exploitation of rights extends to the development and sales of media and non-media commercial spin-off products and merchandising products. Either the media companies themselves produce these products or they are licensed to other external producers (Wasko, 2005).

The Walt Disney Company is by far the world's largest and most influential licensor and generates much more than its licensor competitors, both within and outside of the media sector (see Table 6.4).

A global company like Disney has major advantages compared with national competitors. Their global presence allows them to make "master agreements" with major toy producers such as Mattel. National media players are for the most confined to their national territories, while Disney can spread their costs globally and sell the same products worldwide (Mjøs, 2010b). Disney's latest major $71.3 billion acquisition of 21st Century Fox included Marvel characters such as the Fantastic Four and X-Men. The acquisition further expands Disney's ownership over characters to be licensed.

While Disney Channel and Disney+ are key platforms for distribution of the company's media content globally, Disney licenses the well-known characters of these productions for merchandising worldwide to third parties. The products include toys, clothing, games, furnishings, accessories, health and beauty products, books, food, stationery, footwear, and consumer electronic:

> The Company licenses characters from its film, television and other properties for use on third-party products in these categories and earns royalties, which are usually based on a fixed percentage of the wholesale or retail selling price of the products. Some of the major properties licensed by the Company include: Mickey and Minnie, Frozen, Star Wars, Disney Princess, Avengers, Spider-Man, Toy Story, Disney Channel characters, Winnie the Pooh, Cars and Disney Classics.
>
> (Walt Disney Company, 2020: 13)

Disney also sells products through over 300 physical Disney Stores in the United States, Europe, Japan, and China, and its Disney online store globally.

Table 6.4 The Top Ten Leading 150 Global Licensors, 2020

1. The Walt Disney Company	$54.7B
2. Meredith Corporation	$26.5B
3. Authentic Brands Group	$12.3B
4. WarnerMedia	$11B
5. PVH Corp.	$10.6B (estimated)
6. Universal Brand Development	$7.1B
7. Hasbro	$6.9B
8. ViacomCBS	$5.8B
9. General Motors	$4.62B (estimated)
10. Sanrio	$4.4B (estimated)

Source: License Global, 2020.

Disney's control over rights to stories and characters over time is at the heart of the company's ability to develop and produce media content. Critics point out how Disney's practice of securing rights gives Disney influence and control over significant parts of global children's media and culture:

> Disney's global hegemony in the field of children's media culture is unparalleled. The sheer longevity of Walt Disney's own creations – Mickey Mouse, Donald Duck, Bambi, Dumbo and the rest – has, of course, been achieved through a very calculated programme of re-releasing; but the ability of these animated characters to entertain children across the decades and across cultures remains remarkable. Meanwhile, it is hard to think of a fairy tale or a "classic" children's book which children will not now encounter first (and in most cases *only*) in its "Disneyfied" version. Symbolically – and in many cases legally – Disney now "owns" nearly all the fictional characters who have populated children's imaginations over the past century, from Sleeping Beauty and Cinderella right through to its most recent acquisitions such as the Muppets and the Ninja Turtles. A.A. Milne, Lewis Carroll, Rudyard Kipling, Hans Christian Andersen, J.M. Barrie and (most recently) Roald Dahl are only some of the children's authors whose work has been appropriated by the Disney empire.
>
> (Buckingham, 1997: 285)

Disney's control over rights makes the company able to exploit stories and characters in a range of ways and decide how to introduce them to new generations in new media content formats and distribution platforms.

Public Service Broadcasting in the Global Era

Public service broadcasting is an alternative broadcast model to the dominant commercial model, not least through its funding and role in society, and as a tool for national media policy (Syvertsen et al., 2014). Public service broadcasting thereby also represents an alternative for the media audience— including children, as we shall see. The position of the public service broadcasting system in society, and their legitimacy and state funding in a commercializing media landscape, have been key issues in the international communication context. While many have argued for the strengthening of public service broadcasting, not least during the New World Information and Communication Order (NWICO) debates in the 1970s in the United Nations, the financial support for new publicly owned or state-run broadcasters was limited (Straubhaar, 2007: 65).

Historically, the public service broadcasters in Britain and the rest of Northern Europe, particularly the Nordic region, and other countries such as Japan have been financed by the state with a range of obligations and responsibilities. Their remit has been to provide quality information and entertainment to whole national populations, including children as discussed above, and serve as an arena for debate and fostering a national public sphere (Syvertsen et al., 2014). Furthermore, particularly in Europe and Japan, public service television was established to "ensure national cultural informational sovereignty" (Straubhaar, 2007: 65). Despite its state funding and extensive obligations, the public service broadcaster in these parts of the world is situated at arm's length from the direct influence of political interests and authorities, and has editorial freedom. Such a broadcasting system is considered to have an important role in society and to be an alternative to commercial broadcasting, but also to state broadcasters (e.g., China), as they lie outside the reach of both the state and the market. Public service broadcasters outside of Europe and Japan, such as in New Zealand and Canada, receive less funding. In the United States, the world's largest television market, the US public service broadcasting receives only a small fraction of state funding compared to these countries (Syvertsen et al., 2014).

One of Schiller's key arguments regarding how cultural imperialism manifests itself was the expansion of the US commercial media model internationally. He pointed out that: "The United States communications presence overseas extends far beyond the facilities owned, the exports, and the licensing agreements secured by major American broadcasting companies and electronics equipment manufacturers, considerable as these are. Equally, if not more important, is the spread of the American system, the commercial model of communications, to the international arena" (Schiller, 1971: 93). Some point out how this is exactly what has happened in broadcasting:

> Critics of media imperialism routinely take earlier proponents of media imperialism to task for their apparently simplistic fears of a monolithic US dominance of television worldwide. Yet that is precisely what has happened, not in the form of television imported from the USA [...] but in the form of the global adoption of an approach to television that was invented by US media corporations.
>
> (Boyd Barrett, 2015: 134)

Throughout the twenty-first century, most of the revenue within the audiovisual market stems from the commercial model of broadcasting. In fact, less than 10 percent of global revenue was public funding, which has been stagnant, while the commercial television sector continues to grow and expand.

The difference between countries manifests itself further when comparing the public funding that public service broadcasters across the world receive per inhabitant (see Table 6.5).

While public service broadcasting in the Nordic countries and the UK, but also in other European countries and Japan, remains strong and well funded in an international perspective, the share remains marginal in countries that developed and adopted a commercial broadcasting system from an early stage.

In line with their obligations to provide a media diet to the population and reflect life and society, as well as protect local and national culture within countries, many of the European public service broadcasters have launched dedicated children's television and media outlets for children as a response to and to compete with the major US television and media players (see Table 6.6). The trend in Europe is to create dedicated television and media outlets instead of traditional programming blocks shown on the main television channels of the national broadcasters, and "Digital television packages have boosted the number of dedicated children's TV channels, in particular those operated by private players" (EAO, 2017: 7; see also Iosifidis et al., 2005: 145–6).

Table 6.5 Public Service Broadcasting: Public Funding per Head of Population, 2020 ($)

Norway	128
Germany	118
Denmark	110
Finland	100
Sweden	91
United Kingdom	72
Australia	36
Italy	35
Canada	27
New Zealand	19
United States	3

Source: Adapted from EY, 2020.

Table 6.6 National Public Service Broadcasters' Children's Television Channels in Europe, 2021

Television Channel	Public Service Broadcaster	Country
RTSH	RTSH	Albania
OUfTivi	RTBF	Belgium
VRT Ketnet	VRT	Belgium
CT D	CT Ceska Televizie	Czech Republic
DR Ultra	DR	Denmark
DR Ramasjang	DR	Denmark
KiKA	ARD	Germany
M2	Duna	Hungary
TRTE	RTE	Ireland
RTEjr	RTE	Ireland
Cúla4	Telefis na Gaeilge	Ireland
Rai Yoyo	RAI	Italy
RAI Gulp	RAI	Italy
NPO Zapplin Extra	KRO	Netherlands
NPO Zapp	KRO	Netherlands
NRK Super	NRK	Norway
TVP ABC	TVP	Poland
Tlum HD	Tcifrovoe Televidenie	Russia
Telekanal O!	Channel One–Perviy Kanal	Russia
Mult i muzyka	Tcifrovoe Televidenie	Russia
MULT	Tcifrovoe Televidenie	Russia
Mama	NKS-Media	Russia
Karusel International	Karusel	Russia
Karusel	Karusel	Russia
DTR	RTR	Russia
Super 3	Television de Catalunya	Spain
ETB 3	Euskal Telebista	Spain
Television VASCA, SA		
Clan TVE	RTVE	Spain
SVT Barnkanalen	SVT	Sweden
Cbeebies (Poland)	BBC	UK
CBBC	BBC	UK
Cbeebies	BBC	UK

Source: Mavise, 2021.

However, despite the public service broadcasters' launch of dedicated children's television channels, in Europe, by 2021, the majority of the 451 children's television channels available in Europe originate in the United States, and Disney owns around seventy-one of them (Mavise, 2021). The four US groups that control pan-European children's television are Disney, Viacom, Time Warner, and AMC. Their position is strengthened by establishing their own branded media outlets, first television channels, and, increasingly now, through streaming services such as Disney+. This gives several advantages:

- The opportunity to access a higher share of added value by bypassing the European TV channels.
- A large back catalogue of rights, in some cases fully amortised, and therefore a relatively low market entry cost.
- The possibility to develop a coherent, pan-European brand strategy.

(EAO, 2017: 55)

Despite an overall increase in original children's programming content in Europe, largely due to the US outlets, the number of local content productions may decrease as European children's channels may, for budgetary reasons or to reduce risk, decide to acquire US programming that has been tested and successful in other markets and regions (EAO, 2017: 7).

The Global Online Environment: Concerns and Aspects of Power and Influence

The internet has facilitated personal communication and interaction and opened up new forms of media use, communication, and distribution of user-generated content across national borders in an unprecedented way. Yet, this development raises several issues and questions. Critical scholars question the distribution of influence, power, and inequalities within the global online environment and the actual influence of the media audience and users. This part of the chapter will look more carefully at some of these issues and discuss how today's concerns within international communication in many ways mirror those of the past.

A fundamental issue is the ongoing debate and fight for the values of the internet, described as "a battle for the Internet's core values. Innovators and hackers are fighting to maintain them. Commercial and bureaucratic forces are working to change them in line with their own values. There are a number of ongoing conflicts, all with the Internet's openness as the recurring theme" (Rasmussen, 2007: 16). It is, for example, a question of "What dominant principles, values and perceptions of power are being embedded in our technologically-mediated interactions?" Another critical question is "How is technological innovation in the new media field being structured; by whom and for whom is it being negotiated?" (Mansell, 2004: 103). In response to the rapid emergence of global online players such as Facebook and Google, and their prominent position in the global media and communications landscape, van Dijck expresses the "need for a *critical history* of the rise of social media. Such a history is needed to comprehend current tendencies in the ecosystem in which platforms and ever-larger groups of users operate" (2013: 5).

In this debate, the dominance of the United States is still a concern for critical scholars. Boyd Barrett, who originally coined the term "media imperialism," points explicitly to how the theoretical concept continues to be relevant when explaining the United States' dominant role in information and communication technologies (ICT). The term "media imperialism" originally aimed to explain the American presence and power in the international media market, but this focus "may have distracted attention from the emergence of microprocessor-based computer networking technologies" and the "influence these have exerted on US economic and foreign policies" (Boyd Barrett, 2006: 21). Following this argument, Boyd Barrett emphasizes how one should, in addition to studying the process of the consumption of point-of-consumption content, "be concerned with the technological, administrative and business infrastructures that enable the production and dissemination of point-of-consumption content"—including both hardware and software and their symbiotic relationship (Boyd Barrett, 2015: 4). The corporatization of the internet shows how it is the commercial logic and values that are shaping the internet. While this development creates opportunities for online users, some argue that the enthusiasm for user autonomy masks questions of power and influence, as "Corporate platforms owned by Facebook, Google and other large companies strongly mediate the cultural expressions of Internet users" (Fuchs, 2017: 68).

Platform Imperialism, and Digital and Data Colonialism

The terms "imperialism" and "colonialism" are also used when characterizing the current digital media and communications landscape. The term "platform imperialism" refers to the increasing presence and role of US-based platforms: "U.S.-based platforms in capital accumulation and culture, as exemplified with Facebook and Google, are arguably clear examples of the rise of platform imperialism" (Jin, 2015: 39). These platforms also include the dominant global mobile phone producers:

> The hegemonic power of American-based platforms is crucial because Google, Facebook, iPhone, and Android have functioned as major digital media intermediaries thanks to their advanced roles in aggregating several services. The U.S., which had previously controlled non-Western countries with its military power, capital, and later cultural products, now seems to dominate the world with platforms, benefitting from these platforms, mainly in terms of capital accumulation. This new trend raises the question whether the U.S., which has always utilized its imperial power, not only with capital and technology, but also with culture, to control the majority of the world, actualizes the same dominance with platforms.
>
> (Jin, 2013: 145)

Mirroring earlier notions of cultural and media imperialism, platform imperialism "is not only about material, but also ideological issues" as "platform developers clearly impose their symbolic hegemony to the majority of developing countries that buy and use platforms, and therefore, provide their labor to benefit platform inventers and countries owning these platforms" (Jin, 2015: 39). The United States used military and financial power to influence and control non-Western countries, followed by dominance in cultural media products, and now "dominates the world with platforms," according to Jin: "a handful of U.S.-owned platforms have rapidly expanded their dominance in the global market, which has caused the asymmetrical gap between a few Western countries and the majority of non-Western countries" (Jin, 2013: 161).

Although a number of non-US social media, such as Kakao (Korea), Mixi (Japan), Baidu and QQ (China), and VK (Russia), provide competition for the US digital platforms, they have limited users outside of their domestic market and diaspora. As a consequence, users in other non-Western countries and regions do not have alternative services: "these countries are not able to develop their own platforms due to the paucity of talents, skills, and capital. The asymmetrical power relationship between a few developed countries, mainly the United States, and the majority of non-Western nations has been widening" (Jin, 2020: 55).

Throughout the twenty-first century, "imperialism has continued to evolve," and despite the expansion and growth of the digital economy in countries like China, India, and Korea, there are still "reasonable doubts" as to whether non-Western digital platforms have been able to develop a new global order or "a balance between the West and East." Only a few countries have been able to develop and advance domestic platforms, and it is still the US platforms that have expanded and dominate globally (Jin, 2020: 57).

The related term "colonialism" has also been used to characterize the digital media and communications landscape. The terms "digital colonialism" and "data colonialism" attempt to capture key developments in a global context. "Digital colonialism" aims to conceptualize how a "structural form of domination is exercised through the centralised ownership and control of the three core pillars of the digital ecosystem: software, hardware, and network connectivity, which vests the United States with immense political, economic, and social power" (Kwet, 2019: 4). Companies like Google/Alphabet, Amazon, Facebook, Apple, and Microsoft—but also US intelligence agencies, such as the National Security Agency (NSA)—represents "the *new imperialists*" (Kwet, 2019).

The aim of the term "data colonialism" is "refashioning the very term—colonialism" by using it as a frame in which to understand an emerging form of colonialism in the twenty-first century. Data colonialism utilizes a combination of "the predatory extractive practices of historical colonialism" and "the abstract quantification methods of computing", Couldry and Mejias (2019: 337) argue:

> Through what we call "data relations" (new types of human relations which enable the extraction of data for commodification), social life all over the globe becomes an "open" resource for extraction that is somehow "just there" for capital. These global flows of data are as expansive as historic colonialism's appropriation of land, resources, and bodies, although the epicenter has somewhat shifted.
>
> (2019: 337)

Historically, "the West" was the "pole of colonial power", but data colonialism involves at least two colonial powers: the United States and China: "This complicates our notion of the geography of the Global South, a concept which until now helped situate resistance and disidentification along geographic divisions between former colonizers and colonized" (Couldry and Mejias, 2019: 337).

Global Search Engines: Concerns and Issues

Google, one of the key internet-based companies to emerge in the early 2000s, established its search engine as a global force in just a few years. While hailed as a key example of the opportunities of the Web 2.0 era, a closer look at its business logic, search mechanisms, and dominance raises a number of issues and concerns in a global context. The development of Google gives insights into how different core values attempt to shape the development of the online environment.

A starting point that encapsulates how different motives and core values and interests aim to shape the development and characteristics of the internet is the term "Web 2.0." We have seen how the internet dotcom crash was a major setback for the commercialization of the internet and thereby the ability of commercial values to shape the internet. The internet had become increasingly popular throughout the late 1990s, and the number of users had increased internationally, yet the dotcom bubble burst and this had a devastating effect on internet-related businesses. Yet, the potential for commercial development was not forgotten as the number of internet users continued to increase, and computer hardware and software became more and more advanced, but for many also more affordable.

The new internet, Web 2.0, promised a "new" web in which financial rewards, increased usability, and, importantly, user power and interactivity were at the center of internet development. *Time* magazine's announcement of "You" as "Time's Person of the Year" in 2006 emphasized the empowerment of users, and opportunities for collaboration through services like Wikipedia, Myspace, and YouTube:

> It's a story about community and collaboration on a scale never seen before. It's about the cosmic compendium of knowledge Wikipedia and the million-channel people's network YouTube and the online metropolis MySpace. It's about the many wresting power from the few and helping one another for nothing and how that will not only change the world, but also change the way the world changes. [...] The tool that makes this possible is the World Wide Web. Not the Web that Tim Berners-Lee hacked together (15 years ago, according to Wikipedia) as a way for scientists to share research. It's not even the overhyped dotcom Web of the late 1990s. The new Web is a very different thing. It's a tool for bringing together the small contributions of millions of people and making them matter. Silicon Valley consultants call it Web 2.0, as if it were a new version of some old software. But it's really a revolution.

> (Grossman, 2006)

At the time of *Time*'s article, Google's profits increased at an astounding rate, and the social media Myspace had been bought by News Corporation; these developments were "by many considered as proof of the promises of Web 2.0, and served the interest of both technological, financial, and political stakeholders—

strengthening belief in the internet after the dotcom crisis" (Mjøs et al., 2014). The hype surrounding Myspace, at the time the main internationally expanding social media service, promoted the service as a key tool for users and particularly musicians and bands to help them succeed. This exemplified the "power of Web 2.0" for many and signified the potential of the social media phenomenon in various ways.

Web 2.0 became the most significant buzzword in the revival of the internet throughout the 2000s. The term's function was "simplifying a complex field," the development of the internet globally, "promoting it as something new"—separating the old internet (1.0) and the new internet (Web 2.0)—and, importantly, "justifying strategies and actions"—the investment in the internet and the significant role of the internet in business and society, and for individuals (Mjøs et al., 2014). Still, the enthusiasm and celebrations came at a cost: "The hidden 'magic' of Web 2.0 technologies remains conspicuously unquestioned by all promoters, whether business gurus or cultural experts. They all claim a brave new world where the spirits of commonality are finally merged with the interests of capitalism" (van Dijck and Nieborg, 2009: 870).

In 2005, as US internet search engines began their worldwide expansion, Jacques Chirac, the president of France, argued for a European internet search engine to compete against these new services and Anglo-Saxon cultural imperialism: "We're engaged in a global competition for technological supremacy. In France, in Europe, it's our power that's at stake." Furthermore, Chirac pointed out how "Culture is not merchandise and it cannot be left to the blind forces of the market," and added, "We must staunchly defend the world's diversity of cultures against the looming threat of uniformity" (Chirac, quoted in Litterick, 2005). This part of the chapter takes a critical look at key concerns in relation to the global search engine phenomenon.

By 2021, just a handful of search engines dominate internet use worldwide. The American Google's estimated global market share of searches globally is between 80 and 90 percent, followed by Baidu, the Chinese search engine, Microsoft's Bing, Yahoo!'s search engine, and the Russian search engine Yandex.

The world has never before seen a media and communications entity like Google monopolize information gathering and achieve such market position, formatting and influencing our view of the online world, and embedded so deeply in local and national conditions. Global search engines do not treat all information equally, but sift and select information according to various criteria and principles hidden from public scrutiny. Theologian Philip Clayton describes our online reality as a "Google-shaped world" (Clayton, 2010: 9, quoted in Hillis et al., 2013).

Yet, in contrast to traditional media, global search engines facilitate new online spaces for users that enhance their access to information. These services drive the integration of geographically and culturally specific information and knowledge, and thereby open up for the comparison and challenging of local understandings and definitions in an unparalleled way. In this way, there is an unprecedented collapse of a range of traditional limits and restrictions to knowledge and information. Google alone is available in around 200 languages, and users now have a presence within and access to the global media and communications landscape in a way never seen before in media history: "a profound transformation in the structure of feeling of our common world has taken place" (Hillis et al., 2013: 5). Global media and communications services have never been so global, yet never been so local.

Dataveillance, Algorithmic Injustice, Filter Bubbles, AI-driven Mass Personalization, Micro-targeting Propaganda

However, the global power and presence of Google and other major online media and services raises several questions and concerns. One key concern is the practice and consequences of *dataveillance*. While online surveillance traditionally refers to the monitoring of user data for defined purposes, dataveillance "entails the continuous tracking of (meta)data for unstated preset purposes" (van Dijck, 2014: 205). For example, Google applies dataveillance to make predictive analyses: "Google claims they are much better than state agencies in forecasting unemployment statistics or flu epidemics because their web crawlers can determine when an individual is about to start looking for a new job or starts seeking information about influenza" (van Dijck, 2014: 204). However, this activity has problematic sides, since the different algorithmic criteria, such as how job seeking is defined, and how and by whom data is processed, are not necessarily known to users. This shows how dataveillance has major consequences for the relationship and trust between the digital platforms and authorities and individual citizens (van Dijck, 2014: 205).

Another, related concern is *algorithmic injustice*. Political, economic, and social decisions and choices in society are increasingly made with input from various forms of automated systems and software-aided input (Birhane and Cummins, 2019). "However, automated and standardized solutions to complex and contingent social issues often contribute more harm than good—they often fail to grasp complex problems and provide a false sense of solution and safety" (Birhane, 2021).

While algorithmic tools aim to increase efficiency and precision, they also "embed and perpetuate societal and historical biases and injustices," and indications suggest that "society's most vulnerable are disproportionately impacted" (Birhane and Cummins, 2019). Search engines have long played a role in this development (e.g., Introna and Nissenbaum, 2000). Birhane and Cummins point out that by registering "social and historical behavioural action," computer systems infer individual behavior through "superficial extrapolations," which are then applied to the wider society. This practice has unintentional consequences: "In the process, individuals and groups, often at the margins of society that fail to fit stereotypical boxes, suffer the undesirable consequences. [...] As algorithmic decision-making is deployed across the social sphere in socially contested contexts such as 'acceptable' behaviour, 'ill' health, and 'normal' body type, algorithms make decisions with moral implications, not just value-free categorization tasks, for instance" (2019). The point is that "Categories simplify and freeze nuanced and complex narratives obscuring political and moral reasoning behind a category." As such, tasks such as "identifying and predicting 'employable' or 'criminal' characteristics carry grave consequences for those that do not conform to the status quo" (Birhane, 2021).

Another key concern is the formation of *filter bubbles*. These are digital information enclaves consisting of misinformation and are self-reinforcing groups of hyperpartisans. The formation of such environments is fostered and reinforced by general search engines and news search engines, but also digital recommendation systems and social media. For example, through search engines users get different search results based on online activity. This phenomenon has become well known, not least through scholars such as Sunstein (2001) and Pariser (2011), as Bruns (2019a) points out, but the scope of filter bubbles, how common they actually are, and how they actually work are not clear, as there has been a general tendency to refer to them anecdotally, rather than through empirical evidence, Bruns argues. As such, Bruns argues that single case studies should not be generalized, as they are embedded in complex networks (Bruns, 2019a; 2019b).

Another concern relates to the relationship between *public interest* and the *commercial motives* of search engines. Key to Google's success was its ability from early on to navigate between the pressures for marketization and more idealistic motives and libertarian beliefs. This "hybrid value formation" provided an "efficient and transparent means of ensuring precise results" (Hillis et al., 2013: 38), and this helped Google achieve legitimacy among diverse stakeholders. This ideology was key in shaping the norm of internet search. Still, Google is a dominant force and this raises a number of related issues and concerns. It is a massive global commercial operation, and its aims are not necessarily in line with democratic development and public and local benefit.

Already in 1998, in a paper presenting the very prototype of Google, the authors and founders of Google, Brin and Page, acknowledged the problematic relationship between advertising and online searches. From "historical experience with other media [...] we expect that advertising funded search engines will be inherently biased towards the advertisers and away from the needs of the consumers" (1998). Therefore, Brin and Page argued, "the issue of advertising causes enough mixed incentives that it is crucial to have a competitive search engine that is transparent and in the academic realm" (1998). Google's way of dealing with searches and advertising is by differentiating between "search-engine optimization" and "paid search." The former "aims to exploit so-called organic (nonpaid-for) search results [...] the list of websites that appear when you type keywords into the search box" (Turow, 2011: 65). The latter process, Google's paid-search advertising system, "involves an auction, as companies bid on search words—perhaps thousands of them—to win the right to have its ads appear prominently alongside the organic search results" (Turow, 2011: 66).

Still, this does not mean that users are able to distinguish between the two search forms. According to an early Pew study, as many as 62 percent of searchers are not aware of the difference between paid and unpaid results (Fallows, 2005: ii). A later Pew study showed that 73 percent of users of search engines believe that "most or all of the information they find" through search engine use is "accurate and trustworthy," and 66 percent believe that search engines provide "fair and unbiased" information, according to a Pew study (Purcell, 2012: 3).

The personalization of online searches reinforces the ongoing fragmentation of media and communications use, but also of access to information. This may have consequences for our society and democratic conditions. In a "hypercustomized" media world (Turow, 2011) not only advertising, but also

---

Case Study 6.1 Cambridge Analytica, Facebook, and Global Personalization

A seemingly innocent personality quiz on Facebook was at the center of a scandal that showed how the gathering of user data of up to 87 million social media users, unknown to these users, could easily be used for political gains. The user data was shared with the London-based company Cambridge Analytica, who worked for Donald Trump's election campaign and used it to map individual US voters and develop a software program that could predict and have an impact on their choices through personalized political messages and advertisements

(BBC, 2019; Cadwalladr and Graham-Harrison, 2018). Christopher Wylie, who took part in the data collection with the researcher Aleksandr Kogan and his company GSR, explained: "We exploited Facebook to harvest millions of people's profiles. And built models to exploit what we knew about them and target their inner demons. That was the basis the entire company was built on" (Cadwalladr and Graham-Harrison, 2018).

How is this possible? A key example is how researchers were able to show how the analyses of digital footprints in the form of Facebook Likes revealed that "computers' judgments of people's personalities based on their digital footprints are more accurate and valid than judgments made by their close others or acquaintances (friends, family, spouse, colleagues, etc.) Our findings highlight that people's personalities can be predicted automatically and without involving human social-cognitive skills" (Youyou et al., 2015: 1036). However, the scholars noted that the knowledge and insights from applying these methods "can also be used to manipulate and influence" Facebook users:

> Understandably, people might distrust or reject digital technologies after realizing that their government, internet provider, web browser, online social network, or search engine can infer their personal characteristics more accurately than their closest family members. We hope that consumers, technology developers, and policy-makers will tackle those challenges by supporting privacy-protecting laws and technologies, and giving the users full control over their digital footprints.
>
> (Youyou et al., 2015: 1039)

Despite such calls for privacy protection, this is exactly what the British political consulting company Cambridge Analytica did. It went ahead and exploited these Facebook-based methods to target Facebook users "based on their psychometrics" in support of Donald Trump's presidential campaign: "Building on personality profiles of American voters, they employed a huge number of different messages, including traditional ads and memes, which has sparked controversy and debates about the potential effects and threats of such a form of personalization" (Winter et al., 2021).

The term "personalization" is often used to describe "different types of tailoring strategies" (Winter et al., 2021). In media, the term is "used by contemporary media practitioners to denote the emerging process by which a media organization tailors the content an individual receives based on attributes the organization believes it knows about the individual" (Turow, 2017: 135). While personalization is most common in advertising, it is being adopted throughout the digital media system and increasingly considered a central strategy for advertisers and media and communications services and outlets alike to locate and reach individual users on a worldwide scale: "Personalization is the cornerstone of contemporary algorithmic devices. What we buy, the news we read, the music we listen to and so many more components of our everyday lives increasingly depend on algorithmic suggestions, supposedly tailored to fit our personal interests" (Kotras, 2020). In fact, the global consultancy firm McKinsey points out that the application of personalization strategies "must become the core driver of how companies do marketing": "Personalization is impossible if marketers don't have the means to understand the needs of high-value customers on an ongoing basis. So top marketers are developing systems that can pool and analyze structured and unstructured data, algorithms that can identify behavioral patterns and customer propensity, and analysis capabilities to feed that information into easy-to use dashboards" (Boudet et al., 2019).

Still, some point out that there is an element of hype regarding personalization: "despite claims that this new form of campaigning was a crucial factor in Trump's victory, empirical research showing the effectiveness of *trait-based personalization* in the context of social media marketing is still very limited" (Winter et al., 2021). However, the Cambridge Analytica/Facebook case raises several issues in relation to global personalization. One key issue is how, in the Cambridge Analytica case, Facebook user data were collected, analyzed, and used unwittingly. While users may have "approved" such activity by third parties when registering their profile, in practice the possibilities for misuse and the consequence of such misuse is severe in any case and happens without consent in each case.

news may be tailored to individual users based on information on and profiles of users that few are aware are being continuously created and refined by corporate media and communications players (2011). This brings us to Case Study 6.1.

A highly relevant issue is the application of artificial intelligence (AI) in personalization strategies, or *AI-driven mass personalization* (Hermann, 2021). The massive data processing capacity of AI coupled with the aggregation of enormous amounts of digital and social media data based on the tracking of users highlights the ethical consequences involved, as "AI allows to personalize content at unprecedented speed, scale, intensity and responsiveness" (Hermann, 2021). AI not only opens up opportunities for personalization based on preferences, interests, and demographics, but also on psychological aspects and factors: "AI-powered psychological targeting offers considerable opportunities to tailor (persuasive) appeals to individuals' psychological traits (variability across consumer such as personality traits or values) and states (variability within consumers over time such as mood or emotions) that are computationally predicted from their digital footprints" (Hermann, 2021).

Another issue at stake is the consequences of personalization of media content, services and offers. Increasingly, we receive not only advertising, but also information and media content based on our user data. This tailoring, *hypercustomization*, (Turow, 2006, 2011) means that the big data used to personalize advertising are also used to personalize news, entertainment, and even prices:

> *Personalized* refers to a form of a *deep* personalization—content whose selection has already been *decided for* citizens on the basis of criteria unknown to them and calibrated not to their proximate selection decisions, but to big data–generated *assumptions* about where those citizens would want to focus their attention or where marketers need those citizens' attention to be focused. This development is not the result of conspiracy to remove people from collective experiences. It is instead an unintended side effect—a *negative externality*—of how advertising, big data, and content production have come to coexist over the past two decades.
>
> (Couldry and Turow, 2014: 1712)

This development may have severe consequences and "be erosive of the civic sphere" (Couldry and Turow, 2014: 1712). A further issue at stake is the relationship between *micro-targeting propaganda* and personalization. The distribution of propaganda, part of the media imperialism thesis, continues to be highly relevant in the digital era. Two of the most striking examples of propaganda strategy in the twenty-first century are Cambridge Analytica and the way the Trump campaign of 2016 exploited big data to micro-target propaganda (Boyd Barrett, 2020: 25; see also Case Study 6.2).

Case Study 6.2 "Fake News" and Global Platforms

The worldwide popularization of the internet and the global reach of Facebook and other social media services, as well as messaging apps and search engines, has facilitated rapid distribution of information online, such as news. The targeting tools available have made it possible to reach social media users with unprecedented accuracy and scale. However, such services also facilitate the distribution of information to users that is inaccurate or not even true. "Fake news" has become a phenomenon of the latter type of information:

> [F]ake news appropriates the look and feel of real news; from how websites look; to how articles are written; to how photos include attributions. Fake news hides under a veneer of legitimacy as it takes on some form of credibility by trying to appear like real news. Furthermore, going beyond the simple appearance of a news item, through the use of news bots, fake news imitates news' omnipresence by building a network of fake sites.
>
> (Tandoc et al., 2018)

Fake news can thereby also contribute to challenging the reliability and integrity of ordinary news, as the source and origins of the information distributed can be missing or may be incorrect (Tandoc et al., 2018).

"Fake news" became a buzzword in 2016 during the US presidential election when pro-Trump fake news was distributed widely, and particularly on Facebook (van Dijck et al., 2018; Tandoc et al., 2018). Since then, online fake news has become increasingly mainstream and particularly present and noticeable during major crises and events in world society, for example, during the Brexit process as the UK withdrew from the EU, and throughout the Covid-19 pandemic. In the early part of the Covid-19 pandemic the World Health Organization (WHO) warned against the consequences of an "infodemic": "At its extreme, death can be the tragic outcome of what the World Health Organization has termed the infodemic, an overabundance of information—some accurate, some not—that spreads alongside a disease outbreak. False information runs the gamut, from discrediting the threat of COVID-19 to conspiracy theories that vaccines could alter human DNA" (WHO, 2021).

Social media services, or platforms, do moderate the content that is distributed and exchanged. However, this practice has faced significant criticism and created controversy. Some critics argue that they moderate too much, when censoring images that may have different meanings and significance across the world, while others point out that they moderate too little, as in the case of the flow of misinformation: "In other words, platform moderation practices constitute an intricate balancing act between different actors, interests, and concerns" (van Dijck et al., 2018: 44).

In the wake of the 2016 US presidential election, Facebook and Google took various measures to reduce their role as facilitators for distribution of misinformation, and also launched projects to fund production of news and journalism, provided financing for fact-checking, and deleted information and posts. Still, despite acknowledging the existence of such information and unwanted activity, and the implementation of measures to reduce and prevent it, scholars point out that this problem is far from solved:

> Tech platforms have not always been clear about their stance when it comes to fighting online falsehoods. For example, social media companies suspended outgoing US President Donald Trump's accounts on their platforms after the January 6, 2020 bloody riot perpetrated by his supporters at the US Capitol, but this came only after years of criticism about how the same platforms had allowed Trump to communicate baseless claims.
>
> (Lien et al., 2021)

As such, the relationship between fake news and global platforms, and Facebook in particular, is often problematic. However, the moderation done by these companies "should be understood within the larger commercial regulatory environment of the online ecosystem, in which often contradictory economic, political, and social pressures are at work" (van Dijck et al., 2018: 45). Social media and other platform companies have an economic motivation when deciding whether to limit the activity of distributing and exchanging information and content or not. This would reduce the income from advertisement and other forms of income:

> This economic incentive became particularly poignant during the 2016 US elections when so-called fake news widely circulated across social media platforms. Overall, platforms tend to especially respond to controversy: pressured by users and advertisers, they are usually highly motivated to moderate controversial content and practices. [...] The criteria for filtering content and blocking users are constantly evolving, driven by changing societal concerns and ideals.
>
> (van Dijck et al., 2018: 45)

Still, an important, and often neglected, point is the role of the user and audience. To what extent are they able to judge whether something is fake or real news? If they are not deceived, and do not believe the information is true, the information presented "remains a work of fiction." As such, the audience and users clearly play a role in the creation of fake news:

> It is when audiences mistake it as real news that fake news is able to play with journalism's legitimacy. This is particularly important in the context of social media, where information is exchanged, and therefore meanings are negotiated and shared. The socialness of social media adds a layer to the construction of fake news, in that the power of fake news lies on how well it can penetrate social spheres. Social spheres are strengthened by information exchange, and it may well be that the quality of information becomes secondary.
>
> (Tandoc et al., 2018)

The United States and China: Media Imperialism

The emergence of the concept of BRICS has raised the questions of whether the United States' position globally is being challenged and, if so, what the possible consequences may be (e.g., Thussu and Nordenstreng, 2021). However, scholars do not necessarily agree on this, pointing out that even if the BRICS countries made up a "unified bloc" it would not come close to equaling the structural power of the United States: "Only China might be considered an emerging rival to the United States, but current evidence does not show this. [...] current evidence does not indicate that China is now a substantive rival to the United States. Currently, the United States outmatches China, economically, militarily, and in terms of the centrality and scope of its ICT and cultural industries" (Boyd Barrett and Mirrlees, 2020: 8). China is expanding militarily and has forged alliances and collaborations with around 140 countries across the world through its Belt and Road infrastructure program, as well as scaling up its "soft power" initiatives worldwide, and is experiencing tremendous growth and expansion in its ICT and media sectors, also overseas: "So while we may not yet be living in the 'Chinese Century,' China's military, economic, and cultural rise suggest that the global system may be shaping up to be bipolar" (Mirrlees, 2020: 314; see also Sacks, 2021; Thussu and Nordenstreng, 2021). Still, while China can surpass the United States economically and while "China is developing a media and cultural apparatus to support its nascent imperialist role, it has not yet achieved much in the way of popular acceptance. It is certainly not yet in a situation in which it can hope to supplant the United States as the world's leading power, neither in terms of political and military, nor media and cultural, power" (Sparks, 2020: 283). In fact, Sparks argues that "there are strong reasons for thinking that China will find it very difficult to replicate the success enjoyed by US media and cultural imperialism" (Sparks, 2020: 284). While one may argue that the US empire is in decline, it continues to exist and with its global ICT and cultural industries as central parts of it:

> The future is without guarantees, but if the past is any guide to the future, the US empire will not loosen its grip on the global system's order without first exercising the optimal level of persuasive and coercive power to tighten it. For this reason, the future of the global system is likely to be shaped and reshaped significantly by mounting tensions and conflicts between the United States and China.
>
> (Mirrlees, 2020: 314)

Another concept that aims to make the concept of media imperialism relevant in different media markets across the world is *regional imperialism*. The term implies how large media companies form oligopolies of three to four companies in a regional media market, reflecting the dominant positions of these companies: they "may be regarded as agents of imperialism where they exercise business practices in ways that suppress the viability of smaller media in their own countries of origin so that the diversity and inclusiveness of creative voices is reduced" (Boyd Barrett, 2015: 14). While the media imperialism discourse has often referred to the power of US media companies, regional centers of production and distribution have emerged and consolidated and thereby become "candidates for the status of media imperialist" that have emerged from the South. These represent "newer models of imperialism," some being "regionally hegemonic" (Boyd Barrett, 2015: 118–19).

References

Alexander, A. and Owers, J. (2007) The Economics of Children's Television, pp. 57–74 in J. A. Bryant (ed.) *The Children's Television Community*. Mahwah, NJ: Lawrence Erlbaum.

BBC (2019) Facebook agrees to pay Cambridge Analytica fine to UK. *BBC News*, October 30. https://www.bbc.com/news/technology-50234141 (accessed April 15, 2021).

Birhane, A. (2021) Algorithmic injustice: A relational ethics approach. *Patterns*, 2, 2. https://doi.org/10.1016/j.patter.2021.100205

Birhane, A. and Cummins, F. (2019) Algorithmic Injustices: Towards a Relational Ethics. Presented at the Black in AI workshop, @NeurIPS2019, arXiv:1912.07376 (accessed April 21, 2021).

Boudet, J., Gregg, B., Rathje, K., Stein, E., and Vollhardt, K. (2019) The future of personalization—and how to get ready for it. McKinsey & Company, June 18. https://www.mckinsey.com/business-functions/marketing-and-sales/our-insights/the-future-of-personalization-and-how-to-get-ready-for-it (accessed April 15, 2021).

Boyd-Barrett, O. (1977) Media Imperialism: Towards an International Framework for an Analysis of Media Systems, pp. 116–35 in J. Curran, M. Gurevitch, and J. Woollacott (eds.) *Mass Communication and Society*. London: Edward Arnold.

Boyd-Barrett, O. (1980) *The International News Agency*. London: Constable.

Boyd-Barrett, O. (1998) Media Imperialism Reformulated, pp. 157–76 in D. K. Thussu (ed.) *Electronic Empires: Global Media and Local Resistance*. London: Arnold.

Boyd-Barrett, O. (2006) Cyberspace, globalization and empire. *Global Media and Communication*, 2, 1: 21–41.

Boyd-Barrett, O. (2015) *Media Imperialism*. London: SAGE.

Boyd-Barrett, O. (2020) Media and Cultural Imperialism: Genealogy of an Idea, pp. 11–30 in O. Boyd-Barrett and T. Mirrlees (eds.) *Media Imperialism: Continuity and Change*. Lanham, MD: Rowman & Littlefield.

Boyd-Barrett, O. and Mirrlees, T. (2020) Introduction: Media Imperialism: Continuity and Change, pp. 1–10 in O. Boyd-Barrett and T. Mirrlees (eds.) *Media Imperialism: Continuity and Change*. Lanham, MD: Rowman & Littlefield.

Brin, S. and Page, L. (1998) The anatomy of a large-scale hypertextual web search engine. *Computer Networks and ISDN Systems*, 30, 1–7. https://research.google/pubs/pub334 (accessed June 2, 2022).

Bruns, A. (2019a) How the "echo chamber" and "filter bubble" metaphors have failed us. Paper presented at the IAMCR 2019 conference, July 7–11, Madrid, Spain. https://snurb.info/files/2019/It%e2%80%99s%20Not%20the%20Technology,%20Stupid.pdf (accessed June 2, 2022).

Bruns, A. (2019b) *Are Filter Bubbles Real?* Cambridge, UK: Polity Press.

Buckingham, D. (1997) Dissin' Disney: Critical perspectives on children's media culture. *Media, Culture & Society*, 19, 2: 285–93.

C21 Media (2006) Disney Channel expands to South Africa. August 8. https://www.c21media.net/news/disney-channel-expands-to-south-africa/ (accessed May 15, 2022).

Cadwalladr, C. and Graham-Harrison, E. (2018) Revealed: 50 million Facebook profiles harvested for Cambridge Analytica in major data breach. *The Guardian*, March 17. https://www.theguardian.com/news/2018/mar/17/cambridge-analytica-facebook-influence-us-election (accessed April 15, 2021).

Chalaby, J. K. (2005a) Deconstructing the transnational: A typology of cross-border television channels in Europe. *New Media & Society*, 7, 2: 155–75.

Chalaby, J. K. (2005b) The Quiet Invention of a New Medium: Twenty Years of Transnational Television in Europe, pp. 43–65 in J. K. Chalaby (ed.) *Transnational Television Worldwide: Towards a New Media Order*. London: I. B. Tauris.

Chalaby, J. K. (2009) *Transnational Television in Europe*. London: I. B. Tauris.

Clarke, S. (2015) Disney Channel rolling out in Canada. *TBI Vision*, August 12. https://tbivision.com/2015/08/12/disney-channel-rolling-canada/ (accessed August 31, 2022).

Clayton, P. (2010) Theology and the Church after Google, *Princeton Theological Review*, 43: 2, 7–20.

Couldry, M. and Mejias, U. A. (2019) Data colonialism: Rethinking big data's relation to the contemporary subject. *Television & New Media*, 20, 4: 336–49.

Couldry, N. and Turow, J. (2014) Advertising, big data, and the clearance of the public realm: Marketers' new approaches to the content subsidy. *International Journal of Communication*, 8: 1710–26.

Croteau, D. and Hoynes, W. (2006) *The Business of Media: Corporate Media and the Public Interest*. Second edition. Thousand Oaks, CA: Pine Forge.

De Bens, E. and de Smaele, H. (2001) The inflow of American television fiction on European broadcasting channels revisited. *European Journal of Communication*, 16, 1: 51–76.

Dorfman, A. and Mattelart, A. (1975) *How to Read Donald Duck: Imperialist Ideology in the Disney Comic*. New York: International General.

Dorfman, A. and Mattelart, A. (1984) *How to Read Donald Duck: Imperialist Ideology in the Disney Comic*. New York: International General.

EAO (2017) *Media Ownership: Children's TV Channels in Europe—Who Are the Key Players?* https://rm.coe.int/media-ownership-children-s-tv-channels-in-europe-july-2017-l-ene-/1680788fd1 (accessed April 14, 2021).

European Commission (1984) *Television without Frontiers. Green Paper on the Establishment of the Common Market for Broadcasting, Especially by Satellite and Cable.* COM (84) 300, June 14, 1984. Introduction; Parts One, Two and Three, 47. http://aei.pitt.edu/archive/00001151/01/TV_frontiers_gp_pt_1_3.pdf (accessed June 1, 2022).

EY (2020) *International Perspectives on Public Service Broadcasting: EY Report for Ofcom.* www.smallscreenbigdebate.co.uk/__data/assets/pdf_file/0026/204587/international-perspectives-on-psb.pdf (accessed April 13, 2021).

Fallows, D. (2005) *Search Engine Users: Internet Searchers Are Confident, Satisfied and Trusting— But They Are Also Unaware and Naïve.* Washington, DC: Pew Internet and American Life.

Fuchs, C. (2017) *Social Media: A Critical Introduction.* Second edition. London: SAGE.

Grant, J. (2007) Disney talks Turkey, extends Polish reach. April 30. https://www.c21media.net/news/disney-talks-turkey-extends-polish-reach/ (accessed 21 June, 2022).

Grossman, L. (2006) You—yes, you—are TIME's Person of the Year. *Time,* December 25. https://content.time.com/time/magazine/article/0,9171,1570810,00.html (accessed June 21, 2022).

Hamelink, C. J. (1983) *Cultural Autonomy in Global Communications.* New York: Longman.

Hermann, E. (2021) Artificial intelligence and mass personalization of communication content—An ethical and literacy perspective. *New Media & Society.* https://doi.org/10.1177/14614448211022702

Hillis, K., Petit, M., and Jarrett, K. (2013) *Google and the Culture of Search.* Routledge: London.

Indian Television (2004) Disney Channels to be available in four languages. *Indian Television,* December 14. https://www.indiantelevision.com/headlines/y2k4/dec/dec125.htm (accessed August 31, 2022).

Introna, L. and Nissenbaum, H. (2000) Shaping the web: Why the politics of search engines matters. *Information Society,* 16, 3: 1–17.

Iosifidis, P., Steemers, J., and Wheeler, M. (2005) *European Television Industries.* London: BFI.

Jin, D. J. (2013) The construction of platform imperialism in the globalization era. *tripleC,* 11, 1: 145–72.

Jin, D. Y. (2015) *Digital Platforms, Imperialism and Political Culture.* London: Routledge.

Jin, D. J. (2020) *Globalization and Media in the Digital Platform Age.* London: Routledge.

JTA (2009) Disney to launch channel in Israel. *The Jerusalem Post,* July 30. https://www.jpost.com/arts-and-culture/entertainment/disney-to-launch-channel-in-israel-150322 (accessed August 31, 2022).

Kirchdoerffer, Ed (1998) A Salute to Disney Channel: International: Vive le Mickey. *Kidscreen,* April 1. https://kidscreen.com/1998/04/01/21323-19980401/ (accessed August 31, 2022).

Kotras, B. (2020) Mass personalization: Predictive marketing algorithms and the reshaping of consumer knowledge. *Big Data & Society*, 7, 2. https://doi.org/10.1177/2053951720951581.

Kunzle, D. (1975) Introduction to the English Edition, pp. 11–21 in A. Dorfman and A. Mattelart, *How to Read Donald Duck: Imperialist Ideology in the Disney Comic*. New York: International General.

Kwet, M. (2019) Digital colonialism: US empire and the new imperialism in the Global South. *Race & Class*, 60, 4: 3–26.

License Global (2020) The 150 Leading Licensors. August 19. https://www.licenseglobal.com/rankings-and-lists/top-150-leading-licensors (accessed April 19, 2021).

Lien, C. H., Lee, J., and Tandoc, E. C., Jr. (2021) Facing fakes: Understanding tech platforms' responses to online falsehoods. *Digital Journalism*. https://doi.org/10.1080/21670811.2021.1982398

Litterick, D. (2005) Chirac backs Eurocentric search engine. *The Telegraph*, August 31. https://www.telegraph.co.uk/finance/2921407/Chirac-backs-eurocentric-search-engine.html (accessed March 12, 2014).

Littleton, C. (2021) Disney Plus tops 100 million subscribers worldwide. Variety, March 9. https://variety.com/2021/tv/news/disney-plus-100-million-subscribers-worldwide-1234925654 (accessed June 1, 2022).

Mansell, R. (2004) Political economy, power and new media. *New Media & Society*, 6, 1: 96–105.

Mavise (2021) Database on TV channels, on-demand services and licences in Europe. https://mavise.obs.coe.int (accessed April 14, 2021).

Mirrlees, T. (2020) Not (Yet) the "Chinese Century": The Endurance of the US Empire and Its Cultural Industries, pp. 305–19 in O. Boyd-Barrett and T. Mirrlees (eds.) *Media Imperialism: Continuity and Change*. Lanham, MD: Rowman & Littlefield.

Mjøs, O. J. (2010a) *Media Globalization and the Discovery Channel Networks*. London: Routledge.

Mjøs, O. J. (2010b) The symbiosis of children's television and merchandising: Comparative perspectives on the Norwegian children's television channel NRK Super and the global Disney Channel. *Media, Culture & Society*, 32, 6: 1031–42.

Mjøs, O. J., Moe, H., and Sundet, V. S. (2014) The functions of buzzwords: A comparison of "Web 2.0" and "telematics." *First Monday*, 19, 12. https://doi.org/10.5210/fm.v19i12.4896

Papathanassopoulos, S. (2002) *European Television in the Digital Age: Issues, Dynamics and Realities*. Cambridge, UK: Polity.

Pariser, E. (2011) *The Filter Bubble: What the Internet Is Hiding from You*. London: Penguin.

Purcell, K., Brenner, J., and Rainie, L. (2012) Search engine use 2012. Pew Internet & American Life Project, March 9. https://www.pewresearch.org/internet/2012/03/09/search-engine-use-2012 (accessed June 21, 2022).

Rasmussen, T. (2007) *Kampen om Internet*. Oslo: Pax.

Reuters (2007) Walt Disney launching cable channel in Turkey. April 3. https://www.reuters.com/article/industry-disney-turkey-dc-idUSL0364926320070403 (accessed August 31, 2022).

Sacks, D. (2021) Countries in China's Belt and Road Initiative: Who's In and Who's Out? Council on Foreign Relations, March 24. https://www.cfr.org/blog/countries-chinas-belt-and-road-initiative-whos-and-whos-out (accessed June 22, 2021).

Schiller, H. (1971) *Mass Communications and American Empire*. New York: Beacon Press.

Schiller, H. (1985) Electronic Information Flows: New Basis for Global Dominations, pp. 11–20 in P. Drummond and R. Patterson (eds.) *Television in Transition: Papers from the First International Television Studies Conference*. London: BFI.

Schiller, H. ([1976] 2018) *Communication and Cultural Domination (1976)*. First edition. Abingdon, Oxon. and New York: Routledge.

Schneider, M. (2020) Year in review: Most-watched television networks—ranking 2020's winners and losers. Variety, December 28. https://variety.com/2020/tv/news/network-ratings-2020-top-channels-fox-news-cnn-msnbc-cbs-1234866801 (accessed April 14, 2021).

Smith, E. and White, G. (2011) Disney to Launch Russia Channel. *The Wall Street Journal*, October 28. https://www.wsj.com/articles/SB10001424052970203554104577001733244896716 (accessed August 31, 2022).

Sparks, C. (2020) China: An Emerging Cultural Imperialist, pp. 275–89 in O. Boyd-Barrett and T. Mirrlees (eds.) *Media Imperialism: Continuity and Change*. Lanham, MD: Rowman & Littlefield.

Straubhaar, J. D. (2007) *World Television: From Global to Local*. Los Angeles: SAGE.

Sunstein, C. R. (2001) *Republic.Com*. Princeton, NJ: Princeton University Press.

Syvertsen, T., Enli, G., Mjøs, O. J., and Moe, H. (2014) *The Media Welfare State: Nordic Media in the Digital Era*. Ann Arbor, MI: University of Michigan Press.

Tandoc, E. C., Jr., Lim, Z. W., and Ling, R. (2018) Defining "fake news." *Digital Journalism*, 6, 2: 137–53. https://doi.org/10.1080/21670811.2017.1360143

Thussu, D. K. and Nordenstreng, K. (2021) Introduction, pp. 1–19 in D. K. Thussu and K. Nordenstreng (eds.) *BRICS Media: Reshaping the Global Communication Order?* Abingdon, UK: Routledge.

Tomlinson, J. (1991) *Cultural Imperialism: A Critical Introduction*. London: Continuum.

Tunstall, J. and Machin, D. (1999) *The Anglo-American Media Connection*. Oxford: Oxford University Press.

Turow, J. (2006) *Niche Envy: Marketing Discrimination in the Digital Age*. Cambridge, MA: MIT Press.

Turow, J. (2011) *The Daily You: How the New Advertising Industry Is Defining Your Identity and Your Worth*. New Haven, CT: Yale University Press.

Turow, J (2017) Personalization, pp. 135–7 in L. Ouellett and J. Gray (eds.) *Keywords in Media Studies*. New York: New York University Press.

Van Dijck, J. (2013) *The Culture of Connectivity: A Critical History of Social Media.* Oxford: Oxford University Press.

Van Dijck, J. (2014) Datafication, dataism and dataveillance: Big data between scientific paradigm and ideology. *Surveillance & Society*, 12: 2. https://doi.org/10.24908/ ss.v12i2.4776.

Van Dijck, J. and Nieborg, D. (2009) Wikinomics and its discontents: A critical analysis of Web 2.0 business manifestoes. *New Media & Society*, 11, 4: 855–74.

Van Dijck, J., Poell, T., and De Waal, M. (2018) *The Platform Society: Public Values in a Connective World*. Oxford: Oxford University Press.

Walt Disney Company (2020) Form 10-K. Walt Disney Co, Annual Report. November 25. https://sec.report/Document/0001744489-20-000197/dis-20201003. htm (accessed April 12, 2021).

Walt Disney Company (2021) Disney+ tops 100 million global paid subscriber milestone. Walt Disney Company, March 9. https://thewaltdisneycompany.com/ disney-tops-100-million-global-paid-subscriber-milestone (accessed April 14, 2021).

Wasko, J. (2005) *How Hollywood Works*. London: SAGE.

WHO (2021) Fighting misinformation in the time of COVID-19, one click at a time. https://www.who.int/news-room/feature-stories/detail/fighting-misinformation-in- the-time-of-covid-19-one-click-at-a-time (accessed March 11, 2022).

Winter, S., Maslowska, E., and Vos, A. L. (2021) The effects of trait-based personalization in social media advertising. *Computers in Human Behavior*, 114, 106525. https://doi.org/10.1016/j.chb.2020.106525

Youyou, W., Kosinski, M., and Stillwell, D. (2015) Computer-based personality judgments are more accurate than those made by humans. *Proceedings of the National Academy of Sciences*, 112, 4: 1036–40.

7

The Power of Media Audiences and Users

Empowerment and Autonomy

Throughout the twenty-first century, the worldwide adoption of the internet, and the popularization of smartphones and other digital devices and services, have given unprecedented opportunities for media users to communicate, consume, and distribute media products across the world. Scholarly interest in digital media audiences and users has increased throughout. However, the preoccupation with understanding the media audience and user is not new. The previous chapter showed how the critical political economy tradition, concerned with asymmetric power relations, exploitation of user data, and dominance, stretches from the 1960s up until today. However, as early as the 1970s, scholars began criticizing this tradition for having major weaknesses. It did not give attention to the media audiences. It did not explore how audiences actually engage with media content nor ask the audiences their opinion of the media content they watched. A tradition emerged that aimed to explore these questions, arguing that the media audience was far from passive and powerless, but active, interpretive, and selective in their media use. Scholars within the field of cultural studies pioneered such studies of the media audience: "If, for much of the 1970s, the audience was largely ignored by many media theorists in favor of the analysis of textual and economic structures which were presumed to impose their effects on the audience, the 1980s, conversely, saw a sudden flourishing of 'audience' (or 'reception') studies" (Morley, 1991: 2). As scholars explored the ability of media audiences across the world to interpret and make choices according to their background and cultural and linguistic preferences, theoretical concepts focusing on unequal media flows and structural inequalities were increasingly "criticized as overly simplistic" (Straubhaar, 1991: 39). This chapter first traces the emergence of this audience-centered tradition and moves on to discuss how today's audience is conceptualized, studied, and understood in the context of digital global media and communications. The recent emergence of numerous media audience- and user-centered approaches and concepts such as "participatory culture" (Jenkins, 2006), "produsage" (Bruns, 2008), "creator power" (Cunningham and Craig, 2019a), "mass self-communication" (Castells, 2013), "global mobility" (Mjøs, 2012; Urry, 2007), "co-creation" (Kornberger, 2010), and "crowdsourcing" (Howe, 2006) clearly underlines the continuing preoccupation with the media audience and user throughout the twenty-first century. This chapter will therefore trace the manifestations of such audience-centered thinking and theories throughout the history of international communication and global media.

The Active Audience Emerges

In the mid-1970s, Stuart Hall, at the Centre for Contemporary Cultural Studies, Birmingham University, brought new, critical perspectives on the communication process and media studies, which gave rise to the new audience-centered approaches. In contrast to the macro-concepts such as cultural imperialism and their supposedly devastating effects on media audiences and local cultures, the new approaches focused on the micro-conditions, specifically on understanding media audiences. The key argument was that the media audience was far from passive when engaging with the media, and with television in particular. Nor were they overwhelmed by media, but were in fact able to interpret television programming in different ways. Hall argued in his article *Encoding and Decoding in the Television Discourse* (1973) that television programs could be read in different ways by the television audience. There is an "encoded" intended meaning in a media text based on dominant societal norms and understandings, and audiences may read the text accordingly. However, audiences may "decode" the television programs in other ways, either by accepting the intended meaning, or by making a "negotiated" reading, or even an "oppositional" reading of the same television program.

　　Morley and Brunsdon, also at the Centre for Contemporary Cultural Studies, conducted studies of the audience reception of the British television program *Nationwide*, and showed how groups of audiences with different backgrounds made different interpretations of the program (Brunsdon and Morley, [1978] 1999; Morley, [1980] 1999). The key aim of these studies was to examine "how decodings are influenced and structured by social position, in an overdetermined manner, across a range of dimensions—class, 'race', ethnicity and gender—not class alone" (Morley, 2006b: 108).

The active audience perspective was soon incorporated into the field of international communication in various ways. The perspective suggested that audiences interpreted and even resisted foreign "hegemonic" media texts (Sreberny, 2000: 97). The "cultural imperialism" thesis was criticized for expressing ideas of hegemonic media that are "frozen in the realities of the 1970s, now a bygone era" (Sreberny, 2000: 96).

The audiences of the American television soap series *Dallas*, one of the major international television exports in the 1980s, became a key object of study for the early audience studies within the field of international communication (Katz and Liebes, 1984; [1990] 1993). Confronting the cultural imperialism perspective, Katz and Liebes argued that it had major weaknesses and shortcomings:

> Critical studies of the diffusion of American television programs overseas have labeled this process "cultural imperialism" as if there were no question but that the hegemonic message the analyst discerns in the text is transferred to the defenseless minds of viewers the world over for the self-serving interests of the economy and ideology of the exporting country (Dorfman and Mattelart, 1975). Perhaps so. But labeling something imperialistic is not the same as proving it is. To prove that *Dallas* is an imperialistic imposition, one would have to show (1) that there is a message incorporated in the program that is designed to profit American interests overseas, (2) that the message is decoded by the receiver in the way it was encoded by the sender, and (3) that it is accepted uncritically by the viewers and allowed to seep into their culture.
>
> (Katz and Liebes, [1990] 1993: 4)

Instead, Katz and Liebes argued that contrary to the arguments, represented by Dorfman and Mattelart's *How to Read Donald Duck* (1975): "ideology is not produced through a process of stimulus and response but rather through a process of negotiation between various types of senders and receivers" ([1990] 1993: 4). It is not sufficient to make "abstract generalizations" from analysis of the content of television programs. Instead, one needs to focus on how such content is being understood by the audiences. In regard to the *Dallas* television series, the task is therefore to "observe how the melodrama of a fictional family in Texas is viewed, interpreted, and discussed by real families through out the world" (Katz and Liebes, [1990] 1993: 4). Their original study was designed and conducted in the following way:

> We assembled 50 groups of three couples each – an initial couple invites two others from among their friends – to view and episode from the second session of *Dallas* and to discuss it with us afterwards. The focus groups were of lower-middle class, with high school education or less, and ethnically homogenous.

There were ten groups each of Israeli Arabs, new immigrants to Israel from Russia, first- and second- generation immigrants from Morocco, and kibbutz members.

(Katz and Liebes, 1984: 28).

These groups watched an episode of *Dallas* and the "readings" of the program were compared to those of "ten groups of matched Americans" in Los Angeles. The findings suggested "that television programs do not impose themselves unequivocally on passive viewers," as the "reading" of a television program is characterized by "a process of negotiation between the story on the screen and the culture of the viewers, and it takes place in interaction among the viewers themselves" (Katz and Liebes, 1984: 28).

While *Dallas* may represent certain values, norms, and lifestyles, reception studies of the television series show how television audiences' perceptions, understanding, and interpretation of the programs vary and diverge (Ang, 1985). Furthermore, Ang argues, while academics, policy makers, and other "guardians of the 'national culture'" worry, "a stubborn fixation on the threat of 'American cultural imperialism'" may neglect that American popular media and culture has over decades of consumption become "integrated to a greater or lesser degree into the national 'cultural identity' itself, especially in Western Europe" (Ang, 1985: 3). One of the criticisms of Katz and Liebes' study is that they "effectively 'reduce' their respondents to their ethnic identities," Morley noted, which risks being a "rather essentialist position" (2006b: 108). An important strand of audience research was therefore the more nuanced approaches to the role of media in identity formation. Gillespie's (1995) early study of members of South Asian communities in the UK further highlighted the diversity within the television audience. Aksoy and Robbins' (2000) study of Turkish television audiences in Europe in the mid-1990s showed that they watched a variety of television channels and programs within a "transnational space" as they "are seeking to find a way between their sense of their own Turkish origins and their sense of how they might belong in their host countries" (Aksoy and Robbins, 2000: 345). The point is that "these audiences use television to actively think about their own identities: their identities between places" (Aksoy and Robbins, 2000: 343).

This strand of research has continued since, represented by, for example, Kartosen and Tan's (2013) study of young Asian Dutch and how they "identify with multiple ethnic-cultural 'groups.'" Their ethnic-cultural identification includes the "hostland" (Dutch), the "homeland" (e.g., China), and a "novel pan-ethnic Asian ethnic-cultural identification," and their "Asian ethnic-cultural identification" is articulated using "popular media from other than their homelands." As such, the connection between ethnic-cultural identification and media shows how "ethnic minorities" can "break away from the traditional hostland/homeland dichotomy" (2013: 653). These studies represent key approaches to audiences within the field of international communications.

While media and cultural imperialism perspectives underlined how national cultures were under threat, such views underestimated the significance of local culture and language for media audiences. The growth of national and regional television and the cultural sector in Latin America from the end of the 1960s and throughout the 1980s showed how audiences preferred national and regional television programming with greater cultural proximity or relevance (Straubhaar, 1991). The next chapter will elaborate on this theme, but it is emphasized here that the concept of "cultural proximity" contributed to our understanding of audience preferences and audience patterns in an internationalizing media landscape.

Since the 1970s and 1980s, audience-centered approaches have shaped the field of international communication and global media. With the emergence of digital media and the internet, in particular, interest in the audience has been renewed and given considerable attention.

Active Audience II: The Popularization of the Internet and the Rise of the Digital Media User

While an "active audience" choose films and television programming from a rapidly growing number of television channels, and benefit from watching these media products in numerous ways, such traditional audiovisual spaces still provide limited opportunities for individual media users' actual participation and input. The emergence of the internet and online environment gave rise to optimism on behalf of the media audiences' possibilities for participation and engagement. Early research on what we today refer to as the internet focused on personal representation and possibilities for action within the emerging "cyberspace." Many researchers focused on the potential for such activity, often depicting the future in utopian terms. In the future, individuals would be able to operate and create within this "virtual reality": "In cyberspace the common man and the information worker—cowboy or infocrat—can search, manipulate, create or control information directly; he can be entertained or trained, seek solitude or company, win or lose power ... indeed, can "live" or "die" as he will" (Benedikt, 1991: 123).

In the early phase of internet development in the 1990s, Turkle, along with others, optimistically drew attention to the possibilities for the growing numbers of internet users to operate within this space (1995: 9). The internet would facilitate an arena for human interaction and the creation of communities within this new space: "We have the opportunity to build new kinds of communities, virtual communities, in which we participate with people from all over the world, people with whom we converse daily, people with whom we may have fairly intimate relationships but whom we may never physically meet"(Turkle, 1995: 9–10). As the popularization of the internet intensified throughout the 2000s, the celebration of the increased opportunities for the audiences and their newfound influence has continued. Some consider new media and the internet as having a central place in peoples' lives because it "fulfils the personalization of our needs in a way that past media could never achieve" (Marshall, 2004: 26). Such celebratory accounts emphasize how:

> The user subjectivity of new media with this production ethos is a massive and unparalleled challenge to the traditions of media use that have been in place for most of the previous century. The reception/consumption ethos and dichotomy of the twentieth century has given way to a production ethos of users. In some ways, new media has heralded a transformation of contemporary culture through a democratization of cultural expression.
>
> (Marshall, 2004: 27)

Such beliefs have certainly been fueled by the immense preoccupation in both the internet industry and among practitioners and scholars with the potential significance and implications of the behavior of new media users. Rosen (2012) presents perhaps one of the most celebratory descriptions of the triumph of the new media and internet user. Once, the audience was forced to receive messages and media content from "a few firms competing to speak very loudly while the rest of the population listened in isolation from one another," but the situation has been changed radically:

- Once it was *your* radio station, broadcasting on *your* frequency. Now that brilliant invention, podcasting, gives radio to us. And we have found more uses for it than you did.
- Shooting, editing and distributing video once belonged to you, Big Media. Only you could afford to reach a TV audience built in your own image. Now video is coming into the user's hands, and audience-building by former members of the audience is alive and well on the web.
- You were once (exclusively) the editors of the news, choosing what ran on the front page. Now we can edit the news, and our choices send items to our own front pages.

- A highly centralized media system had connected people "up" to big social agencies and centers of power but not "across" to each other. Now the horizontal flow, citizen to citizen, is as real and consequential as the vertical one.

(Rosen, 2012: 13)

Produsage, Participatory Culture, Co-creation, Mass Self-communication, Creator Power and Global Mobility

The popularization of the internet renewed interest in the media audience and media users. Throughout the twenty-first century, many scholars have attempted to theoretically understand and capture the role of the users within the online environment through a range of new concepts and terms. We consider six such concepts here, which have particular relevance for the international communication and global media perspectives.

The concept of "produsage" attempts to describe a "move beyond the commonplace assumptions associated with traditional concepts of producers, products, and production, and to develop a systematic understanding of the processes, principles, and participants of produsage" (Bruns, 2008: 5). The drivers of the advance of this development, so-called "user-led online environments," are numerous and include social networking sites such as Facebook, LinkedIn, and Orkut, and the various additional features and services that can be incorporated within the social networking environment to enhance users' opportunities. Further examples of the drivers of "produsage" include "collaborate knowledge management" that "is now emerging as a key challenge to the traditional guardian authorities of knowledge" such as Wikipedia (Bruns, 2007). New online sites and services open for producing "a rich and diverse range of user-submitted creative content," and the Creative Commons provides a framework for "re-use and remixing" of various content. Citizen journalism and open source development also represent drivers of the processes associated with produsage (Bruns, 2007).

The concept of "participatory culture," perhaps the most optimistic of the terms, describes how the production and distribution of media content "depends heavily on consumers' active participation." The point is that the concept of participatory culture stands in contrast with traditional understandings of media audiences—or "passive media spectatorship." It is no longer sufficient to distinguish between media producers and media consumers, as one has traditionally done. They do not have different roles but are "participants who interact with each other according to a new set of rules none of us fully understands" (Jenkins, 2006: 3). Media users now have unprecedented opportunities to take part in the production and distribution of cultural and media content within the internationalizing media landscape.

The concept of "co-creation" mirrors the terms "produsage" and "participatory culture." Using branding as an example, Kornberger argues, "consumers are creative and innovative, blurring the old dividing line between production and consumption" (Kornberger, 2010: 159). While the emphasis has been on the company as being in control and creating the brand and its value, brand communities represent a modifying and innovating force through co-creation, as "insiders and outsiders innovate as they gather in communities formed around brands" (2010: 159). The Wikipedia brand exemplifies how users are members of brand communities and contribute in the online open-source environment. From a "co-creation" perspective, then, the brand becomes the interface between production and consumption. However, there are risks attached to the practice of "co-creation" for brands, as these communities "are far from representing cosy communities in which people joyfully congregate around brands." Instead, individuals "might hijack the brand for their own purposes, just like British hooligans hijacked Burberry [fashion brand]" (2010: 145). Brands are not created only at a corporate level or sphere. Instead, as with media content, individuals make their own interpretations of a brand "framed by their cultural, social and political context," forming an "interplay between the authors and readers of brands" (2010: 207).

In contrast to traditional mass communication, described as "one-directional," Castells' concept of "mass self-communication" aims to describe the new opportunities for the media user as a "new form of interactive communication [that] has emerged" which is both "mass communication" and "self-communication" (Castells, 2013: 55). Castells calls this "historically new form of communication *mass self-communication*," whereby internet users can "potentially reach a global audience, as in the posting of a video on YouTube," and at the same time "it is self-communication because the production of the messages is self-generated" (2013: 55). Castells emphasizes that we have moved from mass communication to an "active audience" who engage in "interactive production of meaning." It is "*the creative audience, the source of remix culture that characterizes the world of mass self-communication*" (2013: 132).

The popularization of the internet and, not least, the rise of streaming and social media services, have facilitated personal communication and interaction, and opened up for new forms of user-generated content production and distribution across national borders in an unprecedented way. Some emphasize how power relations in the twenty-first-century screen media industry are challenged and increasingly shaped by the agency and strategies of "social media creators" who utilize streaming and social media platforms to create and globally distribute content they own themselves (Cunningham and Craig, 2019a: 5, 12). In fact, the very power of digital platforms is shaped by "creator power" that is "now exerting significant influence on platform fortunes," and "creators" are now "accorded the status of 'partners' across nearly every platform" (Cunningham and Craig, 2019b).

> The difference offered by the new screen ecology's provision of potential career opportunity, even celebrity status, through amateur hobbyism and personal expression cannot be gainsaid. These creators disrupted the normative route through which media talent is filtered. YouTubers must be seen as a class of content creators who are able to exercise a higher level of control over their career prospects than in previous models of professionalizing talent.
>
> (Cunningham and Craig, 2019a: 12)

The theoretical "new mobilities" framework argues that social science fails to address the emerging practices of mobility in social and cultural life. The "mobility turn" in society is linked to the emergence of "mobility systems." These systems include low-cost air travel, mobile phones, and networked computers. These systems facilitate and increase numerous forms of mobility in society, such as physical or virtual travel and movement and communication (Sheller and Urry, 2006: 207–8; see also Urry, 2007). Global social media is the result of systems like the internet, digital devices, and the popularization of the online environment. Facebook and YouTube are therefore key parts of this "mobility turn." These services enable and facilitate communicative and virtual mobility for individual media users within the global media and communications landscape (Elliott and Urry, 2010: ix; Mjøs, 2012: 147). This is particularly visible within the global social media and music nexus. Placing this nexus within the "mobilities" framework helps to theoretically articulate the logic and characteristics of these online spaces and the user activity of music practitioners and fans within them, referred to as "global mobility" (Mjøs, 2012: 147–8).

The above concepts attempt to describe theoretically the users and audiences within the digital and online environment. The case of music in the digital era highlights the shifting role of the audience and user and some of the tensions that have arisen (see Case Study 7.1).

Case Study 7.1 Music, Digitization, and the Creative Media User

Change is nothing new to the music industry. Radio broadcasting in the 1950s, the cassette tape in 1970s, the compact disc in the 1980s and 1990s, and the deregulation and ownership concentration of the media and cultural industries in the last decades of the twentieth century represented forms of change that impacted on the music industry. Yet, the changes and transformations taking place in the first decades of the twenty-first century, which have impacted across the whole industry (Wikstrøm, 2020: 4), "are even more dramatic than the previous ones," and more fundamental. The relationship between music, the internet, and the user is often characterized by controversy. Some emphasize unprecedented user empowerment for fans and bands alike; others argue that developments are undermining the music industry and copyright. The ability for users to distribute their own music, but also circumvent rights holders of music and other media products from the distribution chain as individual internet users share MP3 files of music as well as other media content, is considered by some as "perhaps the single most important technological concept which has pushed that irreversible process forward" (Wikström, 2020: 153). As the capacity and speed of personal computers increased and were utilized in the developing online environment, peer-to-peer (P2P) networking became more and more prominent among users. In 1999, the technology reached the attention of the wider audience as the Napster software for file sharing became popular and the subsequent legal controversy between Napster and music companies intensified. Although Napster had to close, P2P has since developed into ever more advanced and powerful software and services (Wikström, 2020: 154). In the 2000s, technology enabling various forms of sharing and communication was increasingly becoming part of the global social media environment: "The music sharing and social exchange involved in subcultural peer-to-peer sharing is now becoming part of everyday media experience," via platforms and social media services (Hesmondhalgh, 2009: 63). Since the pioneering social media service Myspace's launch in 2005, social media have facilitated increased opportunities to distribute their own or others' music and for communication;

music artists, bands, and promoters use these services to get in touch with their fans, and fans may link to or communicate back (boyd and Ellison, 2007; Mjøs, 2012; Shklovski and boyd, 2006). At the same time, social media services and legal streaming services are connected, allowing users of Facebook and Spotify to post and distribute playlists from the music service:

> The new version of Spotify [online music streaming service] is really pretty amazing—it shifted the experience so now you connect with your Facebook account to see what all your friends are listening to and all the different music they like and subscribe to. It adds a new element on top of the experience and almost makes it a completely different experience. I'm using it so much more.
>
> (Mark Zuckerberg, founder of Facebook, quoted in *The Guardian*, Kiss, 2010)

The internet and digitization of the sector, the emergence of new media players, convergence between music and other sectors, and the integration of a global music market have created tensions in the current music industry that impact locally, nationally, and internationally. All these tensions relate to the role of, and in many ways increased the influence of, the digital music and media user:

- **Connectivity versus control:** The twentieth-century music industry was based on control over distribution of music between companies and users, and limited contact between the music audiences. The internet has increased "connectivity" between users and the possibility for distribution of music among them (see also Mjøs, 2012). In the current music industry, control is scarce, but the level of connectivity is high (Wikstrøm, 2020: 7).

- **Service versus product:** Previously, music and the medium were integrated in a physical product (e.g., the compact disc, vinyl, and cassette tapes). Today, the two are separated. Charging for pieces of information is difficult, while people are willing to pay for services that give access and guide them through the enormous aggregate of information (Wikstrøm, 2020: 8).

- **Amateur versus professional:** The increased connectivity, free software, and affordable hardware have enabled amateurs to take part in music production, distribution, and remixing of professional music productions. At the same time, many of these users are considered as dedicated music fans who spend the most money on music-related products, and they sometimes come with large online followings. For this reason, the music firms cannot reject them outright, but need to develop a certain bond with them (Wikstrøm, 2020: 8–9).

The music industry has grappled with how to act in the midst of these tensions: "the response of the music industry to Internet distribution, social networking sites, home-copying and the creation of noncommercial distribution mechanisms has been complex and even chaotic" (Lister et al., 2009: 193). In fact, from 2001 to 2014, the revenues of the record music industry declined. Then, in 2014, for the first time, global revenues from digital channels equaled those of the physical format sales, with 46 percent each of total revenues. In 2020, the market grew for the sixth consecutive year, by 7.4 percent. This growth is primarily due to the popularity of music streaming services, and especially paid subscription revenues. By the end of 2020, there were 443 million users of paid subscriptions, and total streaming revenues, consisting of both paid subscription and advertising-based services, grew by 19.1 percent and made up 62.1 percent of the total global recorded music revenues. Revenues from performance rights declined in 2020, largely due to the Covid-19 pandemic (Hesmondhalgh, 2020; IFPI, 2015; 2021).

Alongside the increased corporatization of digital music economy, artists and fans continue to exert influence, produce and distribute, and navigate and operate within the three tensions that continue to exist (connectivity vs. control; service vs. product; amateur vs. professional).

In fact, the barriers to entry in the new digital music economy are negligible, meaning that "every amateur musician and ordinary music fan is able to create, remix and publish music online" (Wikstrøm, 2020: 152). The opportunities for individuals to be creative, communicate, and express themselves through music are unprecedented, and have changed the industry. The emergence of practices such as "audience-driven talent development," "remix culture," and "crowd funding" reflects this development (Wikstrøm, 2020). The rise and dominance of music streaming services has been—and is—controversial, and the consequences unclear, yet some suggest that in fact "more musicians rather than fewer might now be able to earn money from recorded music than in the preceding recorded-music system," but that the "current system retains the striking inequalities and generally poor working conditions that characterized its predecessors" (Hesmondhalgh, 2020). Since the mid-2000s, social media, combined with curated playlists (e.g., Spotify), represent "new gatekeepers" in the digital music economy. While the gatekeepers in the twentieth century were national or regional (i.e., television and radio), the new ones are increasingly global in reach (Wikstrøm, 2020: 170–1).

This has several consequences. Mjøs shows how music artists and other practitioners from the mid-2000s adopted social media—first Myspace, and then, even more so, Facebook—to promote their music and communicate with colleagues and fans worldwide: "Global social media [are] facilitators of new online spaces. While these spaces exist within corporate and contested environments, they provide increased potential for participation of the media audience and users. This development is particularly visible within the global social media and music nexus emerging since 2005" (Mjøs, 2012).

This exemplifies the increased opportunities for music practitioners and fans in the wake of the popularization of the internet and digitization of media and communications. In fact, studies show that: "with the growing influence of social media as tastemakers and gatekeepers, music fans increasingly listen to international music originating from countries that have been considered as 'emerging' music exporters. In other words, the digital music economy is characterized by an increasing lever of *geographical* diversity" (Wikstrøm, 2020: 173). On the other hand, although the "commercially successful music is increasingly geographically diverse, the commercially successful songs sound increasingly the same" (Wikstrøm, 2020: 173).

As with the other theoretical traditions within international communication and global media, the active audience paradigm has also been criticized for a number of reasons since its emergence until today. The next section examines some of the points of concern or critique, some made by audience researchers themselves.

Audience Studies versus Critical Political Economic and More Structurally Focused Approaches

The proliferation of media user and reception studies and the increased attention given to audience-centered approaches risk narrowing the inquiry, according to media audience researcher Morley. There is a danger that "the discursive process of the construction of meanings is frequently analysed without reference to its institutional, economic or material settings" (Morley, 1992: 4). Although political economists do not have an adequate approach or model for the inclusion of the audience perspective, "it does not mean that they are wrong about everything else as well," Morley argues (2006a: 33).

A critique of studies such as Katz and Liebes' *Dallas* study holds that "just in itself, a micro approach is also inadequate to track the fortunes of the television exports of peripheral nature" (Sinclair et al., 1996: 17). Critics further emphasize that a trend in many of the recent studies of audiences is "the romanticisation of the power (and supposed freedom) of media consumers to reinterpret texts at will" (Morley, 2006a: 39). Morley elaborates on this point: "it is still mainly North American programs that people are busily 'reinterpreting'. We should remember that these models of audience activity were not initially designed (however, they may have sometimes been subsequently deployed) to make us forget the question of media power, but rather to be able to conceptualize it in more complex and adequate ways" (Morley, 2006b: 105–6). Therefore, the task is to "balance these two perspectives" and also to distinguish "between empirical situations where one or the other is more applicable, without presuming that either tells the whole truth, for all places and all times" (Morley, 2006a: 39).

Just as the earlier audience studies were criticized for not adequately taking economic, institutional, and political dimensions into account (Morley, 1992), the study of the new media user and audience must also consider these issues carefully. While the term "participatory culture" draws attention to users' increased opportunities for participation in media and cultural production and distribution, some highly critical scholars argue that the concept's focus is too narrow: "Jenkins' definition and use of the term 'participatory culture' ignores aspects of participatory democracy, it ignores questions about ownership of platforms/companies, collective decision-making, profit, class and the distribution of material benefits" (Fuchs, 2017). Fuchs elaborates on his critique of the term "participatory" in relation to the online environment: "Corporate platforms owned by Facebook, Google and other large companies strongly mediate the cultural expressions of Internet users. Neither the users nor the waged employees of Facebook, Google & Co. determine the business decisions of these companies, they do not "participate" in economic decision-making, but are excluded from it (Fuchs, 2017: 68).

Still, Jenkins does acknowledge the existence of unequal power relations and corporate influence, as "Not all participants are created equal." It is a fact that media companies and even people who work there "still exert greater power than any individual consumer or even the aggregate of consumers." Within the processes associated with participatory culture, "some consumers have greater abilities to participate in this emerging culture than others" (Jenkins, 2006: 3). In later writings, Jenkins elaborates in response to critics:

> [W]e need to be working together to broaden who gets to participate, to push back against corporate and governmental policies that constrain our capacity to use new media in the public interest, to identify ways groups are engaging

in active participation in spite of such constraints, and to advocate ways that corporate, governmental and other organizations might better respond to their constituencies.

(Jenkins, 2014: 290)

While "[W]eb 2.0 culture has been overwhelmingly hailed as a culture that celebrates the idea of sharing, participation, and community bonding," van Dijck argues that the problematic side of such a notion and view "is that it does not reveal the way in which connections are engineered and exploited and how it profoundly transforms social norms for (political) communication" (van Dijck, 2011: 173). In order to "understand the dynamics of social media," we need to find "an analytical model that accounts for the complexities of the contradicting interests interpenetrating this new space of mediated communication. Much like Facebook itself, this model will never be finished, as long as its analytical objects keep evolving" (van Dijck, 2011: 173).

The "Newness" of Audience Participation in the Digital Era

Another point of critique in terms of audience perspectives relates to the perceived "newness" of participation in the digital era. As we have seen, a number of concepts have emerged that attempt to conceptualize the user in the internet era. User-generated content (UGC) is one of the most widely adopted, yet some argue that one should be conscious of how concepts connect with earlier audience perspectives: "UGC cannot be detached from the long history of participatory practices within the media. Mainstream media but especially alternative and community media have a long history of organizing participatory practices at the level of content and organization" (Carpentier, 2014: 199). Pointing to the MacBride Commission during the NWICO debate, Carpentier underlines how the audience perspective was emphasized already in the commission's report. According to the report, in response to the lack of opportunities for audience participation, one should encourage alternative forms of communication and media:

As a healthy reaction, a high value should be attached to the many examples of "alternative communication", which operates horizontally instead of vertically and enables individuals to assume an active role in the communication process. Obstacles are numerous, but the imagination of people – particularly many organized social groups, the young and marginal segments – show that print media, local radio, amateur films, citizens' band radio, cable television, even small computers and so on, may become tools for liberating people's initiatives.

(MacBride Report, 1980: 113)

There is certainly a wider range of "participatory practices" within the online environment, but "Arguably, this is more a matter of modality than of novelty," Carpentier argues (2014: 199). Similarly, van Dijck points out the importance of considering a concept like user-generated content in a historical perspective:

> The historical continuity between participation of ordinary citizens in "old media" like television and participation of users in networked UGC sites defies any definition grounded in binary oppositions. Instead, user agency comprises different levels of participation, varying from "creators" to "spectators" and "inactives". The same can be said with regard to the notion of "communities", a term that applies to very different modes of user involvement.

(van Dijck, 2009: 46)

Still, the twenty-first century is characterized by an extensive and rapid increase in the possibilities for mediated interaction and interpersonal communication through digital technologies and online services. This has resulted in a situation where "There have never been more ways to communicate with one another than there are right now" (Baym, 2010: 1).

Social Media and User Power

The emergence and global expansion of social media or "social networking sites" (boyd and Ellison, 2007; Papacharissi, 2009) is one of the most significant developments associated with increased user opportunities and autonomy in the digital era. Many argue that such technologies and services represent unprecedented opportunities for internet users across the globe: "Physical spaces are limited by space and time, but, online, people can connect to one another across great distances and engage with asynchronously produced content over extended periods. This allows people to work around physical barriers to interaction and reduces the cost of interacting with people in far-off places" (boyd, 2012: 53). As such, we need to look closer at the workings of social media to grasp their characteristics, and how they set themselves apart from other media and services. Bechman and Lomborg (2012) provide a definition of social media that emphasizes the role of users through three characteristics:

1. "Communication is de-institutionalized" as users can share and contribute content in contrast to following the rules of corporate media and their control over content.
2. "[T]he user is regarded as producer."
3. "[C]ommunication is interactive and networked" as social media are constructed by the communication between users who shift between being creator of content and communication and receiver of such.

(Bechmann and Lomborg, 2012: 767)

Others emphasize how social media such as Facebook stand out as they are platforms made up of a combination of ICT technologies, media forms, and services that "support cognition, communication/ networking and cooperation (communities, collaborative work, sharing of user-generated and other content)" (Trottier and Fuchs, 2015: 7).

While the definitions and descriptions of social media give emphasis to different aspects and characteristics, they all place the users of these services at the center. As social media has expanded and been adopted by internet users across the world, the key question of the extent to which and how these services actually facilitate audience autonomy has been a key issue.

It is a fact that not everyone has the same opportunities to take part in the "networked publics" and utilize the possibilities of such technologies and services: "an increase in people's ability to contribute to publics does not necessarily result in an increase in their ability to achieve an audience" (boyd, 2012: 54). At the same time the structures of social media are "engineered to control user agency: most platform owners have a vested interest in knowing users' 'true' identity, their preferences, and behavioral data" (van Dijck, 2013: 34). To understand the users of social media one should also taking structural conditions into account when studying user activity and practices (boyd, 2012; Mjøs, 2012; Papacharissi, 2009). This exemplifies why it is difficult to give one answer or make generalizations regarding audience autonomy in the digital era:

[W]e are still standing on shifting ground in our efforts to make sense of the capabilities of digital media and their social consequences. New media are constantly developing, new populations are taking up these new tools, and new uses are emerging. Who is excluded from or enabled by digitally mediated interaction is neither random nor inconsequential. The same tools may take on very different meanings for different populations in different contexts or different times.

(Baym, 2010: 21)

Therefore, it is fruitful to look at specific developments and examples within the global media and communications landscape.

Global Social Change and Social Media

The presidential campaign of Barak Obama in 2008 has been widely referred to as "the breakthrough moment" for the utilization of social media for political election campaigns and purposes (Bruns et al., 2016: 1). While Obama's 2008 campaign contributed to making this use of social media a popular research topic, some argue that it also led to overoptimism regarding the impact of social media use: "The hype surrounding social media in election campaigns is largely a result of the media-friendly success story of President Barack Obama's use of Twitter and Facebook to communicate with young people and hard-to-reach user groups" (Enli and Moe, 2013: 641).

However, since then, the central role of social media in the mobilization of contemporary protests and social movements, from G20 demonstrations to the Arab Spring and from the Occupy movement to Black Lives Matter, has put the perceived power of the activist on the mainstream agenda. In many ways, these recent events and developments have come to represent tests of the degree of empowerment of the digital "active audience." Millions of social media users have taken part in the mobilization of protest and production and distribution of activist material, content, and communication (Poell, 2020; Poell and van Dijck, 2018).

The relationship between ICTs and social movements is not new. The Mexican Zapatista movement's use of the internet is considered pioneering and is described as the "first informational guerilla movement" (Castells, 1997: 79, quoted in Aton, 2002: 133). In 1999, the Independent Media Center (Indymedia) website was formed by a number of activists and independent and alternative media organizations to cover the World Trade Organization (WTO) protests in Seattle, offering reports and audiovisual material through its website. The Indymedia initiative became an reference point for protestors and activists across the world and provided "their own space to provide grassroots coverage of their own protests" (della Porta and Mattoni, 2015: 44). These online initiatives allowed for the distribution of information in support of mobilization:

> It does not come as a surprise, therefore, that mobilisations occurring from 2008 onwards made use of social networking platforms that began to emerge late in

2004: the repertoire of communication, which had quickly included the previous generation of Internet tools and web platforms, expanded again when activists began to employ Facebook, Twitter, YouTube and other social networking sites during their mobilisations.

(della Porta and Mattoni, 2015: 44)

Still, a question that arises is how the new "digitally mediated collective action formations," in which social media are among the key tools, differ from more traditional and conventional mobilizations and protests that are arranged by traditional membership organizations. Some suggest that the key difference lies in the unique characteristics of digital organization, which means one may:

- Scale up more quickly
- Produce large and sometimes record-breaking mobilizations
- Display unusual flexibility in tracking moving political targets and bridging different issues (e.g. economy and environment)
- Build up adaptive protests repertoires, share open-source software development, and embrace an ethos of inclusiveness.

(Bennet and Segerberg, 2013: 25)

The application of digital technology and communication clearly seems to have a number of advantages that sets it apart from traditional collective action and protests. However, there are several aspects that should be taken into account when trying to explain the relationship between social media and the user power represented by social movements:

1. Social media and digital technology are used by activists and opponents alike

Just as social movements use social media, so can authorities. During the uprisings in the Middle East and North Africa, security services not only censored online information but used new technologies to counter and control the opposition and closed services and access to them (della Porta and Mattoni, 2015: 56). The relationship between social movements and the state is a "dynamic relationship of power and counter-power based on actions and reactions that become more intense during the peak of mobilisations" (della Porta and Mattoni, 2015: 58). Yet, there are "vital differences in how dictatorial states steer and control social media activism" (Poell, 2016: 196).

2. Social media are owned by private companies that map users

The most popular social media services are commercial operations whose aim is to increase the number of users and generate profit. As such, they do not cater specifically to the needs of activists. This means that some of their user functions and possibilities may be to the advantage of social movements, while others are less so (Poell, 2016: 202). One of the risks for activists is the mapping of the users' activity, "especially when private corporate interests align with the desire of state repression in times of mobilization" (della Porta and Mattoni, 2015: 59).

3. The interaction between social media and traditional media and non-media organizational tools

While the focus is very much on the role and impact of the use of social media, a danger is that we forget that social media coexists with a number of other media services and outlets, many of which are so-called traditional media. Traditional media "remained central in amplifying the messages of protesters in the Middle East, North Africa, in southern Europe and in North America" (della Porta and Mattoni, 2015: 55). The proliferation of information and content across all distribution and media forms proved difficult for state authorities to curtail.

The internet (and social media) should be considered as part of a wider "electronic complex of informational and communicational possibilities" that is connected with existing technologies and media and communications, forms of face-to-face communication, print, and music, as well as traditional non-media initiatives such rallies and demonstrations. It is in combination with these that the internet's potential as a tool for opposition is evident (Aton, 2002: 133).

4. The temporality of social media

Some argue that protests and activist mobilization using social media create "loosely connected protest networks" that "just as quickly fall apart as they are stitched together" (Poell and van Dijck, 2018). One reason for this is the very logic of social media platforms, which is both an advantage and a disadvantage for activists:

> As social media penetrate deeply into everyday personal communication in ways alternative media have never been able to do, activists can reach people who would otherwise not be reached by activist communication. At the same

time, the interactions and interests that tie dispersed social media users together to form protest movements, generating instant moments of togetherness, tend to dissolve when social platforms algorithmically connect users to the next wave of trending topics.

(Poell and van Dijck, 2018)

While social media introduce and facilitate community features, such as Facebook groups, they need to do so in line with their business model and thereby "sustain their structural commercial appetite for online engagement." This is done by introducing new topics, themes, and stories that appeal to and satisfy the interest of users. Social media both connect and reconnect their users and this makes it challenging to uphold public attention through these services (Poell and van Dijck, 2018).

5. Social change happens through institutions, but changes must start somewhere

In most cases of social movement across the world, "the critical passage from hope to implementation of change depends on the permeability of political institutions to the demands of the movement, and on the willingness of the movement to engage in a process of negotiations" (Castells, 2012: 234). Similarly, commentators on the 2011 uprising in Egypt point to how easy it is to exaggerate the effect of platforms such as social media, as they:

amplify and affectively drive a movement in a manner much grander, versatile, and diverse than previous media permitted, but typically in tandem with some form of offline mobilisation and always subject to context. Perhaps this is where we run the risk of overestimating the ability of social media to determine the outcome of mobilisation.

(Papacharissi and Blasiola, 2016: 218)

By 2021, the democratic goals of the activists behind the Arab Spring of 2010–11 have so far failed to materialize across the region. Protests took place across North Africa and the Middle East, yet only in Tunisia has there been positive democratic developments. The current regimes of several of the countries in which protests took place are now even more authoritarian than the ones prior to the uprisings. However, some scholars argue that the mobilization through, among others, social media is just the beginning of a process of change: "The spirit is out of the bottle. One cannot just go back to stable authoritarian regimes. The youth generation, which ran [the protests], will not accept that a corrupt elite rules with force and with full control over the economy and the country's wealth" (Bjørn Olav Utvik, professor in Middle East Studies, quoted in Lilleslåtten, 2021).

While it is easy to be blinded by the speed and spread of messages, communication, and stories through social media, this activity "is not equivocal to the speed with which institutional change may occur" (Papacharissi and Blasiola, 2016: 219). Online activity is not the same as social change: "Events are instantaneous, revolutions are slow, and change is gradual" (2016: 219).

References

Ang, I. (1985) *Watching Dallas: Soap Opera and the Melodramatic Imagination*. London: Routledge.

Aksoy, A. and Robins, K. (2000) Thinking across spaces: Transnational television from Turkey. *European Journal of Cultural Studies*, 3, 3: 343–65.

Aton, C. (2002) *Alternative Media*. London: SAGE.

Baym, N. K. (2010) *Personal Communications in the Digital Age*. Cambridge: Polity.

Bechmann, A. and Lomborg, S. (2012) Mapping actor roles in social media: Different perspectives on value creations in theories of user participation. *New Media & Society*, 15, 5: 765–81.

Benedikt, M. (1991) Cyberspace: Some Proposals, pp. 119–224 in M. Benedikt (ed.) *Cyberspace: First Steps*. Cambridge, MA: MIT Press.

Bennet, W. L. and Segerberg, A. (2013) *The Logic of Connective Action: Digital Media and the Personalization of Contentious Politics*. Cambridge, UK: Cambridge University Press.

boyd, d. (2012) Social Network Sites as Networked Publics: Affordances, Dynamics, and Implications, pp. 39–58 in Z. A. Papacharissi (ed.) *A Networked Self: Identity, Community and Culture on Social Networking Sites*. New York: Routledge.

boyd, d. m. and Ellison, N. B. (2007) Social network sites: definition, history, and scholarship. *Journal of Computer-Mediated Communication*, 13, 1: 210–30.

Bruns, A. (2007) Produsage: Towards a Broader Framework for User-Led Content Creation, pp. 99–105 in B. Shneiderman (ed.) *Proceedings of 6th ACM SIGCHI Conference on Creativity and Cognition 2007*. Washington, DC: Association for Computing Machinery.

Bruns, A. (2008) *Blogs, Wikipedia, Second Life, and Beyond: From Production to Produsage*. New York: Peter Lang.

Bruns, A., Enli, G., Skogerbø, E., Larsson, A. O., and Christensen, C. (2016) Introduction, pp. 1–4 in A. Bruns, G. Enli, E. Skogerbø, A. O. Larsson, and C. Christensen (eds.) *The Routledge Companion to Social Media and Politics*. London: Routledge.

Brunsdon, C. and Morley, D. ([1978] 1999) *Everyday Television: "Nationwide" (1978)*, pp. 19–110 in C. Brunsdon and D. Morley, *The "Nationwide" Television Studies*. First edition. London: Routledge.

Carpentier, N. (2014) New Configurations of the Audience? The Challenges of User-Generated Content for Audience Theory and Media Participation, pp. 190–212 in V. Nightingale (ed.) *The Handbook of Media Audiences*. Chichester, UK: Wiley.

Castells, M. (1997) *The Information Age: Economy, Society and Culture, Vol. 2: The Power of Identity*. Oxford: Blackwell.

Castells, M. (2012) *Networks of Outrage and Hope: Social Movements in the Internet Age*. Cambridge, UK: Polity.

Castells, M. (2013) *Communication Power*. New edition. Oxford: Oxford University Press.

Cunningham, S. and Craig, D. (2019a) *Social Media Entertainment: The New Intersection of Hollywood and Silicon Valley*. New York: New York UniversityPress.

Cunningham, S. and Craig, D. (2019b) Creator governance in social media entertainment. *Social Media & Society*, 5, 4. https://doi.org/10.1177/2056305119883428

della Porta, D. and Mattoni, A. (2015) Social Networking Sites in Pro-democracy and Anti-austerity Protests: Some Thoughts from a Social Movement Perspective, pp. 39–65 in D. Trottier and C. Fuchs (eds.) *Social Media, Politics and the State: Protests, Revolutions, Riots, Crime and Policing in the Age of Facebook, Twitter and YouTube*. London: Routledge.

Dorfman, A. and Mattelart, A. (1975) *How to Read Donald Duck: Imperialist Ideology in the Disney Comic*. New York: International General.

Elliott, A. and Urry, J. (2010) *Mobile Lives*. London: Routledge.

Enli, G. and Moe, H. (2013) Introduction to Special Issue. *Information, Communication & Society*, 16, 5: 637–45.

Fuchs, C. (2017) *Social Media: A Critical Introduction*. London: SAGE.

Gillespie, M. (1995) *Television, Ethnicity and Cultural Change*. London: Routledge.

Hall, S. (1973) *Encoding and Decoding in the Television Discourse*. Birmingham: Centre for Contemporary Cultural Studies, University of Birmingham. http://epapers.bham.ac.uk/2962 (accessed June 2, 2022).

Hesmondhalgh, D. (2009) The Digitalisation of Music, pp. 57–73 in A. C. Pratt and P. Jeffcut (eds.) *Creativity, Innovation and the Cultural Economy*. Abingdon, UK: Routledge.

Hesmondhalgh, D. (2020) The rise of music streaming services—and criticisms of them. *New Media & Society*. https://doi.org/10.1177/1461444820953541

Howe, J. (2006) The rise of crowdsourcing. *Wired*, June 1. https://www.wired.com/2006/06/crowds (accessed June 2, 2022).

IFPI (2015) *Digital Music Report 2015*. https://www.musikindustrie.de/fileadmin/bvmi/upload/06_Publikationen/DMR/ifpi_digital-music-report-2015.pdf (accessed June 2, 2022).

IFPI (2021) *Global Music Report 2021*. https://www.ifpi.org/ifpi-issues-annual-global-music-report-2021 (accessed June 2, 2022).

Jenkins, H. (2006) *Convergence Culture: Where Old and New Media Collide*. New York: New York University Press.

Jenkins, H. (2014) Rethinking "Rethinking Convergence/Culture," *Cultural Studies*, 28, 2: 267–97.

Kartosen, R. and Tan, E. (2013) Articulating Asianness: Young Asian Dutch and non-homeland Asian popular media. *International Communication Gazette*, 75, 7: 653–71.

Katz, E. and Liebes, T. (1984) Once upon a time, in Dallas. *Intermedia*, 12, 3: 28–32.

Katz, E. and Liebes, T. ([1990] 1993) *The Export of Meaning*. Second edition. Cambridge, UK: Polity.

Kiss, J. (2010) Facebook hack day: Zuckerberg talks up merits of personalization. *The Guardian*, June 21. http://www.guardian.co.uk/technology/pda/2010/jun/21/facebook-zuckerberg-personalising-the-internet (accessed October 11, 2010).

Kornberger, M. (2010) *Brand Society: How Brands Transform Management and Lifestyle*. Cambridge, UK: Cambridge University Press.

Lilleslåtten, M. (2021) 10 år siden den arabiske våren – dette har skjedd [Ten years since the Arab Spring – this has happened]. University of Oslo, Department of Culture Studies and Oriental Languages, April 13. https://www.hf.uio.no/ikos/forskning/aktuelt/aktuelle-saker/2021/10-ar-etter-den-arabiske-varen (accessed April 20, 2021).

Lister, M., Dovey, J., Giddings, S., Grant, I., and Kelly, K. (2009) *New Media: A Critical Introduction*. Second edition. London: Routledge.

MacBride Report.(1980) *Communication and Society Today and Tomorrow, Many Voices One World, Towards a New More Just and More Efficient World Information and Communication Order*. International Commission for the Study of Communication Problems. New York: UNESCO.

Marshall, P. D. (2004) *New Media Cultures*. London: Arnold.

Mjøs, O. J. (2012) *Music, Social Media and Global Mobility: MySpace, Facebook, YouTube*. New York: Routledge.

Morley, D. (1991) Where the global meets the local. *Screen*, 32, 1: 1–15.

Morley, D. (1992) *Television, Audiences and Cultural Studies*. London: Routledge.

Morley, D. ([1980] 1999) *The "Nationwide" Audience: Structure and Decoding*, pp. 119–291 in C. Brunsdon and D. Morley, *The "Nationwide" Television Studies*. First edition. London: Routledge.

Morley, D. (2006a) Globalisation and Cultural Imperialism Reconsidered: Old Questions in New Guises, pp. 30–43 in J. Curran and D. Morley (eds.) *Media and Cultural Theory*. London: Routledge.

Morley, D. (2006b) Unanswered questions in audience research. *Communication Review*, 9, 2: 101–21. https://doi.org/10.1080/10714420600663286

Papacharissi, Z. (2009) The virtual geographies of social networks: A comparative analysis of Facebook, LinkedIn and ASmallWorld. *New Media & Society*, 11, 1–2: 199-220.

Papacharissi, Z. and Blasiola, S. (2016) Structures of Feeling, Storytelling, and Social Media: The Case of #Egypt, pp. 211–22 in A. Bruns, G, Enli, E. Skogerbø, A. O. Larsson, and C. Christensen (eds.) *The Routledge Companion to Social Media and Politics*. London: Routledge.

Poell, T. (2016) Social Media Activism and State Censorship, pp. 189–206 in D. Trottier and C. Fuchs (eds.) *Social Media, Politics and the State: Protests, Revolutions, Riots, Crime and the Policing in the Age of Facebook, Twitter and YouTube.* London: Routledge.

Poell, T. (2020) Social media, temporality, and the legitimacy of protest. *Social Movement Studies,* 19, 5–6: 609–24. https://doi.org/10.1080/14742837.2019.1605287.

Poell, T. and van Dijck, J. (2018) Social Media and New Protest Movements, pp. 546–61 in J. Burgess, A. Marwick and T. Poell (eds.) *The SAGE Handbook of Social Media.* London: SAGE. https://pure.uva.nl/ws/files/19952198/Poell_Van_Dijck_Social_media_and_new_protest_movements_2018_.pdf (accessed June 2, 2022).

Rosen, J. (2012) The People Formerly Known as the Audience, pp. 13–14 in M. Mandiberg (ed.) *The Social Media Reader.* New York: New York University Press.

Sheller, M. and Urry, J. (2006) The new mobilities paradigm. *Environment and Planning A,* 38, 2: 207–26.

Shklovski, I. and boyd, d. (2006) Music as cultural glue: Supporting bands and fans on MySpace. https://www.academia.edu/2672710/Music_as_cultural_glue_supporting_bands_and_fans_on_myspace (accessed June 22, 2021).

Sinclair, J., Jacka, E., and Cunningham, S. (1996) *New Patterns in Global Television.* Oxford: Oxford University Press.

Sreberny, A. (2000) The Global and the Local in International Communication, pp. 93–119 in J. Curran and M. Gurevitch (eds.) *Mass Media and Society.* London: Arnold.

Straubhaar, J. (1991) Beyond media imperialism: Asymmetrical interdependence and cultural proximity. *Critical Studies in Mass Communication,* 8, 1: 39–59.

Trottier, D. and Fuchs, C. (2015) Theorising Social Media, Politics and the State: An Introduction, pp. 3–38 in D. Trottier and C. Fuchs (eds.) *Social Media, Politics and the State: Protests, Revolutions, Riots, Crime and the Policing in the Age of Facebook, Twitter and YouTube.* London: Routledge.

Turkle, S. (1995) *Life on the Screen: Identity in the Age of the Internet.* New York: Simon & Schuster.

Urry, J. (2007) *Mobilities.* Cambridge, UK: Polity.

Van Dijck, J. (2009) Users like you? Theorizing agency in user-generated content. *Media, Culture & Society* 31, 1: 41–58.

Van Dijck, J. (2011) Facebook as a tool for producing sociality and connectivity. *Television & New Media.* https://doi.org/10.1177/1527476411415291

Van Dijck, J. (2013) *The Culture of Connectivity: A Critical History of Social Media.* Oxford: Oxford University Press.

Wikström, P. (2020) *The Music Industry: Music in the Cloud.* Third edition. Cambridge, UK: Polity Press.

The Dimensions of Globalization in the Context of Media and Communications

In recent decades, globalization has been one of the most popular, discussed, and influential terms and concepts in general, and particularly within media and communications. This chapter argues that the term continues to be significant—more so than ever—as the global digital shift accelerates throughout the twenty-first century through spectacular global growth in internet users and smartphone sales, major expansion in online communication, SVOD subscriptions, and take-up of social media and cloud services, and the emergence of global production chains and, importantly, digital advertising—which is expected to count for as much as 58 percent of total global advertising revenue in 2023. The digital shift gathered further pace during the Covid-19 pandemic, as the use of digital media and communications and ICTs for all purposes increased, and has, in fact, been key for society to function, as globalization theorists Steger and James point out: "instances of 'distant socializing' via such digital platforms as Zoom and Google Hangout have exploded" (2020: 188).

The term "globalization" appeared in the Webster Dictionary in 1961, and in the late 1980s and 1990s academic disciplines, including sociology, business studies, anthropology, and geography, became increasingly preoccupied with the concept, but the term also became popular in business, media, and other sectors (Robertson, 1990; 2020). In fact, some argue that in the 1990s the term "skyrocketed to terminological stardom" (Osterhammel and Petersson, 2005: 1). Globalization soon became incorporated into the field of international communication and global media, and many scholars central in shaping the field consider "globalization" as a key term over the two last decades. This chapter introduces key theoretical concepts and perspectives that aim to help us understand the term and its relevance in the context of media and communications.

Despite the widespread adoption and use of the term, the meaning, significance, and nature of globalization are fiercely contested. While the term is praised by some for describing developments in society in a concise way, others consider it an inaccurate term or even hype. Some claim to be pro-globalization while others are anti-globalization. Yet, others say "globalization" is just a new word for something old, while others consider it as describing unprecedented developments in society. The very moment one attempts to define globalization the contested and confusing nature of the concept emerges.

Sociologist Giddens described globalization as a "portmanteau term" lacking a common definition (Giddens, quoted in Rantanen, 2005: 67). Similarly, fellow sociologist Bauman argues that "Globalization is on everybody's lips; a fad word fast turning into a shibboleth, a magic incantation, a pass-key meant to unlock the gates to all present and future mysteries" (Bauman, 1998: 1). Anthropologist Nederveen Pieterse points to the complicated character of the concept: "Globalization invites more to controversy than consensus, and the areas of consensus are narrow by comparison to the controversies" (2004: 8). The diverse and complex nature of the term is mirrored in Nederveen Pieterse description of globalization as "the intersection of many wholes, each with their different centers, organizing logics and worldviews" (Nederveen Pieterse, 2020: 236). Media scholar Sparks (2005: 20) points out how "Opinions differ as to whether globalization is a positive or a negative development, but there is general agreement that whatever is going on is either a symptom or a consequence of globalization." Still, Sparks argues, "There is no single theory of globalization upon which all social scientists, let alone everybody else, are agreed" (2005: 20). In fact, Robertson already pointed this out the 1990s. The term "globalization" had increased in popularity, and it was "in the process acquiring a number of meanings, with varying degrees of precision. This has been a source of frustration—but not necessarily a cause for surprise or alarm—to those of us who had sought earlier in the decade to establish a relatively strict definition of globalization" (Robertson, 1990: 20–1). This mirrors sociologist Sassen, over thirty years later, who underlines how the term "globalization" should not be understood as an encompassing concept. Instead, Sassen argues, there is a need for "always attaching specificities to it," and no "holistic and integrative conceptualizations of globalization" (Sassen, 2021: 793). The point is that "We have not globalized the world—we have globalized a broad range of conditions and possibilities that function inside countries, between countries, across countries. And it is the partial character of these conditions that have given them both their agility and their fragility" (Sassen, 2021: 793).

This chapter does not aim to find an all-compassing definition of the term "globalization." Instead, it narrows its inquiry with the aim of theoretically exploring how we can understand globalization in the context of media and communications. The chapter aims to contribute to illuminating and giving insight into how we can theoretically explain the contemporary characteristics, intensity, and limits of the activity in an increasingly interwoven and connected media and communications landscape, and how the global, regional, national, local, and personal are interlinked. This is a challenging task, as the disagreement surrounding the term "globalization" is also fierce within the field of media and communications. Scholars disagree upon how the process of globalization unfolds, its consequences and what it leads to, and even if it exists. The term relates to both continuity and change. Media scholar Servaes' definition of "globalization" is relatively open and explorative, yet highlights the many-sidedness of the term and the understanding of it: "In general, globalization is considered as the widening, deepening and speeding up of worldwide interconnectedness in all aspects of contemporary social life. But, beyond a general awareness and agreement of this global interconnectedness, there is substantial disagreement as to how globalization is best conceptualized" (Servaes, 2007: 20).

On the one hand, some argue that globalization is not necessarily something new, but rather more of the same. In fact, media scholar McChesney (1999) argues that globalization should be viewed as stronger and more totalizing than the earlier concepts of media and cultural imperialism. While the global and local or national were considered to be in opposition, globally expanding media localize their operations and collaborate with local media. Alternative and noncommercial actors may be important, but they will not be influential compared with the "hegemony of the corporate communications giants" (McChesney, 1998: 41). Furthermore, if definitions of globalization lack a critical stance they "pose a threat to constructing mythologies that only see positive sides of globalization and ignore the negative consequences of contemporary globalization processes" (Fuchs, 2011: 164). We should therefore pay attention to aspects of continuity in terms of power and influence as, for example, the old concepts "of imperialism and capitalist empire have gained importance in critical globalization studies" (2011: 165). A key, recent example is "platform imperialism," exemplified by the US-based global digital platforms, fronted by Facebook and Google: "In the 21st century, again, there is a distinct connection between platforms, globalization, and capitalist imperialism" (Jin, 2013: 167; see also Jin, 2020). A handful of platforms "dominate the global order" and have led to the accumulation and concentration of capital: "This is far from a globalization model in which power is infinitely dispersed" (Jin, 2013: 161).

On the other hand, many argue that globalization is something new and constantly evolving. Globalization is a much more unpredictable, "far less coherent or culturally directed process" in society compared with the earlier concept of "cultural imperialism" (Tomlinson, 1991). This process is again made up of a range of interrelated processes, developments, and concepts. A key concept signifying change is the process of "cultural hybridization"—the mixing of media genres and cultural forms across borders. Some consider it the very logic of globalization (Kraidy, 2005; Nederveen Pieterse, 2004; 2021). The related terms "glocalization" and "localization" are also considered key terms in the globalization discourse as they signify how the global and local are connected in myriad ways (Robertson, 1992; 1995). In fact, Robertson argues, the "glocal turn" characterizes the current state of globalization analysis (Robertson, 2020). Others point to how globalization is characterized by the related process of "counter-flow" of media and cultural products from non-Western regions to the West (Thussu, 2006; 2010).

Some emphasize how the process of globalization of media and communications leads to increased autonomy and power for the digital media users (e.g., Cunningham and Craig, 2019; Jenkins, 2006). Others emphasize the process of "deterritorialization": how cross-national electronic media challenge conventional connections between the territorial and cultural and social life (Morley and Robins, 1995). The process of "deterritorialization" is present in, among others, transnational television and global streaming services, and in global competition and production in the media sector (Chalaby, 2003; 2020; Lodz, 2021). A related concept is that globalization entails time and space compression (Robertson, 1995), a process largely created by the globally expanding media and communications, with consequences for our perception of the world and how we live our lives.

Yet, others argue how globalization is increasingly being shaped by geopolitical shifts and tis may lead to the splitting up and reconfiguration of the global media and communications landscape. The rise of China and India, and the BRICS constellation as a whole and individually, may lead to the "de-Americanization" and even "Sino-globalization" of global media and communications. This may have fundamental consequences for our understanding of globalization (Thussu, 2021; Thussu and Nordenstreng, 2021).

To help explain the concept of globalization, we need to take a historical approach which is sensitive to continuity and change, just as we have done in the previous chapters. This means tracing relevant theoretical developments, terms, and concepts within the field of media and communication together with industry developments.

This chapter emphasizes how the concepts of *connectivity* and *interconnectivity* are central to the wider understanding of the term "globalization" (e.g., van Dijck, 2013; Mjøs, 2012; 2015; Nederveen Pieterse, 2021; Robertson and Buhari-Gulmez, 2016; Tomlinson, 1999). In fact, Robertson suggests, "I would speculate that about 80 percent or even more of writings or pronouncements on globalization have defined it as centered upon the phenomenon of connectivity (or interconnectedness)" (Robertson, 2016: 16). So does this chapter.

This book has shown how global trade in media and cultural products, cable and satellite distribution of television and communication in the twentieth century, and the global digital shift accelerating across the world throughout the twenty-first century, with the popularization of the internet and the emergence of online-based services and companies and the general digitization and maturing of the industry across the world, have created increased connectedness across the world. In fact, Nederveen Pieterse argues, "In the 2000s, the language of globalization became digital and metamorphosed as interconnectedness and connectivity" (2021: 8), and even suggests the use of the term "connectivity" rather than "globalization" (Nederveen Pieterse, 2020: 236). This book does not go as far, but examines how connectedness is created and its characteristics, who constructs, shapes, and benefits from it, and its limits.

In doing so, this chapter on globalization draws on Tomlinson's suggestion that the "broad task of globalization *theory* is both to understand the sources of this condition of complex connectivity and to interpret its implications across the various spheres of social existence" (1999: 2). We can theorize the globalization of media and communications by answering the following questions:

- What are the processes that have created the increasingly global media and communications infrastructure?
- What are the characteristics, intensity, and limits of the specific activities that are taking place within this infrastructure, and how is the supposedly complex connectivity utilized?
- What are some of the consequences of these developments and activities?

We thereby explicitly explore how the globalization of media and communications develops by examining the central economic, political, cultural, and technological processes creating a cross-national and increasingly global media and communications infrastructure, as well as by studying the characteristics of what is taking place within this infrastructure (Mjøs, 2010; 2012).

The term "globalization" in the context of media and communications attempts to capture, conceptualize, and explain key developments. These are the developments that have been central in creating and shaping the international and global media landscape in the twentieth and twenty-first century. These developments have all contributed to triggering and motivating the development and adoption of key theoretical concepts and approaches associated with globalization. Several of the concerns and theories related to the term "globalization" have emerged in relation to the concepts and terms discussed in the previous chapters.

In the following part of this chapter, we discuss key concepts and terms that help define and describe the nuances of the term "globalization"—how it unfolds and its consequences—in relation to media and communications.

Although the concept of *"cultural imperialism"* focused on the US/Third World relationship (Schiller, [1976] 2018), Schiller also warned against the consequences of the uneven cultural power between the United States and Western Europe (1985: 11). In fact, in the mid-1980s, the European Commission was concerned that American films and television programs dominated the European media space (European Commission, 1984: 47). Key terms related to this discussion include *Americanization* and *Westernization*. Media and cultural products were distributed, and corporations expanded worldwide, but in addition, ideologies, such as democratic thinking and consumerism, and popular culture, spread throughout the world: "In the twentieth century, the 'American Century', the US was a major global storyteller, ranging from Washington to Hollywood and popular culture. Familiar storylines are modernization, Fordism, Coca-Cola, McDonald's, Walt Disney, Barbie and CNN. [...] Globalization was cast as neocolonialism, Americanization, Coca-colonization, McDonaldization" (Nederveen Pieterse, 2021: 1). However, some argue that the scholarly significance of terms such as "Americanization" and "Westernization" is debatable:

> The rhetorical appeal of these terms is undeniable. But their scholarly value is limited, especially if they are used to short-circuit analysis of how media and information flows work and how cultures change. These terms rightly draw our attention to the inequalities of power that typify international communication, but they do not adequately describe the nature or the consequences of the flow of media across borders.
>
> (Magder, 2003: 31–2)

If we take these terms at "face value" they may suggest that "we are living in an age of cultural convergence or homogenization, that the media globalization is leading to the formation of a singular global culture" (Magder, 2003: 32). However, such views underestimated the significance of local culture and language and for media audiences' preferences. In the 1970s, this was observed in relation to media productions in South America. Local media products, de Sola Pool argued, have several benefits in comparison to imported media products:

1. They are protected by barriers of language; people would rather see a film made in their own idiom than one with subtitles or even one that is dubbed.
2. They are protected by barriers of social support. Much of the enjoyment of media is discussing them with one's friends. Reading this year's best-seller is a social experience. Top TV shows or movies provide grist for conversation the next day, and that is much of their drawing power.
3. Local products are protected by barriers of culture. Domestic products portray characters eating foods the people eat, wearing the clothes they wear, celebrating the events they celebrate and gossiping about the celebrities they follow.

(de Sola Pool, 1977: 143)

These observations are of considerable significance for understanding the audience in an international perspective. De Sola Pool's early observations represent a precursor to Straubhaar's concept of *cultural proximity*, which aimed to take the audience perspective and preferences into account in relation to the processes of internationalization and globalization. The growth of national and regional television and the cultural sector in Latin America from the end of the 1960s and throughout the 1980s showed how "audiences sought greater cultural relevance or proximity from both national and regional television programs," (Straubhaar 1991: 56) and this represented "a qualitative change in world media relations":

> Although the United States still dominates world media sales and flows, national and regional cultural industries are consolidating a relatively more interdependent position in the world television market. Reflecting and contributing to that industrial change, audiences are seeking greater cultural relevance or proximity from both national and regional television programs. We would expect to see similar changes towards nationalization and regionalization of industries and audiences, some producers and genres fail, and some audiences continue to prefer internationalized producers from outside both nation and

region. We simply suggest a larger gamut of possibilities, from dependence to relative interdependence, in media relations.

(Straubhaar, 1991: 56)

Around the same time as the term "cultural proximity" emerged, Collins (1990: 3–4) pointed out that differences in language and also culture in Europe complicated the creation of transnational television and its audience. Although the global broadcaster MTV thought the television channel's content had a universal appeal, by the mid-1990s managers at MTV realized the need to adjust to more local conditions (Chalaby, 2002: 195). This development was also triggered by the rapid increase in television channels in Europe in the 1990s. This also included a growth in *proximate television*—regional and local television channels adapting to Europe's cultural, linguistic, political, demographic, and geographic diversity (Moragas Spa and Lopez, 2000: 43).

In general, *localization* of imported television programming and television channels is done through dubbing or subtitling programs, the introduction of some local television content, or by adding the name of a country or language to a global brand (e.g., Discovery Channel US, Discovery Channel India, CNN Espanol, CNN Germany). These approaches have long been applied in order to appeal to the cultural and linguistic preferences of segments of the national television audience (Chalaby, 2005a; 2009; Mjøs, 2010; Thussu, 2005). Similarly, recently expanding online services such as Netflix (US) and HBO subtitle films and television programs and series in national languages. This shows how global cultural producers reach "differentiated global market" through the "strategy of glocalisation" (Robertson, 1995: 40). *Glocalization*, originally a term applied in marketing, refers to "global localization"—a process that brings the "macroscopic" aspects of life together with the "microscopic" (Robertson, 1992: 173). Robertson points out that "much of the talk about globalization has tended to assume that it is a process which overrides locality," but this interpretation neglects the significance of the *local* (Robertson, 1995: 26). The term "glocalization" aims to help us "make sense of two *seemingly* opposing trends: homogenization and heterogenization" (Robertson, 1995: 40). Robertson argues, "Put simply, globalization, far from standardizing everything, actually encourages diversification. My own conception of glocalization surely catches these antinomies rather neatly. *To put this another way, it is the local that enables the global to work*" (Robertson, 2020: 33).

While the global television channels adjust to different languages, the popularity of global television formats marked the arrival of a more extensive form of glocalization. As with global television channels, these program forms have an ability to travel across the world while appealing to local or national cultural specificities. However, the local or national cultural content is inserted into a defined and copyrighted global television format concept: "Domestic producers can incorporate local color and global audiences can paradoxically feel at home when watching them. Locality needs to be evicted so it can be reintroduced as long as it does not alter the basic concept" (Waisbord, 2004: 378). While global television channels can only adjust to local preferences—at least in smaller television markets—television formats represented an unprecedented localization within the television industry (Chalaby, 2016; 2020).

The concept of glocalization is just as relevant for global social media. Similar to the global television channels MTV and Discovery Channel, the most ambitious social media platform, Facebook, rolled out through regional or country-specific versions. However, Facebook's approach to glocalization is unprecedented in the way it connects its services to individual users. In recent years, Facebook's extensive language translation and personalization has intensified the connection between locally situated individual users and the global media and communications services through "hyper-localization" and "global personalization" (see Case Study 8.1).

Case Study 8.1 Hyper-Localization and Global Personalization in the Digital Era

Global media and communications services have never been so global, yet also so local and personalized. The possibilities for swift and detailed language localization within the online environment, in the case of Twitter and Facebook with the help of thousands of social media users, are exceptional. Furthermore, the personalization of global social media is unprecedented; users' personal Facebook profiles are placed within a network of their friends' profiles, with constant suggestions for new friends to connect with, and targeted advertisements in their national or local languages, based on the user's activity and preferences. The linking of the global Facebook service with the individual users, along with the ability to localize language, is key to explaining the service's rapid expansion. Similarly, the globally dominant search engine, Google, for example, takes glocalization further as it drives the integration of geographically and culturally specific information and knowledge. Google is available in around 200 languages and the world has never seen a media and communications entity achieve such market positions, monopolizing information gathering, formatting and influencing our view of the online world, and embedded so deeply in local, national, and transnational conditions. However, in contrast to traditional internationally expanding media companies, online services like global social media and global search engines have facilitated new online spaces for users that enhance their access to information. As such, global media and communications services have never been so global, yet never so local or personal. This is achieved through the processes of "hyper-localization" and "global personalization," as this book argues.

Global social media and search engines, fronted by services such as Facebook and Google, have affixed themselves among their users and audiences through catering for local culture, personal tastes, and language. Their localization programs aim to create the links between the local and the expanding social media that are required to conduct corporate activity. In particular, Facebook users' opportunities for personalizing their user profiles show how the service creates a link between the individual user and the expanding service. Despite the difference between global television and the internet, there are several corporate lessons to be learned from the traditional media players and brands. Just as within the television sector, the social media landscape is characterized by the negotiation between the global and the national or local: between globalizing trends and the specific interests of culturally and linguistically diverse markets. Similar to the television channels MTV, Discovery Channel, and CNN, which have been able to secure a worldwide presence since the 1990s, the most ambitious social media rolled out through regional or country-specific versions.

While localization is also the key strategy of the expanding social media platforms, their approaches to localization differ from each other in several respects. The possibilities for swift and detailed localization within the online environment, in the case of Twitter and Facebook with the help of thousands of social media users, are unprecedented. Furthermore, when users log on to global social media, they enter their personal version of the service, consisting of their personal profile placed within the network of their friends' profiles. This, along with the ability to localize, helps explain the rapid expansion and adoption of the largest social media platforms, and contributes to understanding why Facebook and Twitter have expanded through hyper-localization so rapidly.

Perhaps the main reason for Facebook's and Twitter's rapid, global expansion and popularity is their approach to localization: this differs from Myspace, the social media platform that pioneered international expansion and was the first to attract major mainstream attention. As pointed out, localization is the key corporate strategy for traditional global television operators and online entities alike. The choice of localization strategies, then, has consequences for the competition between both local and fellow global operators. When looking at the localization strategies of Myspace on the one hand, and Facebook and Twitter on the other, we see how their approaches differ.

All global social media rely on the contributions, input, activity, and communication of their participants and users in the form of postings of written messages, pictures, and video clips. However, MySpace's approach has clear parallels with the traditional global television channels' localization that its owner, News Corp, has successfully implemented across the world for many years by focusing on developing a physical presence in specific territories, and include local or national media and cultural content in their services (Arrington, 2008). This mirrors the localization strategies of the global cable and satellite television channels. In contrast, Facebook has relied on a more online-based and user-led approach to localization:

> Facebook is taking a radically different approach—tapping users to do all the hard work for them. They are picking and choosing markets (Spanish was opened first, two weeks ago; today German and French were launched) and asking just a few users to test out their collaborative translation tool. Once the tool is perfected and enough content has been translated, Facebook will offer users the ability to quickly switch the language on the site, per their preference.
>
> (Arrington, 2008)

When Facebook localized the service into German, more than 2,000 German-speaking Facebook users contributed to translating the site from English. The translation process took less than two weeks (Facebook, 2008a). Facebook used the same approach when translating the site into Spanish. Close to 1,500 Spanish-speaking Facebook users were involved and helped translate the site in less than four weeks (Facebook, 2008b). There were three key reasons for Facebook's adoption of "community translation":

> *Speed.* Deliver localized sites in a fraction of the time required with conventional methods.
>
> *Quality.* Localize using the terminology that is preferred by the target users.
>
> *Reach.* Bring Facebook to more communities around the world.
>
> (De Palma and Kelly, 2011: 386)

By 2010, Facebook claimed that more than 300,000 Facebook users have contributed to the translation of the site into many languages (Facebook, 2010). In fact, Facebook has not only been translated into the major languages but also caters for minority languages and thereby has, in an unprecedented way, adapted to the different cultural and linguistic specificities across the world. By early 2016, Facebook claimed: "To reach a global audience, Facebook supports 70-plus languages" (Facebook, 2016). While traditional methods for translating a language would take months, the use of "collaborative translation" involved participants or "volunteers [who] completed the Spanish and German localizations in just one week, while the French team took just 24 hours to produce its language variant" (De Palma and Kelly, 2011: 386). Twitter also decided to start to localize its service with the help of its users: "Following a lead from Facebook, Twitter announced that it was crowdsourcing the translations through Tweeter volunteer linguists" (Grunwald, 2010).

Facebook's and Twitter's internet-based strategy seems far less costly and more efficient than that of Myspace. The idea of "crowdsourcing" (Howe, 2006) is accepted by many users of these services despite the fact that they are helping the expansion of a commercial media entity. The service's immersion in local cultures is done mainly through personal communication, language, and text. This stands in contrast to traditional global television channels, as well as to Myspace's approach to localization, relying on a more traditional physical engagement with local culture. As Myspace has scaled back its operations and presence as its traditional localization strategy failed, this has also had an effect on its ability to attract users (Garrahan, 2009).

While the linguistic localization of global social media has enabled these platforms to reach linguistically diverse audiences, the personalization of these services has made them able to come even closer to the individual internet user. With the arrival of advanced multimedia mobile telephones—smartphones—social media were introduced on them as well. The number of mobile social media users has increased rapidly, and by 2021, 98 percent of Facebook users use mobile phones when using the service (Tankovska, 2021).

The ability to create a link between the individual user and the service, for communicative, mediated, and commercial purposes, makes these global social media platforms stand out even more compared to traditional global media, due to their opportunities for global personalization.

The fact that that more than two-thirds of Facebook's and Google's advertising revenue is local further underlines, according to the *Financial Times*, how integrated these globally expanding services are in local conditions through glocalizations strategies (Barker, 2020).

Personalization is often used to describe "different types of tailoring strategies" (Winter et al., 2021). In media, the term "personalization" refers to how a media corporation tailors and distribute media content to users based on information about them that the organization has access to or has gathered (Turow, 2017). Personalization thereby also refers to "the degree to which receivers perceive a message reflects their distinctiveness as individuals differentiated by their interests, history, relationship network, and so on" (O'Sullivan and Carr, 2018).

Through language and algorithms, global social media are "constantly trying to more precisely tailor content to users' specific interests," through, for example, Facebook's News Feed, YouTube's recommended videos, Twitter's top search results, tailored advertisements, and, not least, other users: "personalization involves social media platforms prompting users to explicitly make 'personal' connections and stimulating them to create their persona by constantly posting and sharing new content" (Poell and van Dijck, 2018).

Some argue that globalization is an even more forceful and totalizing concept than those of *cultural imperialism* and *media imperialism*. While traditionally the cultural imperialism thesis viewed domestic and local media as opposing the globally expanding media companies, the former companies began to link up with the latter thorough localizing global media content (McChesney, 1999). In the 1990s, as US media companies were becoming globalized, Schiller's critique extended to this development as well: "Initially this could be seen as American cultural imperialism. More recently, it has become transnational corporate cultural domination" (1992: 39). Still, together, the United States and, increasingly, these transnational corporations represent "systemic power and control" also within the global media sector, through the support of both telecommunications and media and communications software and hardware (Schiller, 1998: 23).

The corporatization and commercialization of the global online environment has prompted scholars to also draw attention to uneven power relations and concentration of capital, and have applied the term "imperialism" to describe these developments. Mirroring the notion of *media imperialism* (Boyd Barrett, 1977; 2015), yet coming across as far more forceful and encompassing than the original term, *platform imperialism* aims to conceptualize the globalization of media and communications (Jin, 2013; 2020). The domination of the US-based global digital platforms, including search engines and social media, and most notably Facebook, Twitter, and Google, is an example of platform imperialism with "hegemonic power", as the United States, who previously exerted their "imperial power" and dominance on non-Western countries militarily and economically as well as through media and cultural products, now "dominate the world with platforms" (Jin, 2013: 145). Platforms, then, exemplify "familiar patterns of asymmetrical power relations between the West and the East" (2013: 167–8). The point here is that US imperialism is continuing throughout the twenty-first century, while the expansion of the digital economy gives China, India and Korea opportunities for further growth: "[T]here are reasonable doubts of whether non-Western digital platforms have built a new global order, and therefore, constructed a balance between the West and the East, because digital platforms have reinforced America's imperialistic power. Although a handful of non-Western countries have advanced their own platforms, American platforms have penetrated the global markets and expanded their global dominance" (Jin, 2020: 57). However, some criticize studies of platforms that focus too much on structures, institutional perspectives, markets, and corporate decision making, and neglect the role of users and cultural practices taking place in the platform environment: "Notably absent is an analysis of how platforms transform cultural practices, and *vice versa*, how evolving practices transform platforms as particular socio-technical constructs" (Poell et al., 2019).

Therefore, some scholars argue that the *audience and user power* of these very platforms, such as social media entertainment platforms (SMEs) like YouTube, represents a major contribution to defining globalization in the context of media and communications.

> It is possible to posit a qualitatively new wave of media globalization based on the global availability and uptake of SME platforms, which is relatively frictionless compared to national broadcasting and systems of film and DVD release and licensing by "windowed" territory. And compared to film and television, there is very little imposed content regulation on the major platforms – some of the world's largest information and communication companies.
>
> (Cunningham and Craig, 2019: 14)

So, while the global expansion of Netflix is dependent on its ability to secure rights to programming, either through acquisition, licensing, or production, the content of SMEs is to a large extent "born global," as these services may facilitate the distribution of the user-generated content worldwide. Such a creator-centric perspective gives rise to a more nuance understanding of globalization in the context of media, culture, and communication: "Due to their vintage, debates in media and communication studies about media and cultural imperialism and globalization can develop a shop-worn quality. Due to the depth with which it studies cultural specificity, anthropology may offer a fresh, and perhaps more nuanced grasp of cultural globalization" (Cunningham and Craig, 2019: 262).

Another key concept for understanding how globalization unfolds, which attempts to take both an audience-centered approach and the macro-perspective into account, is the regional perspective, which considers a region as both "geolinguistic and cultural as well as geographic. A regional perspective on the development of television markets brings to light national similarities" (Sinclair et al., 1996: 23). These similarities may include cultural, religious, or ethnic commonalities and shared histories across regions. Together these similarities form *geocultural* and *geolinguistic markets*: "Most of the main transnational geocultural and cultural-linguistic markets for television in today's world system of television have their roots in the religious and cultural systems that predate European colonialism. [...] In many cases, the colonial experience added new historical ties that pulled neighboring countries together" (Straubhaar, 2007: 43).

These commonalities, developed over time, "define cultural markets, to which television responds. Populations defined by these kinds of characteristics tend to seek out cultural products, such as television programs or music, that are most similar or proximate to them" (Straubhaar, 2007: 43). A further dimension is that geocultural markets have production centers, as Sinclair et al. noted in the mid-1990s: "Mexico and Brazil for Latin America, Hong Kong and Taiwan for the Chinese-speaking populations of Asia, Egypt for the Arab world, and India for the Indian populations of Africa and Asia" (Sinclair et al., 1996: 8, cited in Hesmondhalgh, 2019: 384). In the northernmost part of Europe, Scandinavia exemplifies yet a different type of geocultural and geolinguistic market. Norway, Sweden, and Denmark share cultural commonalities as well as languages that are understood across the national borders (Hilson, 2008: 16). Yet, the Nordic region, which consists of the Scandinavian countries as well as Finland and Iceland, is not a geolinguistic market, as Finnish is not related to the other countries' languages. Still, the Nordic countries have common historical roots, and a strong cultural, political, and economic collaborative system "epitomized in the concept of the Nordic Model" (Syvertsen et al., 2014: 3–4).

However, it is also the case, Jin argues, that "people do enjoy other cultures regardless of different geo-linguistic backgrounds. For example, people in Asia with no Latin American contingency enjoy some Telenovelas, and many fans in Africa and the Middle East enjoy the Korean Wave with no linguistic and cultural commonalities" (2020: 52).

A relevant term in this discussion is *diaspora*. While diaspora have existed throughout history, in the mid-1990s, "satellite distribution has opened up regional and transcontinental geolinguistic markets" that also secured "distribution of television products to diasporic communities, notably those of Chinese, Arab, and Indian origin" (Sinclair et al., 1996: 23). These are ethnic communities that are dispersed throughout the world. As such, these geocultural and geolinguistic markets extend across the world and consist of geographically dispersed people:

> It is possible, for example, to see the USA, Canada, the UK, Ireland, Australia and New Zealand as forming one such geolinguistic region, based on the use of English as a first language, and primarily white, Christian cultural traditions. Another potential region comprises Spain, Spanish-speaking Latin America, plus Spanish-speaking parts of the former Spanish empire and the massive

Spanish-speaking population of the USA. Some might include Portugal, Brazil and the former Portuguese colonies in Africa and Asia in the same "region" within a broader set of countries influenced by Hispanic languages and cultures.

(Hesmondhalgh, 2019: 383–4)

Global media companies, such as the US global television services, have also responded to the rationale of geolinguistic and geocultural markets, and structured their services accordingly (Mjøs, 2010). Miami became the bridgehead for satellite television services, expanding not only into Latin America and Central America, but also the United States and Spain. Miami has a "strategic attraction" for the television industry. Sinclair points out that the market for Spanish-speaking television programming is more regional than national and reaches "across both continents of the Americas and across the borders of their constituent nation-states" (Sinclair, 2003: 221).

Social media platforms have increased the opportunities for communication across geocultural and geolinguistic regions, and, importantly, diasporic communities. For example, Kakao (Korea), Mixi (Japan), and Baidu and QQ (China) are not able to compete globally, but they have "significant roles in their own countries and diasporas" (Jin, 2020: 55). As such, "Digital power engages Chinese speakers and persons of Chinese ethnic origin around the globe; they are connected to the motherland, the home nation, by digital resources" (Zhu and Keane, 2021: 216).

Another concept that aims to show the nuances of the globalization of media and communications is *contra-flow* (Boyd Barrett and Thussu, 1992; Thussu, 2006). It relates to the previous terms discussed, but referred initially to how digital technology, a deregulated television industry, and increasingly affordable satellite television distribution have facilitated flows of media content from the South to the West and other parts of the world. As such, the global media landscape is not just characterized by the dominant flows from the West and the United States in particular. The media industries in China, Japan, South Kora, Brazil, and India contribute to these contra-flows (Thussu, 2005; 2006; 2010), and so does the export of Nordic crime television series (Jensen and Waade, 2013; 2014). There is a "*contra-flow* in media products from the peripheries to the centre of global media production," but also "movements within the South itself" (Thussu, 2010). Thussu divides global media flows into two main categories: the dominant flows and the subaltern flows. "Dominant flows" refer to US-dominated media products such as Disney and Hollywood films and television, as well as internet-based services like Google, while "subaltern flows" can be split into "transnational flows" and "geo-cultural flows" (Thussu, 2010: 4).

The notion of contra-flow has led to a more multifaceted understanding of globalization, and multiple flows crisscrossing the world. However, the extent and actual impact of "counter-flow" is debated. Some scholars provide celebratory statements when describing this phenomenon:

> Bollywood and Hong Kong martial arts movies in Africa, Turkish soaps in Saudi Arabia, Brazilian telenovelas in Latin America and Lusophone Africa and the Korean wave in East Asia. The K wave, Hallyu, in pop, soap operas, movies, TV shows, design and cosmetics is unstoppable. Bollywood and Hollywood have strengthened their cooperation. Hollywood now needs China for blockbuster box office numbers. Dalian Wanda has bought into Hollywood studios. The downstream production of books, film and media is increasingly decentered too.
>
> (Nederveen Pieterse, 2021: 2)

Others are more skeptical, pointing out that Bollywood films, telenovelas, and South Korean productions are still not "widely distributed in the West" (Chalaby, 2020: 376).

Korea's fast-expanding media and cultural industries and distribution to the East and South Asian region on a large scale exemplifies the complexities and realities of "counter-flow." The "one-way flow" of films and television programming from the United States decreased for a time, as many "non-Western cultures" have developed their media cultures, but it is also true that Korean and local media and cultural products are mainly distributed to regional markets and not markets in the West (Jin, 2020: 52).

Another development with consequence for the extent and nature of counter-flow is the rise of China and the other BRICS countries. The distribution of media content from inside the BRICS countries has increased due to the mobile digital technological infrastructure, and a multilingual internet: "[S]uch flows are growing and increasingly being noticed in Western capitals as challenging their traditional communication hegemony. As more people connect, content from BRICS countries is likely to become more visible globally and this may have the potential to contribute to a new global communication order" (Thussu and Nordenstreng, 2021: 7). The social media service TikTok is perhaps the most spectacular example of Chinese "counter-flow" to date (see Case Study 8.2).

The concept of *cultural hybridization* aims to explain a central process in the globalization of culture and media. The term implies that the mixing of culture and language (Nederveen Pieterse, 2004) leads to the emergence of new cultural expressions and forms (Kraidy, 2005; Nederveen Pieterse, 2021; Straubhaar and Duarte, 2005).

Case Study 8.2 TikTok: Globalizing and Localizing Chinese Social Media in the United States

TikTok is ranked as the sixth most popular global social media, with over 50 million daily users and 100 million monthly users in the United States in 2020. In 2020, TikTok was the most downloaded app on both App Store and Google Play—ahead of Instagram, Snapchat, WhatsApp, Facebook, and Zoom (Freer, 2020; Sherman, 2020; Tankovska, 2021).

However, what we today know as TikTok is the result of the merger of several different apps. Musical.ly launched in Shanghai, "but had strong US business links" (Tidy and Smith Galer, 2020) and a considerable user base there. Then, in 2016, the Chinese technology company ByteDance launched Douyin, which had over 100 million users in China and Thailand the same year. In 2018, ByteDance acquired Musical.ly, and merged the two into TikTok (Tidy and Smith Galer, 2020). Since then the Chinese app has expanded globally, and was downloaded 2 billion times by the mid-2020s. The BBC suggest that the reason for its popularity is a combination of music, usability, and technology: "TikTok's secret lies in its use of music and an extraordinarily powerful algorithm, which learns what content users like to see far faster than many other apps. [...] Users can choose from a huge database of songs, filters and movie clips to lipsync to" (Tidy and Smith Galer, 2020).

This global expansion has raised security fears. Most users outside China are not aware that TikTok is Chinese-owned, or of the restrictions users face in China (Zhu and Keane, 2021: 217). The question is, how does the service operate internationally in terms of user data collection and other forms of surveillance?

The Indian government stated, as it banned TikTok and other Chinese apps, that that Chinese apps were "stealing and surreptitiously transmitting users' data" (Tidy and Smith Galer, 2020). In late 2019, the United States started a national security review of the app, and in 2020 President Trump sought to ban both TikTok and the Chinese app WeChat in the United States. Trump stated that these apps represented a threat to "the national security, foreign policy, and economy of the United States," and the US Secretary of State, Mike Pompeo, argued that TikTok was "feeding data directly to the Chinese Communist Party," as reported by the BBC (BBC, 2021; Tidy and Smith Galer, 2020).

In response, TikTok filed a lawsuit against the US government, claiming that the United States did not have any proof that it is distributing data to the Chinese government (Sherman, 2020). A number of US technology companies have considered acquiring the US part of TikTok, but by 2021, President Joe Biden had decided to delay any legal action against the two apps (BBC, 2021).

However, according to the BBC, TikTok gathers information on its users in a very similar way to Facebook and other social media: what videos are watched and commented on, geographical user data, the device being used, and keystroke rhythms when users type.

While TikTok's CEO Kevin Mayer, former Disney executive, gave experts unprecedented access to scrutinize its algorithms and technology, the fears are that the Chinese government will force TikTok to hand over the data they hold. This is grounded in the Chinese National Security Law of 2017, which can order individuals, organizations, or companies to "support, assist and co-operate with the state intelligence work" (Tidy and Smith Galer, 2020).

The concept of the globalization of culture is far more complex than, for example, the concept of "cultural imperialism," as: "cultural experiences, past or present, have not been simply moving in the direction of cultural uniformity and standardization" (Nederveen Pieterse, 2004: 69). As a consequence, the idea of "global cultural synchronisation"—although not being irrelevant—does not properly address the complexity of developments in the world:

> It overlooks the countercurrents—the impact nonwestern cultures have been making on the West. It downplays the ambivalence of the globalizing momentum and ignores the role of local reception of western culture—for example, the indigenization of western elements. It fails to see the influence nonwestern cultures have been exercising on one another. It has no room for crossover culture, as in the development of "third cultures" such as world music. It overrates the homogeneity of western culture and overlooks the fact that many of the standards exported by the West and its cultural industries themselves turn out to be of culturally mixed character if we examine their cultural lineages.
>
> (Nederveen Pieterse, 2004: 69)

The Latin-American television soap *Telenovela* is considered as a classic example of cultural hybridity within television programming (Straubhaar and Duarte, 2005: 223; Tunstall, 1977: 59). The genre is characterized as a mix of Latin American cultural codes and conventions of the North American soap television:

> While history is replete with media texts such as the telenovela that can be described as hybrid, globalization and the commercial imperative to reach large audiences with minimal investment and risk have made hybrid media forms pervasive. In the case of cultures particularly susceptible to the creation

of hybrid forms such as Latin America and Hong Kong, the *longue duree* of history, including colonialism, conquest, and trade, is the scene of a protracted cultural fusion.

(Kraidy, 2005: 8)

The "Korean wave"—popular culture emerging from Korea, in the form of film, television, and music genres—can also partly be understood as a result of the process of cultural hybridization as:

> local cultural agents and actors interact and negotiate with global forms, using them as resources through which Koreans construct their own cultural spaces, as exemplified in the case of rap. By this, we understand that the globalization, particularly in the realm of popular culture, breeds a creative form of hybridization that works towards sustaining local identities in the global context.

(Shim, 2006: 39–40)

In fact, Nederveen Pieterse argues that generally, "Global cultural interplay and mixing" has always happened and is an ongoing process. Digital technologies and media play key roles in facilitating worldwide communication, and air travel is continuing to grow globally: "The salience of the global and the growth of global mixing is not just trendy; it is structurally embedded in the world economy" (Nederveen Pieterse, 2021: 2–3).

A related process—also associated with globalization—is *deterritorialization*. The globalization of electronic media challenges the conventional connection between the territorial and the social (Chalaby, 2003: 462; Morley and Robins, 1995: 132), and "deterritorialization" refers to "the simultaneous penetration of local worlds by distant forces, and the dislodging of everyday cultural meanings from their 'anchors' in local cultural contexts" (Tomlinson, 2012: 1). As such, there is "a weakening or dissolution of the connection between everyday lived culture and territorial location" (Tomlinson, 1999, quoted in Chalaby, 2009: 228).

The plethora of new digital media distribution forms and personal communications systems and platforms may lead to increased deterritorialization as people communicate, form communities, and consume media products online regardless of territory. Deterritorialization can therefore be viewed as both "a perplexing and disruptive phenomenon, and an exhilarating and potentially empowering one in the way in which it can expand the cultural, political, and moral horizons of people beyond their geographical localities" (Tomlinson, 2012: 1). Similarly, Hernàndez i Martí emphasizes to not consider the "deterritorialization of localized cultural experiences as an impoverishment of cultural interaction, but as a transformation produced by the impact the growing cultural transnational connections have on the local realm, which means that deterritorialization generates a relativization and a transformation of local cultural experiences" (Hernàndez i Martí, 2006: 94). Therefore, the process of deterritorialization does not signal the end of local diversity, but "territorial context is no longer—as it may have been in the past—the single most important determinant of our cultural experience" (Tomlinson, 2012).

Deterritorialization also takes place in relation to global cable and satellite television channels and production, and competition within the media and communications sector, The former has a weaker attachment to national territory and culture, as there is an attempt to appeal to cross-national audience segments:

> Transfrontier television networks have a relationship to place and time that is entirely different from that of terrestrial television channels. Traditionally, television has been circumscribed by a national territory and at times played an active role in the construction of national identities. Transnational television channels and networks challenge the bond between the television and the nation-state in way that is best comprehended by the concept of deterritorialization.
>
> (Chalaby, 2009: 228)

Similarly, Netflix and other digital streaming services have the technological tools that "enable them to imagine their subscribers as transnational clusters of tastes and sensibilities" (Lodz, 2021: 207). These audiences "are often not sufficiently popular to be addressed by services aiming for a national 'mass' audience" (Lodz, 2021: 207). Deterritorialization is further found in the competition between producers and aggregators in the media delivery chain as they must increasingly seek across borders for production expertise and compete worldwide for productions: "This entails a deterritorialization of competition: if programme suppliers can, today, fill the schedules of broadcasters and platforms located anywhere, the reverse side of the coin is that they compete for these slots against producers from other countries" (Chalaby, 2020: 382).

Castells' theory of the *network society* (2000; 2013) is one of the more ambitious attempts to create an encompassing theory on the nature and consequences of the various forms of interlinking of the global, regional, national, local, and personal. Information and communication technologies are at the heart of a new form of world society that is characterized by horizontal structures and various forms of networks, in contrast to the historically central institutions and traditional geographical centers. Influence and power has shifted to networks and arrangements that are created for solving different tasks and achieving certain goals: "Networks have become the predominant organizational form of every domain of human activity. Globalization has intensified and diversified. Communications technologies have constructed virtuality as a fundamental dimension of our reality" (Castells, 2013: xliv). However, while Castells underline dramatic change, others emphasize continuity.

The role and destiny of the *nation-state* in relation to media, culture, communication, policies, and economy have been much debated in the context of globalization of media and communications. Some consider it as diminishing (e.g., Castells, 2013; Chalaby, 2009; 2020), while others argue for the nation state's continuing significance and importance in the development of world society and in relation to a globalizing media, cultural, and communication sector (e.g., Flew, 2020; Flew et al., 2016; Syvertsen et al., 2014). Flew, among the latter scholars, argues that "the most obvious weakness of the globalization paradigm" is exactly the view that the nation-state is an institution in decline:

> This is partly because it has consistently underestimated the continuing significance of nation-states and their institutions, particularly in managing and brokering the various forms of political, economic and cultural interconnectedness associated with global interdependence. It has also overestimated the degree to which national cultures and territorially derived forms of identity have continued to have resonance, even as there is greater scope for non-territorial forms of identity to be adopted and to enable political, social and cultural change through the formation of transnational networks and movements.
>
> (Flew, 2020: 34)

However, others argue for the diminishing autonomy and influence of nation-states in the face of globalizing media and communications:

> It is undeniable, however, that the close relationship between media and nation has been unravelling over the past two decades. Globalization and digital technologies are remapping media spaces and contribute to the emergence of new products, practices and experiences. They are not only intensifying trade flows but reshaping national media systems from within by embedding them in production/consumption transnational networks.
>
> (Chalaby, 2020: 373)

Flew and Waisbord call for a nuanced approach that carefully considers the role of the nation-state, and its connection with the local and the global: "There is no inevitable, straightforward shift from the local and the national to the global, particularly in relation to legacy media industries and content. Nor does it seem that the Internet represents a uniform shift toward globalization as demonstrated by patterns of use and governance" (Flew and Waisbord, 2015: 632). We need to move away from bombastically stating that the nation-state is either disappearing or "persisting," and rather study how local, national, and global forces shape media politics and politics (Flew and Waisbord, 2015).

The concept of BRICS (Brazil, Russia, India, China, and South Africa) represents a compelling case in relation to this discussion on the nation-state:

> The primacy of the nation state in providing the infrastructure, legal framework and ownership and regulatory rules and regulations remains in place, despite exceptional growth of online communication in the digital age. Comparative models of media and communication systems have ignored the extraordinary expansion of the media among the BRICS nations, which can provide empirical evidence in the context of digital globalization.
>
> (Thussu and Nordenstreng, 2021: 8)

While the BRICS have for the most part been considered from an economic perspective, with their power and impact as the world's fastest growing economies, fronted by China, some emphasize how BRICS is increasingly shaping the global media and communications landscape (Thussu, 2021; Thussu and Nordenstreng, 2021). BRICS in the context of globalization is of particular interest as it relates to a number of the terms discussed above, in addition to the nation-state: geocultural and geolinguistic markets, regionalization and contra-flow and multiple flows, as well as the concept of the network society and connectivity.

While the United States continues to be the world's foremost exporter of media content, and US companies have an undisputed global presence through ownership, services, and networks, "other players including the BRICS nations [...] have emerged in the last two decades to complement, if not to challenge, the US hegemony in this field. In the so-called 'post-American world', the globalization of media from BRICS nations is arguably the most significant development" (Thussu and Nordenstreng, 2015: 1). As such, scholars argue that the emerging BRICS nations, and particularly China, represent geopolitical shifts and may lead to the reconfiguration of the global media and communications landscape. Could this lead to the "de-Americanization" and even "Sino-globalization" of global media and communications (Thussu, 2021; Thussu and Nordenstreng, 2021)? This may have fundamental consequences for our understanding of globalization:

> [W]hile the internet continues to be dominated by the West, in particular the US, in terms of its infrastructure, economics and governance, this domination is increasingly being challenged by the BRICS countries, notably China, Russia and India. China already have the world's largest Internet population, followed by India, primarily driven by mobile communications. As in the rest of the world, Russia, Brazil, and South Africa, too, have witnessed a major expansion of online communication. With the world becoming increasingly mobile, networked and digitized, the question arises whether BRICS communication flows will help to pluralize and democratize information and communication agendas and create a new communication order, leading to a de-Americanization of the Internet.
>
> (Thussu, 2021: 280)

In fact, some argue that in the twenty-first century, "the tables have turned," and we have moved on from "the American Century" (the period from the middle of the twentieth century when the United States was dominant in the political, economic, and cultural realms), as "Emerging societies and the global South welcome globalization and free trade while in the US and part of Europe globalization is often viewed with discomfort." China's globally expanding Belt and Road Initiative, the new Silk Road, is a clear example of this development (Nederveen Pieterse, 2021: 1).

Critics point out that while "The BRICS grouping" is "a political and diplomatic reality, united by some common aspirations and substantial trade flows," underlying the concept lies "well-known tensions" and differences in the "scale and dynamics" between the countries (Sparks, 2015: 42). The coherence and synchronization of the BRICS members should therefore be considered critically:

> An even closer look at their main social and political structures, and particularly at the nature of the media and of their relationships to social and economic power, reveals differences so large as to call into question the utility of trying to see them as anything other than a somewhat ad hoc grouping of governments that are at least as different as they are similar.
>
> (Sparks, 2015: 42)

This is also the case with media and communications between the countries: "[W]ithin the BRICS countries there is very limited intercultural communication or media exchange: all five are largely dependent for their international-oriented content on US-supplied media" (Thussu and Nordenstreng, 2021: 10–11).

Still, the flow *from* the BRICS countries, and particularly China and India, throughout the world is already considerable and will continue to grow dramatically as the digitization process continues, and may eventually lead to a "new global communication order" (2021: 7). Others are more critical, pointing out that although Chinese apps, notably TikTok, have expanded worldwide, Chinese media and cultural products remain "domestically bound, with little traction beyond China," Zhu and Keane (2021: 217) argue:

> The draconian Chinese government policy that compulsively vets content and reduces content to a mere echo chamber of Party directives remains one of the major obstacles towards making Chinese content appealing globally. Nevertheless, numerous reports are conducted in China each year about why China's cultural power is not as potent as Hollywood's. The blame is usually laid on a misunderstanding by audiences and producers alike; in other words, foreigners don't understand China and are unable to appreciate its culture; and Chinese producers don't understand foreigners' tastes. The elephant in the room left unaddressed is government censorship.
>
> (Zhu and Keane, 2021: 217)

Still, "Notwithstanding its limited global appeal in the global Internet ecosystem, China has more people online than any other nation" (Zhu and Keane, 2021: 217). This leads to one of the major issues in the relation between media, communication, and the BRICS group, along with other countries: how the internet should be regulated and by whom. The regulatory framework relates to the political systems and traditions of the different countries, and these differ both between the BRICS countries, and also in comparison with the United States, which has been central in shaping and creating the internet we know today. Some ask what would happen if the BRICS countries decide to split the internet into national structures, reconfigured according to national specific policies, rules, and values (Thussu, 2015: 259).

Google executives Eric Schmidt and Jared Cohen point out that as states begin to regulate and influence online through filtering and other restrictions, the internet could move from a "global internet" to "a connected series of nation-state networks," and warn against such "balkanization of the Internet":

> The World Wide Web would fracture and fragment, and soon there would be a "Russian Internet" and an "American Internet" and so on, all coexisting and sometimes overlapping but, in important ways, separate. Each state's Internet would take on its national characteristics. Information would largely flow within countries but not across them, due to filtering, language or even just user

preference. [...] The process would at first be barely perceptible to users, but it would fossilize over time and ultimately remake the Internet.

(Schmidt and Cohen, 2013: 72)

While in the mid-1990s, 60 percent of the world's internet users were based in the United States, by 2019, only 7 percent of online users were based in the country. Increasingly, the populations of major countries, particularly China and India, are reconfiguring the internet, leading to the "de-Americanization of the internet." However, this process may be far from straightforward: "[T]he future of the Internet may be messier than this neat binary, with the other BRICS nations (Russia, India, Brazil and South Africa) and major current and emerging global actors—the EU, Turkey, Japan, Iran, Egypt, Nigeria, South Korea and Indonesia—providing multiple levels of digital discourse in a multilingual and de-centred Internet" (Thussu, 2021: 295–6).

References

Arrington, M. (2008) Facebook taps users to create translated versions of site. Spanish, French and German available. TechCrunch, January 21. http://techcrunch.com/2008/01/21/facebook-taps-users-to-create-translated-versions-of-site (accessed March 5, 2010).

Barker, A. (2020) Digital ad market set to eclipse traditional media for first time. *Financial Times*, June 23. https://www.ft.com/content/d8aaf886-d1f0-40fb-abff-2945629b68c0 (accessed March 18, 2021).

Bauman, Z. (1998) *Globalization: The Human Consequences*. Cambridge, UK: Polity.

BBC (2021) US President Joe Biden "pauses" TikTok and WeChat bans. *BBC News*, February 12. https://www.bbc.com/news/technology-56041209 (accessed March 21, 2021).

Boyd-Barrett, O. (1977) Media Imperialism: Towards an International Framework for an Analysis of Media Systems, pp. 116–35 in J. Curran, M. Gurevitch, and J. Woollacott (eds.) *Mass Communication and Society*. London: Edward Arnold.

Boyd-Barrett, O. (2015) *Cultural Imperialism*. London: SAGE.

Boyd-Barrett, O. and Thussu, D. K. (1992) *Contra-Flow in Global News: International and Regional News Exchange Mechanisms*. London: Published in association with UNESCO by J. Libbey.

Castells, M. (2000) *The Rise of the Network Society*. Second edition. Oxford: Blackwell.

Castells, M. (2013) *Communication Power*. New edition. Oxford: Oxford University Press.

Chalaby, J. K. (2002) Transnational television in Europe—The role of pan-European channels. *European Journal of Communication*, 17, 2: 183–203.

Chalaby, J. K. (2003) Television for a new global order. *Gazette*, 65, 6: 457–72.

Chalaby, J. K. (2005a) Towards an Understanding of Media Transnationalism, pp. 1–13 in J. K. Chalaby (ed.) *Transnational Television Worldwide: Towards a New Media Order*. London: I. B. Tauris.

Chalaby, J. K. (2005b) The Quiet Invention of a New Medium: Twenty Years of Transnational Television in Europe, pp. 43–65 in J. K. Chalaby (ed.) *Transnational Television Worldwide: Towards a New Media Order*. London: I. B. Tauris.

Chalaby, J. K. (2009) *Transnational Television in Europe: Reconfiguring Global Communications Networks*. London: I. B. Tauris.

Chalaby, J. K. (2016) *The Format Age: Television's Entertainment Revolution*. Cambridge, UK: Polity.

Chalaby, J. K. (2020) Understanding Media Globalization: A Global Value Chain Analysis, pp. 373–84 in S. Shimpach (ed.) *The Routledge Companion to Global Television*. New York: Routledge.

Collins, R. (1990) *Satellite Television in Western Europe*. London: John Libbey.

Cunningham, S. and Craig, D. (2019) *Social Media Entertainment: The New Intersection of Hollywood and Silicon Valley*. New York: New York University Press.

De Palma, D. A. and Kelly, N. (2011) Project Management for Crowdsourcing Translation: How User-Translated Content Projects Work in Real Life, pp. 379–408 in D. A. De Palma and N. Kelly (eds.) *Translation and Localization Project Management: The Art of the Possible*. Amsterdam: John Benjamins.

De Sola Pool, I. (1977) When cultures clash: The changing flow of television. *Journal of Communication*, 27, 2: 139–49.

European Commission (1984) *Television without Frontiers. Green Paper on the Establishment of the Common Market for Broadcasting, Especially by Satellite and Cable*. COM (84) 300, June 14, 1984. Introduction: Parts One, Two and Three. http://aei.pitt.edu/archive/00001151/01/TV_frontiers_gp_pt_1_3.pdf (accessed May 17, 2022).

Facebook (2008a) Facebook releases site in German. March 2. https://about.fb.com/news/2008/03/facebook-releases-site-in-german/ (accessed June 21, 2022).

Facebook (2008b) Facebook releases site in Spanish; German and French to follow. February 7. https://about.fb.com/news/2008/02/facebook-releases-site-in-spanish-german-and-french-to-follow/ (accessed June 21, 2022).

Facebook (2010) http://wiki.developers.facebook.com/index.php/Internationalization (accessed March 5, 2010).

Facebook (2016) Localization and Translation. https://developers.facebook.com/docs/internationalization (accessed January 7, 2016).

Flew, T. (2020) Globalization, neo-globalization and post-globalization: The challenge of populism and the return of the national. *Global Media and Communication*, 16, 1: 19–39. https://doi.org/10.1177/1742766519900329

Flew, T. and Waisbord, S. (2015) The ongoing significance of national media systems in the context of media globalization. *Media, Culture & Society*, 37, 4: 620–36.

Flew, T., Iosifidis, P., and Steemers, J. (eds.) (2016) *Global Media and National Policies: The Return of the State*. Basingstoke, UK: Palgrave Macmillan.

Freer, A. (2020) TikTok was the most downloaded app of 2020. Business of Apps, December 15. https://www.businessofapps.com/news/tiktok-was-the-most-downloaded-app-of-2020 (accessed March 21, 2021).

Fuchs, C. (2011) *Foundations in Critical Media and Foundation Studies*. London: Routledge.

Garrahan, M. (2009) The rise and fall of MySpace. *Financial Times*, December 4. https://www.ft.com/content/fd9ffd9c-dee5-11de-adff-00144feab49a (accessed May 17, 2022).

Grunwald, D. (2010) Lost in translation? Twitter language crowdsourcing project. January, 26. http://blog.gts-translation.com/2010/01/26/lost-in-translation-twitter-language-crowdsourcing-project

Hernàndez i Martí, G.-M. (2006) The deterritorialization of cultural heritage in a globalized modernity. *Transfer: Journal of Contemporary Culture*, 1: 92–107.

Hesmondhalgh, D. (2019) *The Cultural Industries*. Fourth edition. London: SAGE.

Hilson, M. (2008) *The Nordic Model: Scandinavia since 1945*. London: Reaktion.

Howe, J. (2006) The rise of crowdsourcing. *Wired*, June 1. http://www.wired.com/wired/archive/14.06/crowds.html (accessed June 2, 2022).

Jenkins, H. (2006) *Convergence Culture: Where Old and New Media Collide*. New York: New York University Press.

Jensen, P. and Waade, A. M. (2013) Nordic noir challenging the "language of advantage." *Journal of Popular Television*, 1, 2: 259–65.

Jensen, P. and Waade, A. M. (2014) When public service drama travels: The internationalization of Danish television drama and the production funding models involved. Paper presented at RIPE@2014, August 27–9, Tokyo.

Jin, D. J. (2013) The construction of platform imperialism in the globalization era. *tripleC*, 11, 1: 145–72.

Jin, D. Y. (2020) *Globalization and Media in the Digital Platform Age*. London: Routledge.

Lodz, A. (2021) In between the global and the local: Mapping the geographies of Netflix as a multinational service. *International Journal of Cultural Studies*, 24, 2: 195–215.

Kraidy, M. M. (2005) *Hybridity: Or the Cultural Logic of Globalization*. Philadelphia: Temple University Press.

McChesney, R. (1998) Media Convergence and Globalization, pp. 27–46 in D. K. Thussu (ed.) *Electronic Empires: Global Media and Local Resistance*. London: Arnold.

McChesney, R. (1999) The Media System Goes Global, pp. 78–118 in R. McChesney (ed.) *Rich Media, Poor Democracy: Communication Politics in Dubious Times*. Champaign: University of Illinois Press.

Magder, T. (2003) Watching What We Say: Global Communication in a Time of Fear, pp. 28–44 in D. K. Thussu and D. Freedman (eds.) *War and the Media: Reporting Conflict 24/7*. London: SAGE.

Mjøs, O. J. (2010) *Media Globalization and the Discovery Channel Networks*. London: Routledge.

Mjøs, O. J. (2012) *Music, Social Media and Global Mobility.* London: Routledge.

Mjøs, O. J. (2015) International communication and global media: Continuity of critical concerns. *Communication Research and Practice,* 1, 3: 267–74.

Moragas Spa, M. de, and Lopez, B. (2000) Decentralization Process and "Proximate Television" in Europe, pp. 33–51 in G. Wang, J. Servaes and A. Goonasekera (eds.) *The New Communications Landscape: Demystifying Media Globalization.* Routledge: London.

Morley, D. and Robins, K. (1995) *Spaces of Identity: Global Media, Electronic Landscapes and Cultural Boundaries.* London: Routledge.

Nederveen Pieterse, J. (2004) *Globalization and Culture: Global Melange.* Lanham, MD: Rowman & Littlefield.

Nederveen Pieterse, J. (2020) Global culture, 1990, 2020. *Theory, Culture & Society,* 37, 7–8: 233–40.

Nederveen Pieterse, J. (2021) *Connectivity and Global Studies.* London: Palgrave Macmillan.

Osterhammel, J. and Petersson, N. P. (2005) *Globalization: A Short History.* Princeton, NJ: Princeton University Press.

O'Sullivan, P. B. and Carr, C. T. (2018) Mass personal communication: A model bridging the mass-interpersonal divide. *New Media & Society,* 20, 3: 1161–80.

Poell, T. and van Dijck, J. (2018) Social Media and New Protest Movements, pp. 546–61 in J. Burgess, A. Marwick and T. Poell (eds.) *The SAGE Handbook of Social Media.* London: SAGE.

Poell, T., Nieborg, D., and van Dijck, J. (2019) Platformisation. *Internet Policy Review* 8, 4. https://doi.org/10.14763/2019.4.1425

Rantanen, T. (2005) *The Media and Globalization.* London: SAGE.

Robertson, R. (1990) Mapping the global condition: Globalization as the central concept. *Theory, Culture & Society,* 7, 2–3: 15–30.

Robertson, R. (1992) *Globalization: Social Theory and Global Culture.* London: SAGE.

Robertson, R. (1995) Globalization: Time-Space and Homogeneity-Heterogeneity, pp. 23–44 in M. Featherstone, S. Lash, and R. Robertson (eds.) *Global Modernities.* London: SAGE.

Robertson, R. (2016) Global Culture and Consciousness, pp. 5–20 in R. Robertson and D. Buhari-Gulmez, *Global Culture: Consciousness and Connectivity.* London: Routledge.

Robertson, R. (2020) The Glocal Turn, pp. 25–38 in I. Rossi (ed.) *Challenges of Globalization and Prospects for an Inter-civilizational World Order.* Cham, Switzerland: Springer. https://doi.org/10.1007/978-3-030-44058-9_2

Robertson, R. and Buhari-Gulmez, D. (2016) *Global Culture: Consciousness and Connectivity.* London: Routledge.

Sassen, S. (2021) How to theorize globalization: A comment. *Globalizations,* 18, 5: 792–3.

Schiller, H. (1985) Electronic Information Flows: New Basis for Global Dominations? pp. 11–20 in P. Drummond and R. Paterson (eds.) *Television in Transition: Papers from the First International Television Studies Conference.* London: BFI.

Schiller, H. (1992) *Mass Communications and American Empire*. Second edition. Boulder, CO: Westview Press.

Schiller, H. (1998) Striving for Communication Dominance: A Half-Century Review, pp. 17–26 in D. K. Thussu (ed.) *Electronic Empires: Global Media and Local Resistance*. London: Arnold.

Schiller, H. ([1976] 2018) *Communication and Cultural Domination*. First edition. Abingdon, Oxon. and New York: Routledge.

Schmidt, E. and Cohen, J. (2013) *The New Digital Age: Transforming Nations, Businesses, and Our Lives*. New York: Vintage Books.

Servaes, J. (2007) Introduction, pp. 14–30 in J. Servaes (ed.) *Communication for Development and Change*. London: SAGE.

Sherman, A. (2020) TikTok reveals detailed user numbers for the first time. *CNBC*, August 24. https://www.cnbc.com/2020/08/24/tiktok-reveals-us-global-user-growth-numbers-for-first-time.html (accessed March 21, 2021).

Shim, D. (2006) Hybridity and the rise of Korean popular culture in Asia. *Media, Culture & Society*, 28, 1: 25–44.

Sinclair, J. (2003) "The Hollywood of Latin America": Miami as regional center in television trade. *Television & New Media*, 4, 3: 211–29.

Sinclair, J., Jacka, E., and Cunningham, S. (1996) *New Patterns in Global Television*. Oxford: Oxford University Press.

Sparks, C. (2005) The problem of globalization. *Global Media & Communication*, 1, 1: 20–3.

Sparks, C. (2015) How Coherent is the BRICS Grouping? pp. 42–65 in D. K. Thussu and K. Nordenstreng (eds.) *Mapping BRICS Media*. London: Routledge.

Steger, M. and James, P. (2020) Disjunctive globalization. *Theory, Culture & Society*, 37, 7–8: 187–203.

Straubhaar, J. (1991) Beyond media imperialism: Assymmetrical interdependence and cultural proximity. *Critical Studies in Mass Communication*, 8, 1: 39–59.

Straubhaar, J. D. (2007) *World Television*. London: SAGE.

Straubhaar, J. D. and Duarte, L. G. (2005) Adapting US Transnational Television Channels to a Complex World: From Cultural Imperialism to Localization to Hybridization, pp. 216–53 in J. K. Chalaby, (ed.) *Transnational Television Worldwide: Towards a New Media Order*. London: I. B. Tauris.

Syvertsen, T., Enli, G., Mjøs, O. J. and Moe, H. (2014) *The Media Welfare State: Nordic Media in the Digital Era*. Ann Arbor, MI: University of Michigan Press.

Tankovska, H. (2021) Global social networks ranked by number of users 2021. Statista, February 9. https://www.statista.com/statistics/272014/global-social-networks-ranked-by-number-of-users (accessed March 18, 2021).

Tidy, J. and Smith Galer, S. (2020) TikTok: The story of a social media giant. *BBC News*, August 5. https://www.bbc.com/news/technology-53640724 (accessed March 21, 2021).

Thussu, D. K. (2005) The transnationalization of television: the Indian experience, pp. 156–72 in J. K. Chalaby (ed.) *Transnational Television Worldwide: Towards a New Media Order*. London: I. B. Tauris.

Thussu, D. K. (2006) Contra-flow in Global Media, pp. 11–32 in D. K. Thussu (ed.) *Media on the Move: Global Flow and Contra-flow*. Routledge: London.

Thussu, D. K. (2010) Introduction, pp. 1–10 in D. K. Thussu (ed.) *International Communication: A Reader*. London: Routledge.

Thussu, D. K. (2015) Digital BRICS: Building a NWICO 2.0, pp. 242–63 in D. K. Thussu and K. Nordenstreng (eds.) *Mapping BRICS Media*. London: Routledge.

Thussu, D. K. (2021) BRICS De-Americanizing the Internet? pp. 280–301 in D. K. Thussu and K. Nordenstreng (eds.) *BRICS Media: Reshaping the Global Communication Order?* Abingdon, UK: Routledge.

Thussu, D. K. and Nordenstreng, K. (2015) Introduction: Contextualizing the BRICS Media, pp. 1–22 in D. K. Thussu and K. Nordenstreng (eds.) *Mapping BRICS Media*. London: Routledge.

Thussu, D. K. and Nordenstreng, K. (2021) Introduction, pp. 1–19 in D. K. Thussu and K. Nordenstreng (eds.) *BRICS Media: Reshaping the Global Communication Order?* Abingdon, UK: Routledge.

Tomlinson, J. (1991) *Cultural Imperialism: A Critical Introduction*. London: Continuum.

Tomlinson, J. (1999) *Globalisation and Culture*. Cambridge, UK: Polity.

Tomlinson, J. (2012) Deterritorialization, in G. Ritzer (ed.) *The Wiley-Blackwell Encyclopedia of Globalization*. Chichester, UK: Blackwell. https://doi.org/10.1002/9780470670590.wbeog143 (accessed June 3, 2022).

Tunstall, J. (1977) *The Media are American*. New York: Columbia Press.

Turow, J (2017) Personalization, pp. 135–7 in L. Ouellett and J. Gray (eds.) *Keywords in Media Studies*. New York: New York University Press.

Van Dijck, J. (2013) *The Culture of Connectivity: A Critical History of Social Media*. Oxford: Oxford University Press.

Waisbord, S. (2004) McTV: Understanding the global popularity of television formats. *Television & New Media*, 5, 4: 359–83.

Winter, S., Maslowska, E., and Vos, A. L. (2021) The effects of trait-based personalization in social media advertising, *Computers in Human Behavior*, 114: 106525. https://doi.org/10.1016/j.chb.2020.106525 (accessed April 15, 2021).

Zhu, Y. and Keane, M. (2021) China's Cultural Power Reconnects with the World, pp. 209–22 in D. Thussu and K. Nordenstreng (eds.) *BRICS Media: Reshaping the Global Communication Order?* Abingdon, UK: Routledge.

Index